# COMPUTER KEYSTROKE LOGGING AND WRITING: METHODS AND APPLICATIONS

**STUDIES IN WRITING**
*Series Editor:* **Gert Rijlaarsdam**

**Recent titles in this series:**

SHUM AND ZHANG
*Teaching Writing in Chinese Speaking Areas*

KOSTOULI
*Writing in Context(s)—Textual Practices and Learning Processes in Sociocultural Settings*

RIJLAARSDAM, VAN DEN BERGH AND COUZIJN
*Effective Learning and Teaching of Writing*

**Related titles:**

BROMME AND STAHL
*Writing Hypertext and Learning: Conceptual and Empirical Approaches*

DE CORTE, VERSHAFFEL, ENTWISTLE AND MERRIËNBOER
*Powerful Learning Environments: Unravelling Basic Components and Dimensions*

**Related journals:**

*Learning and Instruction*
*Educational Research Review*
*Assessing Writing*
*Computers and Composition*
*Journal of Second Language Writing*

# COMPUTER KEYSTROKE LOGGING AND WRITING: METHODS AND APPLICATIONS

EDITED BY

**KIRK P. H. SULLIVAN**

*Umeå University, Sweden*

**EVA LINDGREN**

*Umeå University, Sweden*

ELSEVIER

Amsterdam • Boston • Heidelberg • London • New York • Oxford
Paris • San Diego • San Francisco • Singapore • Sydney • Tokyo

Elsevier
The Boulevard, Langford Lane, Kidlington, Oxford OX5 1GB, UK
Radarweg 29, PO Box 211, 1000 AE Amsterdam, The Netherlands

First edition 2006



**British Library Cataloguing in Publication Data**
A catalogue record for this book is available from the British Library

**Library of Congress Cataloging-in-Publication Data**
A catalog record for this book is available from the Library of Congress

ISBN-13: 978-0-08-044934-0
ISBN-10: 0-08-044934-4
ISSN: 1572-6304

For information on all Elsevier publications
visit our website at books.elsevier.com

Printed and bound in The Netherlands

06 07 08 09 10 10 9 8 7 6 5 4 3 2 1

# Table of Contents

Chapter 1

# Keystroke Logging: An Introduction

Kristyan Spelman Miller[1] and Kirk P. H. Sullivan[2]
[1]*The University of Reading, Whiteknights, Reading, UK*
[2]*Umeå University, Umeå, Sweden*

*This chapter introduces the reader to keystroke logging of writing processes as a research method and places this method at the centre of writing research. We overview the features of the keystroke logging software that is currently available, indicate its domain of application and set the stage for the topics interrogated in this volume.*

**Keywords:** keystroke, writing, revision, pause, logging.

## 1 Introduction

At a time when there is much debate internationally concerning approaches to writing research and their applications, this volume aims to contribute to the discussion by defining and illustrating a research method, which is attracting growing interest within the international research community. The approach, called *keystroke logging*, consists of the computer recording of writing activity as writers compose on the computer. As an observational tool, keystroke logging offers the opportunity to capture details of the activity of writing, not only for the purposes of the linguistic, textual and cognitive study of writing, but also for broader applications concerning the development of language learning, literacy and language pedagogy.

The work presented in this volume shares one common focus: the use of keystroke logging in a range of contexts. The purposes of the volume are to bring together work from a number of researchers to present both a retrospective and a prospective view on this approach to writing scholarship. This introductory chapter will define in general terms the main principles of keystroke logging as a research tool, both against the background of the writing process research agenda and in comparison with other methodological tools.

**Computer Key Stroke Logging and Writing: Methods and Applications**

**ISBN: 0-08-044934-4**

*Spelman Miller, K. & Sullivan, K. P. H. (2006). Keystroke logging: an introduction.*
*In G. Rijlaarsdam (Series Ed.) and K. P. H. Sullivan, & E. Lindgren. (Vol. Eds.), Studies in Writing, Vol. 18, Computer Keystroke Logging: Methods and Applications (pp. 1–9). Oxford: Elsevier.*

This will allow us to situate the chapters, which make up this volume, within the broader debate on writing research and in terms of main lines of research in the field and their applications.

## 2 Positioning Keystroke Research

Historically, keystroke logging has its theoretical underpinnings in a cognitive approach to writing, which is concerned with how language users navigate through the task of producing or understanding text. By definition such an approach is concerned with 'what the writer does (planning, revising and the like) instead of [on] what the final product looks like (patterns of organization, spelling, grammar)' (Applebee, 1986, p. 96), that is, presenting a writer- (rather than text-) based perspective on writing.

Focus on the process of writing has been a major force within composition and second-language writing research and pedagogy since the latter part of the last century, although there is controversy and difference of opinion as to its precise definition. Given the various strands of interest, which have emerged over the last few decades (for historical reviews see Grabe & Kaplan, 1996; Johns, 1990 and for an interesting critique of its complex historical development see Matsuda, 2003), 'process' is best understood as an umbrella term, spanning different disciplinary influences and concerns, including expressive, cognitive and social perspectives.

Of these, the cognitive dimension in writing research, appearing from the 1970s onwards, draws heavily on the interests and empirical methods of cognitive psychology. The concern here is with exploring the inner workings of the mind, that is, the component processes which underpin complex mental activity (Kellogg, 1994, p. 10). This perspective views writing as involving a complex set of hierarchically arranged cognitive activities or operations, which appear to be involved in all directed thinking tasks. These include the operations of collecting, generating and organising ideas according to a set of goals, the translating of these into text and the reviewing of both ideas and textual output. In this sense, writing is viewed as an exemplary form of human thinking, involving problem-solving and decision-making within clearly defined goals (Kellogg, 1994, p. 13). Indeed, the cognitive psychological stance (e.g. Nickerson, Perkins, & Smith, 1985) may even suggest that the study of writing opens up a window on the nature of thinking itself.

The origin of this angle on the study of the writing process is often claimed to be the early work of Emig (1971), whose case studies of individual writers used introspective techniques in an attempt to uncover the otherwise hidden process of writing. Other studies by researchers such as Perl (1979), Selfe (1981, 1984) and Sommers (1980) further developed these insights, using similar introspective and observational methods. From the late 1970s onwards, attempts were made to bring together these findings in a coherent model of the cognitive process of writing. The work of Flower and Hayes (1977, 1980, 1981, 1984; Hayes & Flower, 1980, 1983) is best known in this respect, and their attempts at developing a theoretical framework or cognitive model of the writing process are still widely recognised today.

Flower and Hayes's (1980) representation of writing became extremely influential both in research and in pedagogic domains, providing the basis for much discussion of the basic principles of a cognitive process approach to writing, namely that writing is a complex, goal-directed activity, comprising composing processes, which are 'interactive, intermingling, and potentially simultaneous' (Grabe & Kaplan, 1996, p. 91). Despite criticisms about the power of this as a model of writing (see, in particular, North, 1987) on the grounds of a lack of refinement of components, its limited explanatory power and weaknesses in protocol methodology on which the model is based, the framework that it provides for writing research and pedagogy remains of considerable significance. Emphasis on content and involvement over grammar and usage, the development of the writer's voice, response and accommodation towards reactions from the writer's audience, self-expression and procedural features, such as planning, drafting, revising as part of a nonlinear process, are all recognised nowadays as general principles of writing orthodoxy.

Further developments in the model (e.g. Flower et al., 1990; Hayes, 1996; Hayes, Flower, Schriver, Statman, & Carey, 1987; Hayes & Nash, 1996) have led to elaborations of the subcomponents of writing, and, consonant with the general shift of attention towards the social dimension in writing (see Atkinson, 2003; Bizzell, 1982; Tobin, 1994; Trimbur, 1994), a broadening of the more narrowly cognitivist perspective is seen in the work of those such as Flower et al. (1990) who now conceptualise writing as both a 'cognitive activity' and a 'contextually constrained activity' (Grabe & Kaplan, 1996, p. 115). This appears to be in line with widespread calls for a more comprehensive theory of writing to take account of a number of interconnected dimensions, namely cognitive, textual and sociocontextual aspects (Candlin & Hyland, 1999; Cumming & Riazi, 1996; Grabe & Kaplan, 1996; Witte, 1992). We see arguments, such as that made by Reither (1985):

> writing and what writers do during writing cannot be artificially separated from the social rhetorical situation in which writing gets done, from the conditions which enable writers to do what they do, and from the motives writers have for doing what they do. (p. 621)

echoed in later statements by those such as Candlin and Hyland (1999), concerning the socially situated nature of writing:

> writing research needs to move beyond a focus on the page or the screen to explore the uses to which writing is put, and to offer candidate explanations of how these uses may engender particular conditions of production and interpretation of texts in context. [...] Every act of writing is thus linked in complex ways to a set of communicative purposes which occur in a context of social, interpersonal and occupational practices. (p. 2)

The acknowledgement that writing research and pedagogy are now moving to embrace diversification and a genuine multidimensionality, as articulated in Matsuda's (2003) reference to a movement 'towards the era of multiplicity' (p. 79), is to be welcomed. It allows the broadening of the research agenda to include cognitive, textual and social dimensions, legitimising concerns not only with the detail (in some senses abstract and largely asocial) of internal, individualistic and cognitive processing but also with the textual output of the processing, and with the social context in which this processing takes place. Each of these perspectives, with differing emphases, is reflected in the research presented in this volume.

## 3 Keystroke Logging: Main Features

We began by defining keystroke logging as a research method, which entails the observation of the writing process. Techniques for the observation of writing have been reported for many years (most notably by Matushashi from the 1980s onwards), as offering an alternative to the method of eliciting direct, subject-generated data from writers in the form of introspective protocols (or think-aloud verbalisations). As a research methodology, the think-aloud technique, although strenuously supported by some following Ericsson and Simon (1984/1993), has also been criticised on the grounds of reliability and validity (Cooper & Holzman, 1983; Kowal & O'Connell, 1987; Russo, Johnson, & Stephens, 1989; see Smagorinsky, 1994, pp. 3–89; Stratman & Hamp-Lyons, 1994 for overviews of opinion). Questions are frequently raised about the incomplete nature of the elicited verbalisations (subjects, perhaps on instruction, include only a narrow range of thoughts) and their partial nature (consciously or unconsciously aimed at meeting the needs of the researcher). Russo et al. (1989) also discuss the issue of reactivity, that is, the disruptive nature of the think-aloud method, which potentially interferes with or disrupts the very behaviour it is intended to expose.

Given the potential shortcomings of verbalisation, observation that generates indirect but detailed information concerning the activity of writing has met favour with some researchers as an alternative method of data elicitation. Following the use of rather unsophisticated direct observation and video-recording methods (e.g. Matsuhashi, 1981; Zamel, 1983), the advent of computer-based technology has made available more versatile and discrete methods to record the progression of the writing event unobtrusively without the intervention of video recorder or researcher–observer.

One computer recording technique reported by Levy and Ransdell (1994, 1996a), Levy, Marek, and Lea (1996) and Owston, Murphy, and Wideman (1992) involves 'hidden' video recording using a signal splitting and converting device as subjects write on a word processor. This involves the real-time recording of the writing process without the physical presence of a video camera through the storage and conversion of information on the computer screen to a video image on a video recorder. This output may be remotely watched and analysed, and in one study (Levy et al., 1996) it was used to prompt retrospective comments by writers during replay.

This use of computer-based recording to elicit retrospective protocols has prompted discussion of the use of this technique in writing process research. Arguments are put forward by some (e.g. Greene & Higgins, 1994; Schumacher, Klare, Cronin, & Moses, 1984) in favour of retrospective accounting on the grounds that problems of reactivity are avoided. Greene and Higgins, for example, claim that retrospective accounts, as a direct method of data elicitation, have 'the advantage of allowing writers to explain and reflect on their decisions without interfering directly with their attention to the task' (p. 118). However, strong evidence is put forward by others (e.g. Levy et al., 1996) that retrospective accounts should be viewed more cautiously. Levy et al. (1996) claim that 'retrospective accounts of composing details are fraught with construct validity problems' (p. 553) because of the subjects' memory constraints, and in the worst case may 'hardly differ from guessing behavior' (p. 555). However, they go on to suggest that under certain conditions, in particular by preparing the writer in practice sessions and re-creating the conditions of the original writing session during the retrospective phase, accurate recall of the writing event may in fact be supported. Keystroke logging emerges as a strong alternative computer-based tool for recording the writing event. The advantages of keystroke logging in providing an unobtrusive means of recording are well documented elsewhere (see Pennington, 1999; Severinson Eklundh & Kollberg, 1996a, 1996b; Spelman Miller, 2000a; Strömqvist & Ahlsén, 1999; Van Waes, 1991).

In brief, the electronic recording of all operations (including keypresses, editing functions and cursor movements) made by the writer as he/she writes on a word processor allows the storage and subsequent retrieval of a large number of features of the writing activity, such as the fluency of the writing (where and when pauses occurred, and their duration) and the sequence of actions during writing (to do with text production and activities such as scrolling, navigating with the cursor and deleting). The output of the logfile is a highly detailed record of the temporal features of the writing activity, which provides a rich source of online data for analysis. Figure 1 provides an illustration of a logtext recorded using the logging software JEdit (Cederlund & Severinson Eklundh, nd.; Severinson Eklundh & Kollberg, 1996b).

```
112.6 | The_first_school_we_begin_in_is_called_Primary_C1⌫School<2.3>
136.4 | ._You_start_when_your1⌫'re_<4.3>7<2.5>_y<2.2>ears_old_in_the_!1⌫
165.8 | 1st_grade._Then_you_go_in_that_scj1⌫hool_<2.9>for_<3.3>9_years._
193.4 | <2.4>Whw1⌫en_you're_<3.1>15_to_16_tears_you_quit_that_sd1⌫
218.3 | chool_and_you_begin,_if_you,_wan't_to<6.2>9←1⌫9→<3.2>
246.5 | ,_in_the_Gymnasiun1⌫m<2.7>._There_you_can_choose_what_line_or_<2.6>
272.9 | program_you_want_to_studu.2⌫y,_depending_on_whar1⌫t_ you_like_and_
299.8 | <2.1>are_inr1⌫terested_n1⌫in<4.1>.<2.0>¶<3.5>A_schoolyear_<7.1>
333.2 | contains_two_terms._One_autun1⌫mn_1⌫term_<2.4>and_one_summerterm
358.3 | <2.3>.<2.8>_Between_those_two_terms_you_have_one_<2.0>
381.7 | christmasholiday_1⌫_for_two_weeks_and_one_summerterm_for<2.0>8⌫
406.8 | holiday_for<6.5>ten_weeks<2.2>9←_9→.<5.3>
434.3 | _On_the_terms_you_have,_especially_on_the_springterm,_<2.2>
459.9 | many_different_<2.6>"littlcholidays"_<6.3>too_<8.7>⎘ittle|holid6⌫small
497.2 | 15→¶<4.8>You_go_in_school_from4⌫five_days_a_week<28.3>6⌫
553.6 | of__the_seven_days_of_a_week._The_other_days,_saturday_and_<2.0>
581.1 | sunday,_you_are_vree_from_school,_a1⌫you_normally_sleep_and_<4.8>
610.5 | ⎘are_v|ree_f1⌫f⎘_days|,_sat⎘_and_|rest_yourself_on_those_days<3.1>.
631.7 | <2.4>_And_those_are_the_m1⌫<3.6>
645.0 | most_popular_days_of_the_week,_atleast_the_students_think.<12.2>¶
679.3 | <11.8>⎘too.¶You_g¶⎘_in.¶A_sch¶⎘hink.|¶¶¶<8.5>A_schoolday_begins_at_
711.9 | <5.0>around_eight_a1⌫o'clock_in_the<2.0>
```

Figure 1: An example of a JEdit logfile. Pausological information is presented as bracketed numbers (e.g. <3.2> representing a pause of 3.2 s); cursor movements are indicated by the left/right/up/down arrows; backspace deletions are indicated by the crossed arrow symbol; space bar presses are indicated by the _ symbol; and all other characters (letters and punctuation marks) are also shown. The running time of the writing event (in seconds) is given down the left-hand margin.

A number of different keystroke logging programs based on these principles are reported in use in the literature. Bridwell, Sirc, and Brooke (1985) and Bridwell-Bowles, Johnson, and Brehe (1987) report on an early use of keystroke recording using the program 'Recording Wordstar' in a series of investigations of word-processor writing at the University of Minnesota. Since then, various text editors have been designed for keystroke recording on different systems.

The research reported in this volume uses four of the currently available keystroke logging tools: JEdit (Chapters 8 and 9), ScriptLog (Chapters 4, 7 and 10), Inputlog (Chapter 5) and Translog (Chapter 6). In this chapter, we provide a detailed overview of functionality of JEdit and introduce ScriptLog, Inputlog and Translog. The reader looking for more information about ScriptLog, Inputlog and Translog is directed to Chapter 4 and http://www.scriptlog.net, Chapter 5 and www.inputlog.net, and Chapter 6 and http://translog.dk, respectively.

JEdit is written for Macintosh computers and can be downloaded at http://www.nada.kth.se/iplab/trace-it/index.html. In addition, for logging the writer's interaction with the JEdit word processor, JEdit includes a statistics module that generates descriptive statistics about the writing session. The JEdit logfile can be displayed as shown in Figure 1 or used to reply the writing session.

The JEdit software has a further element of versatility: in addition to displaying the logfile, allowing the writing session to be replayed and displaying some statistics concerning the writing event, there is also the option to use the data stored in JEdit to analyse revision episodes. JEdit data can be converted via a MID (Move–Insert–Delete) file into a representation of revision operations known as S-notation (Severinson Eklundh & Kollberg, 1992, 1996b). On the basis of a set of rules for the identification and interpretation of revisions (deletions and insertions), S-notation allows the writing event to be represented in terms of the text alterations made in chronological order. In other words, the revision type, the extent and the point of initiation are explicitly indicated. This greatly facilitates the interpretation of text operations from the logfile data. A keystroke log analysis program, Trace-it (Nilsson & Kollberg, 1994; Severinson Eklundh & Kollberg, 1996a), allows the S-notation to be presented interactively. That is, the writing session may be replayed revision by revision, so that the analyst or the writer can review the session, considering each revision individually and its impact on the text produced. Some basic statistics are also provided on-screen by the software concerning the frequency of revision types and the distance of the revision from the point of inscription. This interactive replay facility has an easy user interface and can be used to elicit retrospective commentary by writers concerning points of decision-making during the writing session.

While working with keystroke logging, the distinction between an 'elementary' and an 'interpreted' revision (Severinson Eklundh & Kollberg, 1996a) needs to be understood. For example, in S-notation, and used when the number and type of revision is presented in the descriptive statistics module of Trace-it, an elementary revision is defined as a single insertion or deletion; it is not possible for the computer to interpret intentional relations between insertions and/or revisions. Hence, the substitution of one word for another word will involve at least two elementary revisions: one of deletion and one of insertion. A human interpreter of the same logfile would describe this sequence of deletion and insertion as a single revision rather than as two revisions, that is, as a substitution. When the human interpreter has classified the revision in a log, they become interpreted revisions. The number of such revisions is often, but not necessarily, less than the number of elementary revisions. The procedure and the criteria for transforming elementary revisions into interpreted revisions should always be made clear when reporting research results using keystroke logging data.

ScriptLog (Strömqvist & Karlsson, 2002), Inputlog (Leijten & Van Waes, 2005) and Translog (Jakobsen, 1999), in contrast to JEdit, are developed for the PC and run in Windows environments. All of these programs log the writing activities that take place when a writer is composing text on a computer. As in JEdit, every keyboard and mouse action and their temporal distribution is logged. The structure of the logfiles is different (see Chapter 4: Example 1 for an example of a ScriptLog logfile). ScriptLog, in common with JEdit, includes a basic descriptive statistics module and currently only logs all keystrokes and mouse actions within its own integrated word-processing module. It is here that Inputlog distinguishes itself from other current keystroke logging programs. Inputlog is able to log user activity in any Windows-based program. ScriptLog, on the other hand, distinguishes itself by its integrated experimental setup facility and integration with eye-tracking equipment. Translog distinguishes itself through its development for translation research.

In summary, we can say that keystroke logging programs are software that generate copious amounts of recorded data consisting of information concerning pausing (where and when pauses occurred, and for how long) and the history of all keyboard actions including text production and commands such as scrolling, navigating with the cursor and deleting. Such data in logfiles may then be trawled for evidence of temporal aspects of writing (see Wengelin, Chapter 7; Spelman Miller, Chapter 8), including pause location and features of formulation processes.

## 4 The Structure of the Book

This book provides state-of-the-art research from a number of contexts using four keystroke logging tools: JEdit, ScriptLog, Inputlog and Translog, but can only touch selectively on the many applications of keystroke logging with respect to both first-and second-language writing, the writing of those with reading and writing difficulties, the writing of expert and novice writers in professional contexts and in specialist skill areas such as translation.

The book is divided into four sections. Section 1 introduces the reader unfamiliar with writing research to the complexities of written text production and provides the grounding in the field that is necessary to access the methods section of the book (Section 3). In Chapter 2, Kristyan Spelman Miller in her chapter 'The pausological study of written language production' guides the reader through the body of research into temporal aspects of language and written text production of writing. In Chapter 3, Eva Lindgren and Kirk Sullivan introduce the reader to the complexities of writing and the analysis of revision.

In Section 2, we gain our first glimpse of the detail and the complexity generated by the data keystroke logging. This section provides the reader new to keystroke logging an overview of the research topics that can be investigated using keystroke logging and the opportunity to gain state-of-the-art insight into the PC-logging tools: ScriptLog and

Inputlog. In Chapter 4, Sven Strömqvist and his research group, based at Lund University in Sweden, present their work with ScriptLog demonstrating how keystroke logging can be applied in writing research and how the work with ScriptLog is currently being extended to include eye-tracking data. This chapter is well suited for teaching and could be used in a class, examining the differences between speech and writing or discussing writing difficulties. This chapter also describes the tool ScriptLog in detail, permitting comparison with the description of JEdit and Trace-it in this chapter, Inputlog in Chapter 5 and Translog in Chapter 6.

In Chapter 5, Mariëlle Leijten and Luuk Van Waes present the technical and functional characteristics of Inputlog and provide a preview of their plans for the future development of Inputlog. This chapter provides the more technical reader with a grounding in the complexities of how a keystroke log is designed and the issues that need to be resolved to program successful keystroke logging software. In Chapter 6, Arnt Lykke Jakobsen presents Translog, its development, functionality and how it can be used to study translation.

Section 3 assumes that the reader is familiar with both writing research and keystroke logging tool. The reader unfamiliar with these areas is directed to Sections 1 and 2 of this book, respectively. All readers should bear in mind while reading the chapters in Section 3, and research elsewhere that is based on keystroke logging, that the medium of the computer and the particular writing tool used affects and mediates the writing processes. There is a large body of research into the effect of the computer medium on writing behaviour (e.g. Bridwell-Bowles et al., 1987; Daiute, 1986; Haas, 1989; Hawisher, 1987; Hill, Wallace, & Haas, 1991; Joram, Woodruff, Lindsey, & Bryson, 1990; Lutz, 1987; Owston et al., 1992; Van Waes & Schellens, 2003) and the reader needs to bear in mind while reading these chapters and similar papers that the findings of keystroke logging research cannot by default be generalised to other writing media.

Section 3 contains the central methods section of this book. Chapters 7–9 address three core aspects of writing research using keystroke logging: the study of pause location, pausing in relation to planning and discourse production, and revision behaviour. In Chapter 7, Åsa Wengelin examines pauses in writing, showing how corpus linguistics methods can be applied to logged data to examine pause behaviour during writing and to examine the writing processes of different writer groups and how writing can be affected by different writing tasks. Her application of corpus-based methods permits the rapid analysis of large amounts of logged data.

In Chapter 8, logfile data are used to establish patterns of pausing associated with planning locations and revision activity. The context for Kristyan Spelman Miller's study is a comparative analysis of first- and second-language writers on two writing tasks. The locations of pausing are considered in terms of not only their grammatical characterisation but also their discoursal function in serving to introduce, maintain or close the topic, and interesting patterns of pausological behaviour are identified across the first- and second-language writers.

In Chapter 9, Eva Lindgren and Kirk Sullivan examine revision and how online revisions can be categorised. Given the centrality of the study of revision in writing research, there is considerable scope for the analysis of online revision using keystroke logging, and Lindgren and Sullivan's chapter, which focuses on the development of a taxonomy for online revisions, the LS-taxonomy, is clearly grounded in the large body of writing revision literature. Of particular note in this chapter is the discussion surrounding revisions at the point of inscription or precontextual revisions and how these revisions may be studied.

The final section of this book, Section 4, shifts the outlook of the book away from the focus on methodology of Section 3, and back towards using keystroke logging for applied research and pedagogy. Birgitta Englund Dimitrova in Chapter 10 presents the application of keystroke logging in the context of expert and novice translators. This study analyses differences between professional translators and students in how they segment the writing process. The professionals were found to divide their writing process into fewer and larger segments than was done by the students. Interestingly, pause length did not correlate with translation experience, yet facilitation effects were found for all subjects, leading to fewer and larger segments towards the end of the task.

In Chapter 11, Sullivan and Lindgren initially report on an interesting area of application of keystroke logging in the promotion of self-assessment and reflection in language learning. This develops ideas presented elsewhere (e.g. Lindgren, 2004; Sullivan & Lindgren, 2002) in which the replaying of the writing event facilitates reflection through peer-based intervention. Three educational domains are considered: first-language writing, second-language learning and writing, and the translation of texts from one language to another. They then shift their discussion to another application area for keystroke logging. They consider how keystroke logging can be used to investigate theories that are not primarily to do with writing, but for which writing provides a window into the theory: Pienemann's (1998) Processability Theory is considered by Sullivan and Lindgren as an example of a theory that can be investigated with state-of-the-art keystroke logging techniques. In the final part of Chapter 11, Sullivan and Lindgren consider how keystroke logging's capabilities can be extended to provide a bright future for this technology.

All four sections of this volume point to a stimulating agenda for research on language learning, use and pedagogy, and one which develops apace with the shifting emphases in writing research in general, while remaining firmly positioned within cognitive theory.

Chapter 2

# The Pausological Study of Written Language Production

Kristyan Spelman Miller
*The University of Reading, Whiteknights, Reading, UK*

*The aim of this chapter is to present an overview of the theoretical background to keystroke logging research, drawing substantially on the psycholinguistics literature which has traditionally considered temporal aspects of language production from the perspective of speech. From a general consideration of temporal aspects of language production we explore accounts of planning in writing. This provides a necessary theoretical context within which to interpret pausological data such as that elicited through keystroke recording. Critical issues concerning methods and categories of analysis are discussed, focusing in particular on pause definition and the characterisation of pause location.*

**Keywords:** keystroke, pausing, productivity, fluency.

## 1 Introduction

The positioning of keystroke research within writing process research has been clearly articulated in the previous introductory chapters. It is the purpose of this chapter to explore the psycholinguistic basis for the investigation of planning, formulation and revision processes of written language production. Mainstream psycholinguistics has a long established history of focus on spoken language production, but has traditionally given much less attention to the temporal aspects of writing. This chapter argues for the relevance of such a theoretical framework for the type of investigations made possible in keystroke logging research. The definition of temporal variables underpinning fluency provides a backdrop to later discussions in this volume (Wengelin, Chapter 7; Spelman Miller, Chapter 8) of planning and pausing behaviour within different writer contexts.

**Computer Key Stroke Logging and Writing: Methods and Applications**

**ISBN: 0-08-044934-4**

*Spelman Miller, K. (2006). The pausological study of written language production. In G. Rijlaarsdam (Series Ed.) and K. P. H. Sullivan, & E. Lindgren. (Vol. Eds.), Studies in Writing, Vol. 18, Computer Keystroke Logging: Methods and Applications (pp. 11–30). Oxford: Elsevier.*

# 2 Temporal Aspects of Language Production

## *2.1 The Definition of Temporal Variables*

The study of temporal variables in the production of speech has long been an established area of specialised activity within psycholinguistics (Griffiths, 1991). The investigation of temporal aspects of speech, or pausology, owes much to the work of Butterworth (1980), Dechert and Raupach (1980a, 1980b), Deschamps (1980), Grosjean (1980), O'Connell (1980), and others, in the late 1970s and 1980s, although their work was heavily motivated itself by earlier research, mostly notably that of Blankenship and Kay (1964), Goldman-Eisler (1961, 1968), and Maclay and Osgood (1959). Over the past two decades, pausology has continued to have an impact both within and beyond the domain of psycholinguistics and speech production. Substantial work has been carried out, for example, in speech pathology, and aphasiology, and in applied linguistics, especially second language research.[1]

The focus of investigation is the 'variables which pertain to timing in language (utterance rate and duration, frequency and duration of pauses)' (Grosjean, 1980, p. 39), although this notion has been extended by some to include other performance phenomena such as filled pauses and false starts. In general, then, attention is on the 'overt, measurable indications of processing activity' (Chafe, 1980, p. 170), the measurable features of the real-time processing of speech production.

In general, research into temporal features of speech production is concerned with the following variables:

(1) *speech rate*: measured in words per minute, or more precisely, syllables per second, obtained by dividing the total number of words (or syllables) by the total speaking time; a similar measure, the phonation-time ratio (Grosjean, 1980), indicates the amount of time spent articulating as a percentage of the total speech time;
(2) *articulation rate*: this is the phonation rate of the speaker (syllables per second) and is obtained by dividing the total number of syllables by the speaker's articulation time (i.e., total speaking time minus the pause time);
(3) *silent pause occurrence*: this includes the length, distribution and frequency of silent pauses (where no phonation occurs); a further issue is the length of speech runs between two pauses, usually measured in syllables.
(4) *hesitation phenomena*: including features such as drawls (syllable lengthening), repetitions, false starts and filled pauses (such as er, ah, um, and so on). Other more verbal elements such as well, y'see, I mean. y'know, may also be included (Garman, 1990). Grosjean (1980) refers to these hesitation phenomena as secondary variables, since they do not have to occur in speech and often do not, as in the case of very fluent speech.

Even within such a clearly delimited area, issues of nomenclature and categorisation arise. It may be argued, for example, that hesitation phenomena are somewhat different

[1]For overviews of the extensive work in these areas, see collections of papers in Butterworth (1980), Dechert and Raupach (1980a, 1980b), and discussion in Griffiths (1991).

from the other temporal variables in not being strictly related to time measurement, and therefore should not be included. The term 'hesitation' also carries with it a negative connotation of disfluency or deficiency in speech (Chafe, 1980; O'Connell & Kowal, 1980), although the phenomenon to which it refers is clearly a natural feature of the flow of normal speech production. To add to the terminological confusion, 'hesitation phenomena' is sometimes used to refer to all features of real-time production (Chafe, 1980; Garrett, 1982, p. 23), or used interchangeably with another term, 'nonfluency' (Garman, 1990; Garrett, 1982). For the purposes of the discussion that follows, we will take an inclusive view of hesitation phenomena or non-fluencies in the definition of temporal variables, although our own research will be restricted in focus to pause-related phenomena.

A further terminological difficulty arises in the distinction between pauses that are silent and those that are filled. Garman (1990) notes that such an opposition may in fact be difficult to maintain: some silent pauses occur with the so-called filled pauses, rendering the use of the term 'filled' rather misleading. Garman (1990, p. 117) prefers the notion of pauses being partially filled, for example with 'breaks' (non-vocalisation), 'pause fillers' (such as *um*, *er*) and/or 'pause words' (such as *well*, *y'see*) (1990, p. 117).

## *2.2 The Significance of Non-Fluency*

Having defined the notion of temporal variables, we should briefly consider the significance of these phenomena as 'naturally displayed sources of evidence' (Garrett, 1982, p. 23) of language processing. Chafe (1980) has referred to 'pauses, changes of direction, and retracing of steps' as evidence of the speaker's route to achieving 'the adequate verbalization of his thoughts' (p. 170). In providing valuable insights into 'the psychological processes involved in "performance"' (p. 170), these features are therefore fundamental to our understanding of the 'creative act' of speaking (p. 170).

Typically, speech is associated with certain situational and functional characteristics: spontaneity, interactiveness, transience, which impose processing demands on both producer and receiver. The time-related constraints on the production of speech are summed up by Garrett (1982) as 'imposed by the relation between rate of output speech and rate of planning processes' (p. 23). These demands relate, then, to the role of the speaker and listener in operating in real-time. In reflecting these demands, pauses are generally acknowledged (Goldman-Eisler, 1972) as serving three functions:

- physiological, in allowing the speaker to break between strings of sounds;
- cognitive, in allowing the speaker to plan the message; and
- communicative or rhetorical, in allowing the speaker to chunk the message and demarcate sense groups for the listener to process.

In this way, non-fluencies appear to serve both speaker- and listener-oriented functions (Garman, 1990, p. 117), although in fact these functions coincide or overlap with each other. A silent pause, for example, may be interpreted as associated with speaker-based difficulties in formulating the message, and/or as serving listener-oriented needs to structure the message. The reality is that it is difficult to disentangle specific functions.

From the perspective of writing (which cannot be concerned with the direct interaction between producer and receiver), the most interesting and relevant function of non-fluency to explore is that concerned with planning. This does not, of course, mean that alternative interpretations of the functions of pausing in writing are not possible, and we need to be conscious of the status of such phenomena in writing as only indirect evidence of planning. At this point, however, it is necessary to turn to questions concerning the definition of planning and the distribution of pauses as indices of such activity.

### *2.3 Non-Fluency and Planning*

The association between non-fluency and planning processes of speech is widely discussed in the psycholinguistics literature.[2] Of particular prominence in this discussion is the work of Goldman-Eisler (1968, 1972), whose influential hesitation model draws on non-fluency data as evidence from which to develop a model of language production. The planning processes to which Goldman-Eisler refers are concerned with message planning at the conceptual (content) level, and for abstract syntactic form and lexical choice. Using evidence from pause occurrence, in particular, concerning the rate and locus of hesitation, Goldman-Eisler distinguishes between creative, voluntary and automatic, routinised aspects of language production. Her findings suggest that syntactic organisation and articulation are associated with the automatic stages of language production, and lexical selection and conceptual planning with the creative or voluntary stage. With respect to these latter two determinants of pause, lexical uncertainty and conceptual complexity, Goldman-Eisler notes increased frequency and duration of pausing as difficulty of encoding increases. In spontaneous speech, alternating cycles of hesitant and fluent phases of speech appear, corresponding to phases of different types of planning activity: that is, in general terms, hesitant phases where non-fluencies appear to cluster are interpreted in terms of opportunities for forward-planning. There are dangers, however, in overgeneralising this account of non-fluency, as Levelt (1989, p. 128) and Garman (1990, p. 125) point out. Cognitive load induced by increased topic difficulty (e.g., changing from a descriptive to an interpretive task) may give rise to increased non-fluency.

The alternation of hesitant and fluent phases in production is also documented in the work of Henderson, Goldman-Eisler, and Skarbek (1966), who similarly interpret these cycles as fluctuations between phases when the speaker's attention is on goal elaboration and information retrieval or on local-level concerns in the delivery of the message. These observations are confirmed in later work by Butterworth (1980) and Beattie (1983), who introduce the terms macroplanning and microplanning to refer to these different types of conceptual and local-level planning. In the section below we will further elaborate this distinction between different types of planning.

---

[2]For fuller discussion, see, for example, Garrett (1982, pp. 28–36), Levelt (1989) and Garman (1990, pp. 372–376).

## *2.4 Types of Planning*

The previous discussion has already briefly introduced the notion of planning. A simple definition of planning centres on the idea of the speaker retrieving items from his/her relevant linguistic system in line with the intended communicative goal. Discussing planning within a broad model of language production, Faerch and Kasper (1983), for example, state that:

> In the planning phase, the language user selects rules and items which he considers most appropriate for establishing a plan, the execution of which will lead to verbal behaviour which is expected to satisfy the original goal (1983, p. 25)[3]

In such a representation, the notion of a plan is introduced as the outcome of the planning phase, but is only vaguely characterised. In their discussion, Faerch and Kasper (1983, p. 23), move from talking of the development of 'a plan', to describing 'hierarchically ordered level*s* of plan*s*' [my italics] consisting of discourse plans, sentence plans, constituent plans, and articulatory programme. What is more, it is suggested that the plan, as the output of planning, controls the execution phase (Faerch & Kasper, 1983, p. 24), but it is not clear at what point between planning and executing specific formulation of the message takes place. In other words, in this, as in many discussions of planning, it is not clear where the boundary lies between planning and translating or message formulation.

This problem is addressed in Levelt's (1989) well-known model of language production. In this model, the planning (or conceptualisation) component comprises two distinct phases: macroplanning, which consists of 'the speaker's elaboration of a communicative intention by selecting the information whose expression may realize the communicative goals' (p. 3), and microplanning, that is, the assignment of 'an informational perspective for an utterance' (p. 3). The output of these two stages of planning, the preverbal message, is then fed into the formulating component, which 'translates a conceptual structure into a linguistic structure' (p. 11) through grammatical and phonological encoding processes.

The establishment in this model of the planning component, the conceptualizer, as distinct from the formulator and articulator, thus allows for a clearer characterisation of the planning process. Questions continue to be raised, however (see, e.g. Garrett, 1990, pp. 280–281) concerning the separability of message and sentence formulation, and by extension concerning the organisation of the language production model into these distinct preverbal message and verbal formulator components.

## *2.5 The Location of Pauses*

Brief consideration of the research reported above (Beattie, 1983; Butterworth, 1980; Goldman-Eisler, 1968; Henderson, Goldman-Eisler, & Skarbek, 1966; and so on), may

[3]Kellogg (1994) presents a similar definition with reference to planning in writing. He describes the planning phase as concerned with 'creating and organizing ideas and setting goals to achieve [during composition], such as choosing an appropriate tone for a given audience' (p. 27). Section 3.2 will consider planning in writing in greater detail.

have suggested tendencies for pauses related to macroplanning and microplanning to be associated with specific locations in the message string. Attempts to explore such associations, however, reveal a more complex reality, with different types of planning tending to co-occur at particular locations. In this section we shall attempt to explore some of the significant research that will inform the exploration of pause location in our study.[4]

The location of non-fluencies may be characterised in terms of correspondence with the structural composition of the message, be it grammatical or phonological. Of particular relevance to our study of pausing is the correspondence between pause location and grammatical structure. A general claim which is widely reported is that non-fluencies commonly occur at clause and sentence boundaries. Goldman-Eisler (1972), for example, found that the longest pauses appeared between sentences or before coordinated clauses, and the shortest within clauses. This finding would appear to associate long pausing with points of macroplanning.

Beyond that, however, it is also likely that some microplanning occurs at these major boundary points. Major constituent (clause) boundaries may function as 'frame-joints' (Garrett, 1982), and pauses associated with local syntactic selections for these specific frames may cluster at these locations (Garman, 1990, p. 376). Constituents within the clause, however, also attract pauses. A study of impressionistic non-fluency locations in spontaneous speech (Garman, 1990, pp. 120–124) suggests that certain clause-internal locations (e.g., following an utterance initial connective, and before an adverbial constituent) are more susceptible to non-fluencies than others. Other positions, too, within the subject noun phrase attract pausing. Garman discusses this with reference to lexical selection: 'Filling a frame, word by word, yields pauses that tend to gather at prelexical points' (1990, p. 376). Such a finding echoes the claim of Maclay and Osgood (1959) that pauses appear more before content words than function words.

Closer investigation not only of pause location but also of pause duration should provide more insight into the relationship between non-fluency (or, more simply, pausing) and grammatical structure. Several studies (e.g., Gee & Grosjean, 1983; Grosjean & Deschamps, 1975; Grosjean, Grosjean, & Lane, 1979) are concerned with characterising 'performance structures', or hierarchical sentence structures, obtained from pausing during reading aloud and from parsing sentences. In particular, such studies investigate the potential (non-)correspondence between 'clusterings of words imposed by the pause durations' and 'formally motivated clusterings (phrase markers)' (Grosjean et al., 1979).

In this research, groupings of elements into hierarchical structures are determined on the basis of pause length: the smaller the pause length between constituents (represented numerically as a percentage of the total pause duration in the sentence), the 'tighter' the connection between constituents to form a group. By way of example, let us consider the following sentence (Example 1) from Gee and Grosjean (1983, p. 422):

(1) John **10** asked **17** the **3** strange **8** young **5** man **25** to **5** be **3** quick **19** on **5** the **0** task

[4]The categories of pause location used in our study are described in Section 4.

The inserted pause values show, for example, that the elements *the* and *task*, *the* and *strange*, *be* and *quick* form tight clusters, but that *quick* and *on* or *asked* and *the* do not. On the basis of such pause data, then, comparisons may be made between the structures obtained through reading aloud and through parsing and the grammatical structures. In general, similar structures are found from data from both sources, suggesting that performance structures of sentences are not task specific. On the relation between these performance structures and syntactic structure, however, a number of interesting mismatches occur, which may be associated with the need to balance the weight of constituents within the performance structures. In the sentence above, for example, the sentence falls into two main sections, John asked the strange young man and to be quick on the task. Also, contrary to the expectations on the basis of grammatical structure, the noun phrase the strange young man forms two clusters, the strange and young man. In many cases, this need to balance constituent length gives rise to cases such as the displacement of a pause between subject noun phrase and verb to another position (e.g., before or within the noun phrase object). The conclusion from this seems to be, therefore, that performance structures from this type of data are determined by the dual demands on the speaker 'to respect the linguistic structure of the sentence and the need to balance the length of the constituents in the output' (Grosjean et al., 1979, p. 75). We should note, however, an important caveat with respect to the data sources on which observations are made in this research. In focusing on the oral reading of written sentences, rather than on spontaneous speech samples (as in Goldman-Eisler, 1972;[5] Hawkins, 1971), the researchers are not concerned with planning pauses but rather with the rhythmical chunks of production.

Our discussion of pause location so far has focused on its relation to grammatical structure, since this will be the starting point for the analysis of pause location in our written data. Other alternative approaches, which consider the correspondence between units of production and prosodic structure,[6] would need to be addressed, of course, in an examination of spoken language processing. From the point of view of our own study, however, such approaches are not considered of central relevance. We do note, however, the arguments put forward by Chafe (1988) for the existence of 'covert prosody' in written text. Drawing on analyses of the pausing and prosody of readers when reading aloud or repunctuating a text, Chafe notes similarities and discrepancies between the intonation, accent and hesitations assigned to the text by the reader (based on the intonation unit[7] in speech) and the original punctuation units marked in the text. Such a study, he suggests, reveals the covert prosody of written text, which is only partly supported or reflected in the overt

[5]Note, however, that the speech sample has been criticised as biased towards highly skilled 'academic' speech (de Beaugrande, 1984, p. 160).

[6]The description of such units in speech has been extensively reported elsewhere (see, e.g., Boomer, 1965; Brown & Yule, 1983; Halliday, 1967).

[7]Chafe's 'intonation unit' is related to flow of information, with each unit typically verbalising a single new item of information. Hesitations in speech production are described as 'perchings' or brief resting places associated with the activity of bringing information into consciousness. In other words, the occurrence of many hesitations (or non-fluencies), may be attributable to the speaker's activity in finding the next focus: in 'deciding what to talk about next' and also in 'deciding how to talk about what they have chosen' (1980a, p. 171).

markings of punctuation. Whether or not such prosodic units may be uncovered in written text, however, it is clear that the function of pauses in reading aloud is not identical to that of pausing for planning in spontaneous speech. As in the case of the studies of performance structures arrived at through parsing and reading aloud tasks, therefore, we should be cautious in interpreting these findings. They may reveal interesting insights into the rhythms of reading, but may not help us in accounting for the occurrence of pausing in spontaneous language production. It is this issue which our study of written text production will address.

To sum up so far, the discussion above has presented an overview of a number of general theoretical themes underlying keystroke research. First, we have outlined the notion of temporal variables in speech production, which have been the subject of substantial research interest in a number of different contexts. Of these variables, pause phenomena appear to offer particularly interesting insights into planning, which occurs at different levels. Interest in identifying the location of pausing has led us to explore the match between pause occurrence and structural (grammatical) junctures. Throughout this discussion we have been aware of the variety of data sources used in pause studies (spontaneous production, rehearsed speech, oral reading, tasks of varying cognitive demand, and so on) and we note also the wide inter-subject variability, both within and between languages (Griffiths, 1991).[8]

Against this general background of pausological research, we will turn now to the application of such an area of interest to the study of written rather than spoken language production. In the next section we will seek to establish the relevance of this research orientation in the study of the real-time processing of written language, before focusing on the nature of planning within process models of composing as a framework for interpreting temporal aspects of production.

## 3 The Pausological Study of Writing

### *3.1 Pausing in Written Language*

The previous section has presented and argued the importance of the study of temporal variables in spoken language production. With respect to written language production, however, the real-time study of production processes from a temporal perspective has received much less research attention. This perhaps reflects a more general under-representation of written language concerns in psycholinguistic studies. As Bonin and Fayol (1996) point out, ‘writing production has traditionally been a stepchild of psycholinguistics, while substantial studies have dealt with oral production’ (p. 145). We will argue here, however, that the investigation of the real-time activity of writing from the point of view of temporal aspects of production offers a fruitful line of research. In so doing, we pick up on the suggestion made more than a decade earlier by de Beaugrande (1984) that such an approach may

[8]See, for example, collections of cross-linguistic studies in Dechert and Raupach (1980a, 1980b) and the discussion in Griffiths (1991). For examples of recent studies on non-fluency in nonnative speakers see Johnson and Chambers (1997), Lennon (1990), Moore (1997), Riggenbach (1991), and Van Gelderen (1994).

throw light on 'the complex correlations between the real time of writing and such mental events as phrasing, memory search, decision, feedback, conceptual integration, updating, and so forth' (p. 168).

It is, of course, obvious that the functional and situational characteristics of typical written language production differ from those of speech in ways, which are highly relevant to the study of real-time production processes. In particular, with the reader spatially and temporally distanced from the writer and the activity of writing, neither the producer nor the receiver is under the same pressures to handle the processing load under conditions of immediacy. Similarly, there are not the same reciprocity demands on the producer to adjust the message to the feedback signals of the receiver (i.e., through online elaboration, expansions, clarifications, and so on), as in spontaneous, interactive speech.

The writer may not be operating under the same processing conditions as the speaker, but he or she is still involved in managing the pressures of producing text, of moving from communicative intention to production in real time, however. As process models of written text production typically portray, there are three main subcomponent processes, planning, formulating or text generating and reviewing or text interpreting, which the writer will move between in a non-linear, cyclical manner (Flower & Hayes, 1980). In other words, planning will not only occur before composing begins, but will also occur throughout the writing episode, as the writer responds both to the text produced so far and to considerations of the communicative goal in the light of audience, purpose and topic, and so on. In such cognitive process models, therefore, planning is of central importance.

In the investigation of planning, the occurrence of pausing is important since it offers insights into the allocation of attentional resources in the writer during composition (see, e.g. Kellogg, 1994 and Torrance & Jeffery, 1999). In other words, the processes of writing may be tracked through measures of time spent processing and cognitive effort expended, in a way that reveals important information concerning the distribution and sequencing of these underlying processes. One approach to the tracking of writing processes is through the analysis of pauses, that is, of time spent not producing or reviewing text. As 'observable clues to the covert cognition processes, which contribute to discourse production' (Matsuhashi, 1981, p. 114), pauses therefore offer a potentially valuable source of information about otherwise hidden processes. In a more recent comment, Chanquoy, Foulin, and Fayol (1996) neatly summarise the claim that 'the duration and frequency variation of pauses may indicate modulations of the cognitive cost required by the operations in the production' (p. 36).

The association between pausing and planning must be carefully handled, however. Pauses offer only indirect evidence of underlying cognitive processes and their function must be interpreted or inferred. Pauses may be associated with activities or processes other than forward planning. For example, 'look back' (de Beaugrande, 1984, p. 161), or reading previously produced text, may also occur during periods of pausing. This raises the problematic issue of the distinction between processes such as planning, formulating and revising: is it possible to delimit the boundaries between forward and backward-looking planning, which may both be concerned with goal-setting and idea generation? We return to the definition of the planning process in writing (Section 3.2 below). In addition to planning-related processes, time-off writing may also be explained in terms of a range of activities unrelated to the task at hand, such as responding to distractions or interruptions, or daydreaming. The indirect nature of the evidence offered by pauses into planning processes is thus underscored, but the potential significance and importance of these overt, measurable features acknowledged. In the following section we explore in more detail the definition of planning in writing in the light of recent discussions in the literature.

### *3.2 Planning in Writing*

As the substantial literature on models of composing suggests, planning plays a prominent role in accounts of writing processes. Planning appears to take up a considerable proportion of composing time,[9] and seems to be of importance in distinguishing between the behaviours of good and poor writers (Bereiter & Scardamalia, 1987). Both the nature of planning and the relationship between planning and success in writing have been reported on extensively in the past two decades (for reviews of types of plans see Flower, 1989; Flower & Hayes, 1984; for discussion of the relation to quality of texts produced, see Bereiter & Scardamalia, 1987; Kellogg, 1987, 1988, 1990; Piolat, 1999; Torrance, 1996; Torrance & Jeffery, 1999; Torrance, Thomas, & Robinson, 1994).

A simple definition of planning, is offered by Hayes-Roth and Hayes-Roth (1979) as 'the predetermination of a course of action aimed at achieving a goal' (pp. 275–276). As a type of 'preparatory reflection' (Hayes & Nash, 1996, p. 29), planning involves reflection on both the means of achieving the goal and the goal itself. The outcome of this process, the plan, is 'a set of suggestions for how the task should be accomplished in the action space' (p. 32). In writing, planning does not necessarily precede action, as it does in other types of planning situations (e.g., planning an event such as a wedding occurs exclusively before the event itself). Rather, planning and action are often interleaved (see, e.g. the study by Lansman, Smith, & Weber, 1990 of the planning behaviour of 18 adult writers using a computer, in which the majority of subjects were found to interleave planning with writing). Explanations for this are to do with the need to overcome memory limitations (i.e., the difficulty in remembering long plans) and the need for on-going checking of how the plan is working out (Hayes & Nash, 1996).

Different types or categories of planning are proposed to account for the range of plans writers make. The Flower and Hayes' (1980) model establishes the function of planning as taking 'information from the task environment and from long-term memory and to use it to set goals and to establish a writing plan to guide the production of a text that will meet those goals' (p. 12). This process consists of generating (retrieving information from long-term memory, organising (selecting the most useful retrieved information and organising this into a writing plan), and goal-setting (establishing criteria for later evaluation processes).

Flower and Hayes (1980, pp. 44–46) propose three major kinds of plans that writers generate: plans to do, plans to say and composing plans. The first type, plan to do, is rhetorical, or non-content, since it is concerned with responding to a rhetorical problem by addressing goals and communicative purpose. A plan to say, 'a simplified or abstract version of the information you want to convey' (p. 45), is a plan of content, and may consist

[9]Gould (1980, p. 112) reports that planning takes up on average two-thirds of composition time regardless of composition method and writer's experience with the method.

of a variety of forms such as notes or sentence outlines. Composing plans are procedural, focussing on the strategies required to produce the text.

In a revised taxonomy, Hayes and Nash (1996) present a new categorisation of planning, which in some ways bears strong resemblance to that of Flower and Hayes (1980). Similar to the category of composing plan, process planning refers to the writer's planning of how the task itself is to be addressed, for example through thoughts such as 'I'm going to write this tomorrow', 'First, I'll read the text through, then I'll edit it' (Hayes & Nash, 1996, p. 43). Process planning is distinct from text planning, which is concerned with 'what the planned text will be like' (p. 43). Text planning is further subdivided into conceptual, abstract planning, and language planning, which details specific language for the task. The first of these categories, abstract planning, in general terms corresponds to Flower and Hayes' (1980) categories of planning to do and planning to say.

The inclusion by Hayes and Nash (1996) of language planning within their categories of planning reveals an important difference between their taxonomy and that of Flower and Hayes in terms of the boundaries between components of the writing process. For Hayes and Nash, language planning consists of the specification of language for direct use in the text, whereas in the 1980 model this appears to be part of the translating process. Hayes and Nash (1996) themselves recognise the difficulties associated with these unclear boundaries: 'The connection between language planning and text production often appears to be so close that one might question whether or not a valid distinction can be made between them' (p. 43).

A further feature of Hayes and Nash's (1996) taxonomy is the definition of the category of abstract planning to include both non-content and content planning. Whereas Flower and Hayes (1980) suggest that only planning to do addresses the rhetorical problem space (with planning to say involving the creation of an abstract version of that information), Hayes and Nash argue that both non-content and content choices are determined by considerations of rhetoric. In other words, for Hayes and Nash, both content planning and non-content planning are abstract and conceptual. The output of both requires considerable expansion into finished text, whereas the component of language planning leads directly to text.

Table 1 below summarises the main labels presented in this discussion of the two influential taxonomies of Flower and Hayes (1980) and Hayes and Nash (1996). Other researchers such as Bereiter and Scardamalia (1987) make different distinctions between types of planning, in particular with regard to the distinction between conceptual planning and content generation, and the boundaries between planning and text production. For our purposes here, however, we limit our summary to the major categories discussed above, and then propose to relate these terms to the labels frequently used in the broader psycholinguistics literature (Section 2.4 above), namely microplanning and macroplanning. For reasons of consistency we may also wish to add a further label, metaplanning, to refer to procedural planning concerned with the process of composing. Although the taxonomies necessarily differ in their definitions, we also add a fourth column to indicate very generally the main focus of each type of planning.

The summary table (Table 1) suggests a correspondence at a general level between the components of the conceptualiser (Levelt, 1989) that is, macro- and microplanning components, and the categories of abstract planning specified by Hayes and Nash (1996). The output of these conceptualiser processes is a preverbal message, which is then fed into the

Table 1: Summary of major planning categories.

| Focus | Hayes and Nash (1996) | Flower and Hayes (1980) | Alternative terms (following Beattie, 1983; Butterworth, 1980; Kellogg, 1994; Levelt, 1989; etc.) |
|---|---|---|---|
| Procedure | Process planning | Planning to compose | Metaplanning |
| Abstract/ rhetorical/ conceptual | Non-content planning | Planning to do | Macroplanning |
| Abstract/ conceptual/ (rhetorical) | Content planning | Planning to say | Microplanning |
| Language | Language planning | [Translating] | [Formulating] |

formulator for grammatical and phonological encoding. The extent to which a clear distinction may be made between microplanning and formulating reflects similar earlier comments by Hayes and Nash concerning the boundaries between language planning and text production.

One final issue which is addressed by Hayes (1996) concerns the definition of the scope of planning. Hayes's reworking of the 1980 cognitive model of writing replaces the term planning with a broader concept, that of reflection. This suggests that planning, as an aspect of problem-solving, is but one of a number of reflective processes, including decision-making and inferencing. The broadening of this notion brings together a number of similar and related processes under one label, and acknowledges more explicitly the potential interrelatedness of aspects of idea generating and evaluative, interpretive processes. This goes some way to addressing concerns voiced earlier (Section 3.1 above concerning 'look-back') that the component processes of planning, formulating and revising are less than adequately defined and differentiated in the Flower and Hayes (1980) model.

This overview of categories of planning provides a framework within which to interpret the pausological data elicited in keystroke research. In giving specific attention to planning and text production processes, such research responds to the need to consider planning processes in relation to the textual output, in other words, to address 'the critical juncture between planning and translating' (Witte & Cherry, 1986, p. 127). One significant issue for investigation in this domain is the way in which the writer frames material for his/her reader (Bracewell, Frederiksen, & Frederiksen, 1982; Flower & Hayes, 1981; Witte & Cherry, 1986). Flower and Hayes talk of the writer's strategies to 'find a focus' in terms of selection and sequencing of topics both at the sentence and discourse level. Witte and Cherry report on an exploratory attempt to identify such strategies of topic selection and focus on the basis of data from think aloud protocols. Through the investigation of framing decisions (to do with topicalisation) they claim they are able to clarify

> how writers conceptualize a rhetorical situation — including the rhetorical problem — develop frames consistent with the conceptualization, and make framing decisions at both the level of the sentence and the level of connected discourse. (p. 144).

The investigation of the planning and text production processes of writers with specific reference to framing decisions appears, therefore, an interesting focus for on-line writing research.

The approach to the real-time study of writing processes we are concerned with in this book is keystroke logging. In the section below we will briefly position this research against a range of alternative approaches to the study of composing, in an attempt to highlight features of this research tool.

### *3.3 Early Research on Pausing in Writing*

Although our discussion so far has focussed attention on pausing as evidence, albeit indirect, of cognitive processes of writing, this is not the sole data source that may be used. Studies of cognitive processes have drawn on a variety of sources of information, both direct and indirect (elicited directly from the writer him/herself or arrived at through observation or analysis by a researcher other than the writer), and elicited in real-time (online) or outside the time frame of the composing activity (off-line). Table 2 presents a summary of these different research methods adapted from Sanders, Janssen, Van der Pool, Schilperoord, and Van Wijk (1996, p. 474) and Jansen, Van Waes, and Van den Bergh (1996, p. 234).

Until attention shifted in recent years to the study of online activity of writing, the product of writing, the text, was the main focus of research activity.[10] Over the past two decades, however, with the development of interest in process studies, online methodologies have been developed as a means of opening a window on the cognitive processes of real-time text production. The methodology most favoured by researchers has been think aloud verbalisation, which involves the writer producing verbal commentary on his/her thoughts and actions as the task is being performed. As a direct, subject-generated elicitation tool, verbalisation has received much attention in the literature, and its strengths and weaknesses, including that of reactivity, have been well rehearsed (for discussion, see Spelman Miller, 1999, 2000a).

As an alternative to verbalisation, the recording of pauses offers a means of eliciting data online without involving the writer in producing speech while writing. The data elicited, however, provide only indirect evidence of underlying cognitive processes: the functions of pauses need to be inferred and interpreted by the analyst. Although such an analytical approach is well established in the study of spoken language production (see Sections 2.1–2.3, and 2.5), its application to written language is less widely discussed.

---

[10]For a comprehensive review of approaches to textlinguistic research, see Grabe and Kaplan (1996, pp. 36–59).

Table 2: Methods of researching composing (adapted from Janssen et al., 1996; Sanders et al., 1996).

| | **Direct observation** | **Indirect observation** |
|---|---|---|
| On-line (synchronous data collection) | Concurrent think-aloud | Pause analysis |
| Off-line (asynchronous data collection) | Retrospective interview | Text analysis |

However, a seminal pausological study of writing conducted by Matsuhashi (1981) is important in setting the scene for much of the later development of interest in the field. In her 1981 study, Matsuhashi uses video-recorded observation of the writing event, to elicit a real-time record of the temporal progression of the text, providing data concerning the flow of production and breaks in this flow as text alterations are made. This provides a combination of 'a detailed description of written discourse with an observational measure of the writing process — pause time' (p. 114). Pauses, or 'moments of physical inactivity during writing' (p. 114), are visible traces of non-writing activity during production, and as such offer measurable clues to the covert cognitive processes, in particular, planning activity, underlying discourse production.

Matsuhashi's (1981) study focuses on the writing behaviour of a small number of skilled first language writers of English ($n = 4$) who are New York high school students. The aim of the research is to investigate how the writers plan during the production of a number of tasks that differ in discourse purpose (reporting, persuading, generalising essays). In order to explore the potential influences on planning and decision-making of these different discourse demands, Matsuhashi sets about to measure the duration of pausing at specific locations within the linguistic string. Her assumption is that pause-time (associated with planning and decision-making) will vary according to the demands of the task set.

Location of pauses is specified in terms of position prior to a number of language units that correspond either to T-unit[11] boundaries, or to constituent or item boundaries within a T-unit. Location, therefore, is seen primarily in terms of the clausal or supra-clausal unit of the T-unit, and the language unit then interpreted in terms of a number of discourse, propositional and lexical categories. For example, a T-unit at which pausing occurs may be described in terms of its relation to other T-units (superordinate, subordinate, coordinate), its sentence role, its position at the opening of a paragraph or not, and whether or not it opens with an initial modifying structure (a constituent left of the subject noun phrase). Within the T-unit, items attracting pauses may be described in terms of certain features of lexical cohesion, whether or not these items are content words, and whether or not they coincide with certain constituent boundaries.

A number of implications may be drawn from this study for further research, both in terms of the general orientation of the work and the specific methods and categories of analysis. First, the general results reveal interesting effects of discourse type on pause

[11]T-unit (Hunt, 1965) is defined as a single independent clause plus any subordinate clauses attached to it or embedded in it.

length. It appears that mean pause time is shortest in the production of reporting (rather than persuading or generalising) discourse, and at the level of T-unit type, the longest pauses occur prior to generalising superordinate T-units. This suggests that the step-by-step organisation of content of reporting essays, in contrast to the other more matrix-like organisational demands of the generalising and persuading essays, has an effect on the thinking and writing processes of the writers. This difference is reflected in planning processes, with more abstract units of discourse requiring more planning time.

Second, with respect to pause duration and location in general, the paragraph is seen as a particularly important locus of planning and decision-making. For all discourse types, pauses before paragraph openings are longer than before non-paragraph openings. Pause length is also much greater between rather than within T-units, suggesting that T-unit boundary pauses reflect the decision-making that occurs before the sentence begins. Planning may not be complete in advance of a given T-unit or sentence, however, and within a given structural, propositional or information unit, specific item choices may lead to particularly long pauses at certain locations. Although statistically significant findings were not achieved with respect to pause duration within T-units, possibly owing to the overly broad categorisation of the syntactic units within the T-unit, informal analyses reveal a number of interesting issues. For example, relatively long pauses occasionally occur after the first (function) word in a clause or phrase, suggesting that although the structure for the clause or phrase has been decided on, specific semantic and lexical planning of the unit may not be complete before writing begins. This seems to be the case particularly in generalising texts. Other findings concerning longer pauses prior to certain content words suggest additional time for specific propositional and lexical search, and also prior to new subjects as opposed to lexically cohesive (same-word) items.

In sum, Matsuhashi's study offers a useful starting point for the analysis of pausing, with specific reference to the effect on planning of different discourse types. From this, several key issues emerge, which need to be addressed in further research. In particular, we focus on (1) the specification of pause location below the level of the T-unit, and (2) the interpretation of pausing for planning.

**3.3.1 Specification of pause location below the level of the T-unit** Matsuhashi herself indicates the potential inadequacies of her analytical categories below the level of the T-unit (1981, p. 127). The refinement of such a categorisation would therefore appear useful. For example, we note the case of the category referred to as the initial modifying structure ('any constituent to the left of the subject noun phrase of the main clause' (p. 121)). This category, which encompasses a wide range of structures including single words, phrases, and clauses, could be unpacked in a way which differentiates, for example, pre-modifying clausal structures, from conjuncts and disjuncts.

Matushashi's treatment of content words may also be reconsidered. In the following example from the study (1981, p. 128), 'the day before school started was nervous wreck day for me', a lengthy pause of 14.6 s is noted between *started* and *was*. In Matsuhashi's analysis, this function of this lengthy pause is interpreted either as reflecting extra planning time needed to make decisions concerning the propositional or lexical content of the following predicate, or as serving to 'reconnect' with the subject (*the day*) which has become separated from the verb by the additional constituent (*before school started*). An alternative, potentially neater, way of viewing this case, however, might be to propose the notion of a location related to the thematic structure of the sentence. In other words, the extended pause after *the day before school started* may be seen to occur at a location which is discoursally significant, following the establishment of the subject theme of the sentence that serves to frame the rest of the sentence. Pause location, then, may be viewed in terms other than strictly syntactic ones, related to the discourse perspective of the message.

A further issue, which may be considered, is the development of additional categories of pause location to account for potentially significant pauses occurring, for example, within words or at other locations such as at page breaks. In brief, a broader and more comprehensive range of locations may be devised in future analyses of pause location.

**3.3.2 Interpretation of pausing for planning** The interpretation of pauses for planning has already been highlighted as a problematic issue, and the ambiguity of possible functions of pauses is mentioned by Matsuhashi as an area of concern for her study: '[planning for paragraphs] provides the writer time to review what has already been written as well as time to plan ahead for the next section of the text' (1981, p. 130). To some extent the redefinition of planning in Hayes's (1996) paper has addressed the difficulties in distinguishing planning and reviewing processes: by introducing a broader umbrella term, reflection, planning as problem solving is seen as closely related to notions of evaluative decision-making and inferencing. Revision is also remodelled as a composite of text interpretation, reflection and text production (p. 15). Sensitivity to the range of functions of pausing, therefore, remains important in future analyses.

A further issue arises in the interpretation of the level at which planning is occurring. Since pause location is characterised in terms of position prior to a unit of language, it is difficult to interpret the level or levels at which planning may be occurring. In other words, if we take the example of a pause at a T-unit boundary, it is of course possible that planning is occurring simultaneously at the level of discourse, proposition, information focus, grammatical and lexical selection. By defining location in terms of position prior to a certain unit there is also the danger of associating pausing with forward planning only rather than look back. One suggestion for future analysis might therefore be to consider pause location more sensitively in terms of position between units rather than simply prior to them.

**3.3.3 Summary** In conclusion, then, Matsuhashi's (1981) paper provides an important basis for the study of pauses as observational measures of writing behaviour. Subsequent applications of observational pause analysis to the investigation of revision processes are reported in Matsuhashi (1982, 1987) and Matsuhashi and Gordon (1985), and the procedural framework for observation has informed the development of computer-based observational tools (Severinson Eklundh & Kollberg, 1992, 1996b; Strömqvist & Ahlsén, 1999; Van Waes, 1991, 1992; and so on) to be outlined below. Matsuhashi's work sits alongside other complementary work on temporal aspects of writing during the same period of the late 1970s and early 1980s. Prominent in this field is Gould (1978, 1980) who reports on findings from video observation concerning the proportion of time spent planning during composition in a number of different conditions (producing a range of letter types and messages by hand, dictation and typing on a word processor).

### *3.4 Other Studies of Pause Location*

Other interesting work since the 1980s has continued to use video observation of the writing process to elicit pausological data. Of particular relevance to our interests in developing locational categories, Chanquoy et al.'s (1990, 1996) work describes the pause behaviour of 10 university students using five categories of pause location: paragraph, sentence, clause, phrase and word. On the basis of analyses comparing pause duration and location at these linguistic boundaries, they report a correlation between increased length of pause and higher syntactic units (paragraph, sentence and clause). Shortest pauses are associated with non-(sentence) initial locations, following such elements as complement, determiner, pronoun or preposition and preceding a noun or verb. This suggests, they claim, that 'the cost of the processing carried out for each level varied according to the position of the unit in the hierarchy of units' (1996, p. 42). Regression analyses, however, revealed that syntactic location of pauses explained only a small part of the variance. The high degree of individual variation between subjects needs to be taken into consideration.

Phinney and Khouri's (1993) study comparing the writing behaviour of four English as a second language subjects using both the word processor and pen and paper included, among other analyses, a discussion of temporal features, such as total time spent on the different activities of composing, revising/editing, and planning. They also investigated the mean frequency and length of pauses in the subjects' writing in terms of the following locations: before punctuation, before a sentence/clause boundary, before a paragraph, word internally, and at a word boundary. Their results confirm the general tendency for shorter pauses at word internal and word boundary locations, and longer pauses at the higher level units. Both frequency and length of pausing appeared to be influenced by the level of word processing experience of the writers and their English language proficiency. These factors will need to be addressed in the design of further study.

Other studies have addressed pause location from a syntactic perspective. Schilperoord (1996) collected data from professionals dictating letters and subjected them to pause analysis according to location within and between 'minimal constituents', between clauses, sentences and paragraphs. Although these data differ in that they were not produced during writing, the results point to a similar effect of location type on mean pause length: higher level locations such as paragraph and sentence generate a higher frequency of pauses and pauses of greater length mean pause durations from the corpus of 20 texts produced by the six subjects are shown in Table 3.

Similar to the findings of pausing in speech reviewed earlier, these results are explained as reflecting 'a "cascade"-like hierarchical structure of the internal organization of plans and knowledge representations' (Schilperoord, 1996, p. 31). They also fit within the view of writing as a goal-directed process (Flower & Hayes, 1981): pauses reflect processes of 'activating conceptual and linguistic knowledge in order to accomplish particular goals' (Schilperoord, 1996, p. 32). At the top level activation of goals for paragraphs is associated with increased pause length and greater variability in duration, since the activation processes are less constrained by previously activated knowledge structures. Where more constraints are in place (at lower levels), pause duration will decrease as less cognitive effort is needed to activate a piece of knowledge (Schilperoord: *ibid.*). This work also points to the connection between processing and text-specific factors to do with content

Table 3: Schilperoord's (1996, p. 29) findings relating to pause duration by location form the corpus of twenty texts produced by the six subjects.

| **Locations** | **Mean pause durations (s) (and standard deviations)** |
|---|---|
| Paragraph | 8.272 (0.429) |
| Sentence | 2.611 (0.089) |
| Clause | 0.763 (0.053) |
| Constituent | 0.312 (0.019) |
| Word | 0.245 (0.013) |

and structural complexity. In particular, the link is made between greater text variance at the level of paragraph planning and the demands of conceptual, macroplanning activity.

Results from both studies lead to important conclusions (Sanders et al., 1996, p. 490). As anticipated, pause time is 'not randomly distributed across location types', but affected by hierarchical structure. In particular, the longest pauses are associated with transitions between main (topic) lines, where most cognitive effort is required, and the shortest pauses with locations within the segment.

### *3.5 Keystroke Studies and the Investigation of Pauses*

The availability of keystroke recording as a tool for the collection of pausological data has, of course, opened up the possibility of close analysis of the distribution of pausing, that is, the location of non-fluency within the text string. Studies such as Warren's (1996) follow the earlier direction of Matsuhashi (1981, 1982, 1987) in defining pause location principally with reference to the T-unit. Her comparative study of L1 and L2 writers focuses on T-unit junctures often quite broadly defined around the occurrence of major punctuation marks. Results suggest some limited differences in the use of the T-unit juncture for longer pausing, with L2 writers marking these locations slightly more frequently. Interestingly, in the cases where L1 writers do not pause at T-unit boundaries there is often a run-on into the next sentence, with the next likely spot for pausing to occur being in post-theme or post copula position. Jansen et al's (1996) study of Dutch students using Keytrap (Van Waes, 1991) similarly investigates pause length at major syntactic locations: between paragraphs, between sentences and within sentences, and discovers that pauses within sentences are shortest and longest between paragraphs. In a second study reported in the same paper (1996) they modify the analysis to include locations within and between word groups. Again, the smallest pauses are associated with the smallest linguistic unit (locations within word groups). These findings echo those reported above.

Other researchers, such as Strömqvist, Ahlsén, Wengelin, Grönqvist, and Hagman (1999) using Scriptlog, offer a more extensive treatment of pause location in terms of a number of microcontexts defined by such features as location before and after punctuation marks ('major delimiters': the full stop, exclamation mark and question mark; and 'minor delimiters': the colon, comma and semi-colon) and before and after spaces. Wengelin (this volume) presents a comprehensive list of that has been used in the automatic analysis of pausing and flow of production in the writing of four groups of subjects in Sweden: dyslexics, deaf, aphasics and controls (see Wengelin [this volume] for details). The findings suggest different writing profiles for the different subjects concerned. For example, the dyslexic writers pause more frequently than the controls in the word internal location. Furthermore, although mean pause time is generally similar for both groups, pauses by dyslexic writers are longer in locations between sentences and before a punctuation mark, reflecting their slower, more effortful reading of the text produced so far at sentence boundaries. For different reasons, the aphasic writers also produce a greater number of pauses than controls, and their writing is characterised by slow production rate and longer pauses especially at low levels. The deaf writers appear to produce text at the same rate as the controls, and pause more at the start of a new sentence to plan the new string.

To conclude, both keystroke logging and video observation provide useful means of investigating the distribution of planning time at macro and micro levels. Issues identified above concerning problems with Matsuhashi's (1981) exploratory study of pausing still need to be addressed, however. Researchers have defined pause location with different degrees of specificity, but in general have depended on syntactic criteria or the surface appearance of character strings for their identification. The description of pause location in other terms remains a challenge to be addressed. The interpretation of the function of pausing for forward and backward-looking purposes also remains a concern, although most of the recent discussions refer only to pausing in terms of forward planning. Further investigations might seek to clarify, where possible, the likely function of pauses, for example through reference to later actions taken on the text.

## 4 Conclusion

In the introduction to a seminal collection of papers, Rijlaarsdam, Van den Bergh, and Couzijn (1996) point to current trends and future directions for writing process research. Of the 'central questions', which such research should address is the identification of general patterns of cognitive activities during writing by focusing on the temporal organisation of cognitive activities (1996, p. xviii). In this chapter I have argued, against the general background of interest in the temporal organisation of language production, and in particular of the association between pausing (or non-fluency) and planning processes, that the pausological study of writing through keystroke logging offers an important contribution to our understanding of language processing, and thus to the type of question raised in Rijlaarsdam's discussion. However, we have also demonstrated that there is scope for the refinement and elaboration of existing frameworks for the description of pausing, in particular in terms of the location of pausing behaviour, an issue which will be addressed in a later chapter (Spelman Miller, Chapter 8, this volume).

To conclude, the discussion of observational studies of pause behaviour in this chapter confirms the relevance of pausological research as a means of investigating cognitive planning processes in writing as well as in speech. Importantly, it also helps to identify priorities for a research agenda for keystroke logging research which underpins the chapters of this volume. Of key concern throughout is the need for further definition of pausing and revision, and the investigation of these behaviours from the perspective of individual variation depending on writer context and background.

Chapter 3

# Writing and the Analysis of Revision: An Overview

Eva Lindgren and Kirk P. H. Sullivan
*Umeå University, Umeå, Sweden*

*This chapter introduces the reader to the complexities of revision analysis and problematises the issues surrounding the development of revision taxonomies, 'online' revision analysis and the categorisation of online revisions. For the reader unfamiliar with the writing process, the chapter begins by overviewing the writing process. This introduction to the writing process provides the reader unfamiliar with writing and revision processes with a ground for understanding of the complexity of revision and the overview of revision presented in this chapter. After reading this chapter, the reader will have the necessary understanding of the writing and revision processes to follow the arguments relating to the development of an online revision taxonomy and online revision categorisation presented by Lindgren and Sullivan (this volume, Chapter 9).*

**Keywords:** writing process, revision process, online revision, revision types, revision analysis.

## 1 Introduction

Writing is a complex task. During composition, writers have to simultaneously consider what to write and how to express these ideas linguistically in a way that is appropriate for both the topic and the intended reader. In course of constructing text, writers constantly plan, review and formulate the developing discourse; these are processes that often leave traces as pauses and revisions in the output.

The writing process is not a static process. Each writing condition promotes writers to plan, review and formulate their texts differently; this difference is reflected in the way the writers use, among other things, pauses and revisions. Thus, although two writers' final texts composed under identical conditions may be similar in quality and structure, the

**Computer Key Stroke Logging and Writing: Methods and Applications**

**ISBN: 0-08-044934-4**

*Lindgren, E. & Sullivan, K. P. H. (2006). Writing and the analysis of revision: An overview In G. Rijlaarsdam (Series Ed.) and K. P. H. Sullivan, & E. Lindgren. (Vol. Eds.), Studies in Writing, Vol. 18, Computer Keystroke Logging: Methods and Applications (pp. 31–44). Oxford: Elsevier.*

processes behind the creation of each of these texts could have included significant differences in terms of pause and revision behaviour. One writer could have planned most of the text prior to starting transcription, while another writer could have started transcription at once and created the content while writing (see Galbraith, 1999; Kieft, Rijlaarsdam, & Van den Bergh (submitted) for in-depth discussions on differences in writer approach). The interactions between the processes of writing that leave traces as pauses and revisions have been shown to vary between writing situations depending on, among other things, the writing medium (Haas, 1989, 1996; Van Waes, 1992; Van Waes & Schellens, 2003) and the genre (Severinson Eklundh, 1994).

This chapter begins with an overview of the writing process before turning to focus on the revision process; factors that influence the writing and revision processes are outlined. Thereafter, the issues associated with the categorisation of revisions are discussed prior to a presentation of the particular issues associated with 'online' revision analysis.

## 2 The Writing Process

Several models of the writing process have been developed since the early 1980s (Bereiter & Scardamalia, 1987; Chenoweth & Hayes, 2001; Hayes, 1996; Hayes & Flower, 1980; Kellogg, 1996; Van Wijk, 1999). At a general level, all of these models can be viewed as positing that the writing process is composed of a component that plans the text under construction, a component that translates ideas from conceptual to linguistic form and a component that evaluates concepts and forms, and revises them if necessary. Writers use these components actively and in various combinations throughout writing to progressively create a text that meets their conception of topic, task and audience.

The interaction between planning, formulating, evaluating and revising results in a recursive process of change and learning as writers move around their compositions abandoning existing ideas and structures, creating new ideas and structures. In the course of writing, writers strive to present their intentions as accurately as possible in text. Yet, as it is not always an easy task to formulate and write down the intended content perfectly on the first attempt, several attempts and sets of changes might be necessary before a version is reached that is accepted by the writer. During this process of change, content may also alter as the transcribed output provides the writer with a new input that develops and redirects the original intentions of the writer. The way in which changes made during a text's creation lead to new intentions for the text led Flower and Hayes (1981) to describe the writing process as a learning experience in which writers learn about their texts and their goals during composition. More recently, Galbraith (1999) described content generation as a knowledge-constituting process in which content can be generated in different ways. In his description, Galbraith highlights how on-going learning triggered by writing plays an active role in promoting recursive change and in re-creating concept and form:

> It [content] can be retrieved from episodic memory or it can be synthesised in the course of translation. [...] content is produced as a consequence of a dialectic between the writer's implicit disposition and the emerging text. (p. 146)

Galbraith's (1999) description of the writing process posited how differences in writing approaches were functions of different cognitive behaviours because of writer's personality. The writing process is, as with all cognitive tasks, dependent upon and influenced by external factors such as writing language (primary, first, second, third, etc.), working memory capacity, fluency and 'situational variables' (Faigley & Witte, 1981, p. 410). These factors all interact and impact upon the revision process.

Writing language impacts upon the complexity of text generation. One's first language (L1) is no simple task. In a second language (L2), the process is complicated by the problem of finding the appropriate lexicon and syntax for the ideas L2 writers wish to express. Zimmermann (2000) called this process 'translating'. The translating process, like writing *per se*, is dependent on features such as the writer's cognitive capacity, the linguistic complexity of the text being written, the graphomotoric level (in hand writing) and the writer's typing skills (in computer writing).

Regardless of whether a writer is working in their L1 or L2, the more linguistically proficient the writer is, the more automatized the retrieval of the language needed for writing will be (Alamargot & Chanquoy, 2001). Once language and linguistic features have become automatized, they are stored in long-term memory. This reduces the likelihood that working memory will become overloaded, as the writer no longer has to use working memory with the features that have become automatized.

Similarly, the more proficient a writer becomes graphomotorically, or in typing, the more automatized the transcription process will become and more space will be available in working memory to store information about and elaborate upon the goals and the content of the text (Graham & Harris, 2000; Graham, Berninger, Abbot, Abbot, & Whitaker, 1997; McCutchen, 1996, 2000). As long as a writer has a low degree of automatization for language and linguistic features and for the motor activity of writing (pen-and-paper or typing skills), the likelihood of working memory overload is high, as the writer has to simultaneously actively consider motor activity, linguistic demands, the content and the goals of the composition.

One effect of automatization is fluency, which can be defined as a process that implies little conscious attention (Schmidt, 1992). Chenoweth and Hayes (2001), in their study of L1 and L2 writing, found that "... increased experience with a language was associated with increased fluency in writing that language" (p. 93) and that "... in less experienced writers, the writing process was frequently interrupted by revision" (p. 96). Their more experienced writers were more fluent and revised less than the less-experienced writers. Thus, a lack of fluency can result in lexical search and repairs of surface errors, which constantly interrupt the process of constructing meaning in the written text. In an L1, the automatization process is likely to be more fully developed and the language more fluent than in an L2. This results in fewer interruptions in the writing process. Writers' higher linguistic fluency in their L1s leaves more space in working memory to focus revision on meaning than during writing in an L2, where writers are likely to focus more on the form of their texts (see Chenoweth & Hayes, 2001; Kellogg, 1996; Van Gelderen & Oostdam, 2002). However, it is important to distinguish, as Van Gelderen and Oostdam pointed out, between writing quickly and accessing linguistic knowledge at a fast rate. Writing quickly is not, by itself, an indication of fluency.

Comparing the writing processes of young and inexperienced, experienced, L1 and L2 writers, the factors that have been considered thus far, Zimmermann's translating factor and the concepts of automatization and fluency, provide possible explanations for a range of writing and revision characteristics. These include findings which show that L2 writers revise more frequently than L1 writers (Silva, 1993; Thorson, 2000), that L2 writers show a similar surface level focus to that of young and inexperienced writers (Bereiter & Scardamalia, 1987; Flower & Hayes, 1981; Matsuhashi, 1987) and that L2 writers restrict their attention to the linguistic demands of writing more frequently than L1 writers (Broekkamp & Van den Bergh, 1996; Chenoweth & Hayes, 2001). The factor working memory overload has been posited by McCutchen (1996, 2000) as an explanation for why young and L2 writers tend to revise more on a form (or surface) level than experienced writers with greater experience.

However, as mentioned earlier, situational variables (Faigley & Witte, 1981, p. 410), as well as the constraints of writing language, working memory capacity and fluency, are factors that influence the writing process. These situational variables also have to be considered and integrated into a model that can account for differences in writing and revision behaviour, both within and between writers. Situational variables include factors such as writer motivation, the reason for writing, the writing medium, knowledge of writing task, genre and audience and time on task. The impact of situational variable of task has been shown by Lindgren (2004) and Van Waes and Schellens (2003) to often result in different revision patterns. Similarly, it has been shown (Galbraith, 1999; Van Waes, 1992; Van Waes & Schellens, 2003) that different writers employ different revision strategies in similar writing tasks. The writing and revision processes, thus, vary within and between writers.

### *2.1 Between and within Writer Variation*

The way in which text is planned is one example of a process that is undertaken differently depending on the writer, the text type and the writing mode. The writer's personality is one factor that can affect the writing process; Galbraith (1999) distinguished between high and low self-monitors as representing different types of writers. High self-monitors are characterised by idea generation prior to text transcription. Low self-monitors, on the contrary, are characterised by generating fewer ideas prior to writing than the high self-monitors; these writers, instead, create the content of the text primarily during writing.

Different writing profiles that are not necessarily related to personality can also be distinguished. Examples of such writing profiles are 'sculptors' and 'engineers' (Kieft et al., submitted). The sculptor is similar to the low self-monitor and represents a writing profile in which the writing itself is used as a tool to create the text. The contrast is the engineer who is similar to the high self-monitor, characterised by advanced planning.

The sculptor and the engineer writers are likely to produce different pause and revision patterns. The sculptor corresponds with what Van Waes and Schellens (2003, p. 845) defined as 'Fragmentary stage 1 writers'. These writers devote little time to initial planning but produce many short pauses during writing and revise most while composing a first draft of their text. Engineers, on the other hand, are more similar to Van Waes and Schellens' (2003) 'initial planners', who produce long pauses primarily during the initial phase of the writing, pause above average and make few revisions.

In their study of the effect of writing mode on writing profiles, Van Waes and Schellens (2003) defined five writing profiles and identified several significant differences between pen-and-paper writing and computer-based writing (see also Haas, 1989, 1996; Van Waes, 1992). Writers used pauses and revisions as well as recursiveness differently in the two writing modes. On the whole, pauses were longer in the pen-and-paper mode yet more frequent in the computer mode. Writers were also inclined to revise and pause throughout their writing when using the computer, while pen-and-paper-based writing was characterised by longer initial planning and substantial revision at the end of the composition period.

Van Waes and Schellens (2003) also found that 17 of their 19 writers adjusted their writing strategies to the writing mode. The preferred writing style in the pen-and-paper mode was characterised by initial planning together with substantial revision after a first draft was completed. In the computer mode the preferred writing style was more fragmentary; most revisions were undertaken during the creation of the first draft of the text. Further, the pauses made by the writers were more frequent but not as long as in the pen-and-paper mode.

The process of formulating text took different shapes in the two writing modes. In the pen-and-paper mode the writers paused longer, but less frequently before formulating text than in the computer mode. When using the computer, the writers revised more on the level of form when they reformulated text or corrected spelling and grammar. This could be explained, as suggested by Van Waes and Schellens (2003), by the computer medium facilitating revision in a way that pen-and-paper writing does not:

> During the writing process, writers are aware of the fact that, at any moment during writing, they can alter their text without creating an illegible jumble of crossed out and inserted words. This means that writers can start typing a sentence without knowing how it will end. (p. 848)

It is, thus, likely that the formulation process, *per se*, is similar in the two writing modes but represented differently in terms of pauses and revisions in the output. The differences found between the modes concerning formulation pauses and revision of form could be due to the fact that in the pen-and-paper mode it is less 'costly' to try out a formulation before it is written down than edit it afterwards, whereas the computer, as pointed out by Kollberg (1998) encourages writers to try out formulations with their fingers, resulting in revision.

In order to study the differences in text development between and within writers in detail, revisions and pauses need to be studied in the context in which they occur. Keystroke logfiles provide accurate records that facilitate detailed analysis of how discourse is constructed online and in which textual contexts writers revise.

## 3 The Revision Process

As pointed out by Hayes (2004), early models of the revision process focused either on revision made to previously written text (see Hayes, Flower, Schriver, Stratman, & Carey, 1987) or on revision undertaken while text is being produced (i.e. Scardamalia & Bereiter, 1983). More recent models of revision (Chenoweth & Hayes, 2001; Van Gelderen & Oostdam, 2004) account both for revisions that occur in the course of writing and for revisions that occur in previously written text.

Noticing of items potentially in need of revision can be triggered by a wide range of features (Flower, Hayes, Carey, Schriver, & Stratman, 1986; Hayes et al., 1987). Through re-reading of previously written text or in the course of transcription, writers can notice problems, such as a formal spelling mistake or a mismatch between the written text produced thus far and the overall plans and goals for the text (Chenoweth & Hayes, 2001). Revision can also be triggered when writers discover new opportunities in their texts (Hayes, 2004). When thoughts are put into words, they provide the writer with a new input that may be a source for noticing a mismatch or a trigger for new ideas (Galbraith, 1999; Hayes, 2004).

When a writer has noticed a mismatch, a decision has to be made, first, whether to revise and second, where to locate the revision (Flower et al., 1986; Hayes et al., 1987). For example, if the noticed item is a grammatical mistake in the written text, the revision would be undertaken in the externalised text. However, if the noticed item is a mismatch between the written text and the mental representation of it, the writer has to decide whether to revise the plans and goals, the written text or both. When noticing is a result of the written text providing the writer with new input, new ideas are the outcomes of a mental revision process. In this case, the revision takes place in the mental representation of the text and can be followed by revision of the written text. Hence, the function of revision in writing can, in general terms, be described as improvement or verification of the external text or as improvement or verification of the internal representation of the text (Chanquoy, 2001; Faigley & Witte, 1981; Hayes et al., 1987; Rijlaarsdam, Couzijn, & Van den Bergh, 2004).

Improvement and verification of externalised text includes a wide range of revision types. Correction of surface elements, such as spelling or grammar, for example, is a common revision type as is meaning-related revision that concerns the content of the text (*cf.* 'surface and text-base changes' in Faigley & Witte, 1981 and 'surface and semantic revisions' in Chanquoy, 2001). Revision of externalised text also includes changes of a more pragmatic character, such as style and audience orientation.

Improvement and verification of the internalised text representation includes both revision of a conceptual character and revision of a formal character made to pre-text units. Revision of a conceptual character can be exemplified by revision of plans and ideas, and typically occurs in the planning phases of writing. Pre-text revisions are revisions of linguistic formulations that have not yet been externalised as written text.

Since there are several functions of revision, such as to correct mistakes in the written or pre-written text, to adjust a mismatch between the internal and external representations of the text and to assist in planning and formulating, revisions can occur at any point in the writing process (Flower et al., 1986) and can be viewed as a result of other cognitive activities. Re-reading and evaluating the previously written text can trigger the revision process when a mismatch is detected (Hayes, 2004; Rijlaarsdam et al., 2004). Furthermore, the transcription process can itself trigger revision of plans and ideas of both pre-text and externalised linguistic units in the course of writing (Chenoweth & Hayes, 2001; Hayes, 2004).

Revision of an on-going text production entails the revision of both complete sentences or phrases and the partly written words externally as well as internally. Kellogg (1996) described the timing of revision, or editing, as occurring either before or after text has been written down, that is executed.

> Writers can in theory edit ideas, organizational schemes, writing goals, and sentences heard as inner speech or pre-text before execution. Editing may also occur after the writer has read the sentence, paragraph, or larger units of text already produced. Such editing after execution may be juggled with production or delayed until after a writer has completed a section of text. (p. 62)

Factors that affect revision are reading and cognitive resources (Alamargot & Chanquoy, 2001; Hayes, 1996; Kellogg, 1996). In order to revise previously written text writers need to possess the necessary reading skills as well as sufficient working memory capacity. Kellogg (1996) described editing that is preceded by reading as a process that assists in the shaping of the output both in terms of planning and in terms of translating. Planning and translating are, according to Kellogg, two of the most demanding elements of the writing process. Thus, conceptual revision of previously written text, preceded by reading is a cognitively costly venture that cannot go on in parallel with other processes. This means that in order to revise in previously written text, the transcription process has to stop before the revision can be carried out; the revision would be preceded by a pause. When revisions are 'juggled with production', writers conduct them at the point of inscription and the revisions can be carried through without any re-reading of written text.

### *3.1 Revision Types*

Although it is apparent that different types of revision activities go on during writing, it is difficult to make a clear distinction between these activities. However, two major revision categories can be clearly distinguished in revision models: internal and external revisions. Internal, or mental, revision traditionally entails overall, conceptual revision as well as conscious evaluative revision and revision of pre-text. External revision traditionally entails visible changes made to written text. Both internal and external revisions include several revision types (Hayes & Flower, 1980; Scardamalia & Bereiter, 1983).

Flower and Hayes (1984) described the representation of meaning generated during planning in writing as a continuum. At the one end of their continuum is the sensory perception and non-verbal imagery and at the other the formal prose in a textualised form. Revision can similarly be described as a continuum in which conceptual revision of overall goals and plans are at the one end and the visible external revisions at the other end of the continuum.

Along the revision continuum, a great variety of revision types can be recognised. While generating text, the images, plans and goals as well as written text are re-created and changed. Some changes are internal, such as the re-creation of images or goals, and referred to as 'reviewing' (Flower & Hayes, 1981) or 'revision' (Allal, 2000; Rijlaarsdam et al., 2004). Other revisions, such as changes of written words are external and are undertaken as a result of either internal revision or almost automatically; these revisions have been referred to as 'edits' (Flower & Hayes, 1981; Wengelin, 2002), 'changes' (Faigley & Witte, 1981) or 'transformations' (e.g. Rijlaarsdam et al., 2004). However, not all changes along the revision continuum are easily defined or categorised. A change of the overall plan can be triggered and undertaken through changes in the written text, and formulated text can be changed internally before it is written down.

One revision type that lies on the borderline between internal and external revisions is pre-text revision. This is a revision where the writer 'rehearses' a formulation in the head before it is transcribed into text. Pre-text differs from non-linguistic mental representations of text in that it consists of semantic and syntactic components, in the form of, for example, clauses or sentences (Witte, 1987).

Another revision type that, similar to the pre-text revisions, is located somewhere on the borderline between internal and external revisions is revision at the point of inscription (Matsuhashi, 1987). This type of revision is referred to here, and in Lindgren and Sullivan (this volume, Chapter 9), as 'pre-contextual' revision. Pre-contextual revision is defined as changes made to written text before a full context is externalised at the point of inscription; formulations and content elaborated upon by writers to shape the progressing discourse at the point of inscription.

Although internal and external revisions can be similar in character, internal revisions are not directly accessible as they occur internally; this inaccessibility makes them problematic both to define and to analyse. Wengelin (this volume) and Spelman Miller (this volume) suggest that pauses can be an indicator of internal revision. However, defining which pauses represent internal revision and which do not is problematic without additional information from the writers in the form of, for example, verbal protocols.

In order to account for the difficulty in drawing the line between the function of 'internal' and 'external' revisions in on-line writing, we use the broad definition of revision made by Fitzgerald (1987, p. 484): "Revision means making any changes at any point in the writing process". Similar definitions have been used by Alamargot and Chanquoy (2001); Hayes (2004); Van Gelderen and Oostdam (2004).

According to Fitzgerald's (1987) definition, no distinction is made between internal and external types of revisions in terms of their function as modifiers of concepts or form. Thus, revisions of plans and ideas can take place internally as well as externally. Likewise, revision of form can occur internally as pre-text revisions or externally as pre-contextual or contextual revision. The different location possibilities are illustrated in Figure 1, which was developed in conjunction with Marie Stevenson (Stevenson, Schoonen, & de Glopper, submitted).

Figure 1 shows how revisions are first defined according to whether they are internal or external; internal revisions occur mentally within the writer and external revisions are visible in the written product. Both revision types include form revision and conceptual revision. Internal revision is divided into pre-linguistic and pre-text revision. Pre-linguistic revision includes revisions of a conceptual character such as revision of plans or ideas. Pre-text revision includes conceptual as well as form revision. External revisions are categorised as pre-contextual revision and contextual revision, depending upon where they occur in the externalised text. Both of these types of external revisions include revision of typography, form and concept. As revisions occur on a continuum, it is problematic even with the revision scheme to categorise some revisions. For example, a revision at the end of the on-going text production when only a part of the proposed text has been externalised can represent a revision unit that consists of pre-text and pre-contextual revision.

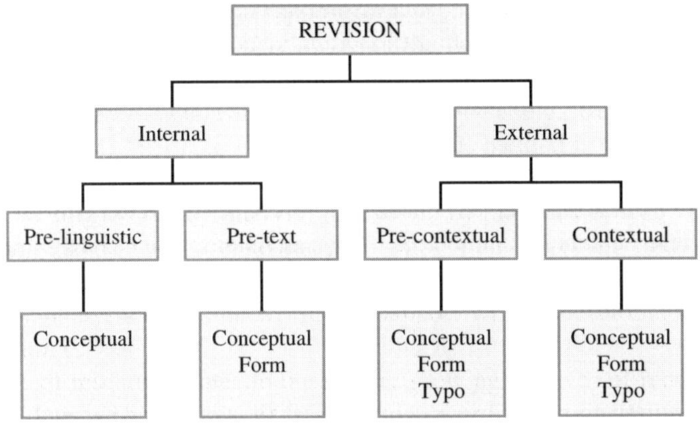


Figure 1: Division of revisions according to type and location.

## 4 Revision Analysis

The nature of the revisions writers makes to their compositions over the period of text gestation provides the research insight into the text's progression. The location of revisions, for example, shows how writers move their points of focus during text composition; this can be viewed as the route writers take through their texts. The actions writers perform during composition can, for example, hint at the writers' developing ideas and associated shifts in text focus (see Allal, 2000).

Several taxonomies for writing revision have been developed since the early 1980s. The taxonomies are in most cases, as Matsuhashi (1987) described it, either product- or process-oriented.

### *4.1 Product-Oriented Revision Taxonomies*

Product-oriented taxonomies focus on the effect of a revision on the written product. Revisions are defined according to their operation, that is, insertion, deletion, substitution, their syntactic level — word or sentence — or according to the object of revision, which is spelling, content or text organisation (Allal, 2000; Bridwell, 1980; Chanquoy, 2001; Faigley & Witte, 1981; Sullivan, Kollberg, & Pålson, 1998; Wengelin, 2002).

Faigley and Witte (1981) developed a product-oriented revision taxonomy based on a study of two drafts of compositions written by different types of writers. The drafts were written using pen and paper. The day before the writing of the first draft the writers received instructions of the writing task and could take notes and plan in advance. The revisions made during the writing of the first draft, differences between the first and the second draft, and in-process revisions made during the writing of the second draft were coded according to "whether new information is brought to the text or whether old information is removed in such a way that it cannot be recovered through drawing inferences" (p. 402).

The Faigley and Witte (1981) revision taxonomy has been one of the most influential in the field of revision analysis. In their taxonomy, Faigley and Witte divided revisions into two super-categories 'surface changes' and 'text-base changes', depending upon whether the revision brought new information to the text or not. Table 1 gives an overview of the taxonomy.

Faigley and Witte (1981) further divided the super-category surface changes into two sub-categories: formal changes and meaning-preserving changes. The former contained revisions that left the content unaffected, such as revisions of spelling, grammar, punctuation and format. Meaning-preserving changes included additions, deletions, substitutions, permutations, distributions and consolidations that did not include formal changes and did not alter the concepts already present in the text.

> *Additions* raise to the surface what can be inferred [...] *Deletions* do the opposites so that a reader is forced to infer what had been explicit [...] *Substitutions* trade words or longer units that represent the same concept [...] *Permutations* involve rearrangements or rearrangements with substitutions [...] *Distributions* occur when material in one text segment is passed into more than one segment [...] *Consolidations* do the opposite. Elements in two or more units are consolidated into one unit. (p. 403)

The super-category text-base changes was divided into micro- and macro-level changes. The former was defined by Faigley and Witte as a revision, which did not affect the summary of the text or the reading of other parts of the text. The latter category, macro-level

Table 1: Faigley and Witte's revision taxonomy (1981).

| **Surface changes** | **Text-base changes** |
|---|---|
| Formal changes | Micro-structure changes |
| Spelling | Additions |
| Grammar | Deletions |
| Tense | Substitutions |
| Number | Permutations |
| Modality | Distributions |
| Abbreviation | Consolidations |
| Punctuation | |
| Format | |
| Meaning-preserving changes | Macro-structure changes |
| Additions | Additions |
| Deletions | Deletions |
| Substitutions | Substitutions |
| Permutations | Permutations |
| Distributions | Distributions |
| Consolidations | Consolidations |

changes, was defined as revision that affected the reading of other parts of the text as well as the summary of the text. In both categories the same six sub-categories as those in the meaning-preserving categories were used. Yet, here the sub-category revisions affected the meaning of the text.

Several later revision taxonomies have been developed along the same lines. One example is the taxonomy used by Chanquoy (2001), which categorised revisions both according to their effect on the text, whether the revision affected the text on a surface or on a semantic level and whether the outcome of a revision was correct, erroneous or neutral, that is whether the revision corrected a mistake in the text, created a mistake in the text or did neither.

Allal (2000, 2004) elaborated on the Faigley and Witte idea of defining external revisions according to operation and object. She narrowed the operation categories into four: addition, deletion, substitution and rearrangements, and adjusted the object category. Instead of defining the object of revision as surface or text-base, she divided revisions according to 'semantics', 'spelling' (including lexical and grammatical aspects) and 'text organisation'. Text organisation included revisions that affected the connection and cohesion of the text. An example of such a revision is the replacement of a noun phrase 'the postman' with the pronoun 'he' (Allal, 2004). This is a valuable contribution to revision analysis as it defines revisions not only according to whether they affect the content or not, but also according to their discoursal effect on the text.

Allal's revision taxonomy further included additional information about the level of language included in the revision and the relationship between revision and language conventions. The latter category corresponds with Chanquoy's (2001) notion of whether the revision corrected a mistake in the text or not. However, Allal (2000) developed the idea into a discussion of the writer's options when revising. Some revisions that were carried out corrected a mistake in the text in order to fulfil the linguistic requirements of the language and were labelled 'conventional'. These revisions were further coded according to whether they were correctly or incorrectly carried out. Other revisions undertaken affected the text on other levels as they, for instance, developed the topic, directed the text towards the audience or clarified unclear passages. These revisions were not necessary in order to adjust the text towards conventional language rules and were, thus, labelled 'optional'.

### *4.2 Process-Oriented Revision Taxonomies*

Process-oriented taxonomies focus on revisions in real time and categorise revisions according to the time and place where they occurred within the writing process. One example is the categorisation of revision in order to examine writers' thought process and focus of attention reflected in the content, process and discourse perspectives on revision. Matsuhashi (1987) divided the content of revisions into 'Conceptual plans' or 'Sequential plans', according to the writer's focus of attention. The Conceptual plans included revision that reflected global discourse planning and text evaluation as well as sentence level planning of, for example, idea testing. The Sequential plans were defined as 'Textual sentence plans' and concern revisions for semantic relationships, grammaticality and correctness. In order to study the recursiveness of the writing process, Matsuhashi (1987) developed an analysis scheme that defined the location of revisions, that is where and when in the writing process revision occurred.

Another line of process-oriented revision analysis investigates the context and location of various processes, including revision, involved in writing (Breetvelt, Van den Bergh, & Rijlaarsdam, 1994; Couzijn, Van den Bergh, & Rijlaarsdam, 2002). Revision activities are related to the cognitive activities preceding and following the revision as well as the timing of the revision within the writing process, that is whether the revision occurs in the beginning, middle or towards the end. The effect of revision can vary according to its preceding processes as well as to the point where it was undertaken (Breetvelt et al., 1994; Couzijn et al., 2002).

## 5 On-Line Revision Analysis

As Faigley and Witte (1981) pointed out the categorisation of revisions is no simple task. This is true regardless of whether a product or process approach is adopted for revision analysis. When categorising online revision activity, features that complicate the analysis, which were not encountered by Faigley and Witte, arise. When analysing a pen-and-paper written text with revisions indicated as crossed out or inserted text, the revisions can only be put in the context of the final text product. Further, it might not be possible to know the exact order of the revisions undertaken if the writing session has not been recorded. In writing, revisions occur within a developing context. Keystroke logging is an approach that affords the researcher the possibility to analyse revision activity on-line; this affordance complicates revision analysis.

In order to study discourse as it develops, revisions need to be analysed in the context of the text written thus far, that is the text written up to and no further than the point of the revision. Flower and Hayes (1981) and Galbraith (1999), among others, have argued how that throughout the writing process, planning, monitoring and reviewing interact with the text produced thus far in such a way that in the light of what writers learn about their own texts during writing, plans and goals can be changed according to new ideas writers come up with in the course of producing text. Thus, if the text, and the goals for the text, can change throughout writing, the final text product does not necessarily correspond with the plans the writer had for the text at any earlier point during writing process. Hence, if a revision undertaken at the beginning of the text is analysed according to the final text product, the interpretation is undertaken according to the goals the writer had for the text at the end of the writing process, which may or may not be in accordance with the writer's goals at the point of revision. However, if a revision is interpreted only according to the text written thus far, the analysis of the revision is framed only by the writer's goals for the text at the point of revision and not by the writer's goal upon text completion.

In her study of online revision, Matsuhashi (1987) developed a revision taxonomy from writing data collected in video-recorded pen-and-paper sessions. She found that many revisions occur at the end of the current text, "shaping at the point of inscription" (p. 204). She noticed that writers explore various ways of continuing their compositions and often the only data available to the researcher are partially written words and phrases, which are deleted and replaced by other words and phrases.

> At the point of inscription the writer continually makes decisions, pushing the text forward, evaluating the plan for the text, revising the plan, or altering the text. (p. 204)

Analysing revisions at the point of inscription according to the text written thus far is problematic, as those revisions are only preceded, and not followed, by context. The text following a revision at the point of inscription can help in designating a category to the revision. However, at the point of revision the text to follow might not be clear to the writer. The revision can be a part of the shaping of the next text item to write, and as such the revision is both a result of previously written text and a creator of future text. Since the future text, at the point of inscription, is not yet externalised it is not possible to know what the writer is intending to write after the revision has been executed. In order not to impose one's own interpretation of the writer's intentions upon the interpretation of the revision, online revisions should only be analysed with reference to the preceding text and the text written thus far.

To date, few revision taxonomies have been developed that account for the online features of text creation. Some keystroke logging software packages provide combined product and process-oriented revision analysis tools. The discourse and/or syntactic level of the revisions are analysed automatically by the program; these can be combined with information about the time of occurrence and the location of the revision within the text (Kollberg & Severinson Eklundh, 2001; Strömqvist & Ahlsén, 1999). Such software has been used in studies of, for example, revision in L2 writing (Thorson, 2000), the relation between pauses and revision (Wengelin, 2002), and emerging discourse structure (Severinson Eklundh & Kollberg, 2003). However, in terms of providing information about the effect revision has on the developing text, automatic analysis is limited. Manual and complementary data-collection methods are needed to interpret keystroke-logged revision data and categorise revisions according to a revision taxonomy.

One automatic notational system that builds upon keystroke logged data and can be used to assist in analysing online revision, as is demonstrated by Lindgren and Sullivan (this volume, Chapter 9), is S-notation. As overviewed in Chapter 1 (Spelman Miller & Sullivan, this volume) and shown in Chapter 1, Figure 2, S-notation indicates both the position where the writer stopped to revise and the location where the revision took place. S-notation, together with step-by-step replay function that is part of Trace-it (Kollberg, 1998; Kollberg & Severinson Eklundh, 2001), has been used in several revision studies (e.g. Lindgren & Sullivan, 2002, 2003; Stevenson et al., submitted; Sullivan et al., 1998) and has been found to assist the researcher with the revision analysis task.

## 6 Summary

This chapter has given the reader an overview of factors that are integral to the writing process and discussed issues relating to the categorisation of revisions undertaken by writers. In particular, this chapter has prepared the reader for the issues relating to online revision and the aspect of logged data that need to be considered when developing an online revision taxonomy such as the one developed by Lindgren and Sullivan (this volume,

Chapter 9). Together with Spelman Miller (this volume, Chapter 2) and Strömqvist, Holmqvist, Johansson, Karlsson, and Wengelin (this volume, Chapter 4) the reader will now be able to fully appreciate the ideas presented by Lingren and Sullivan and contribute to the development of the analysis of on-line revision.

Chapter 4

# What Keystroke Logging can Reveal about Writing

Sven Strömqvist, Kenneth Holmqvist, Victoria Johansson, Henrik Karlsson and Åsa Wengelin
*Lund University, Lund, Sweden*

*Writing is a dynamic activity. In order fully to appreciate that fact, we have to analyse writing as it unfolds in real time. The present paper gives a bird's eye perspective on the budding paradigm of using keystroke logging as a window on the online process of writing. First, methods and tools for designing writing experiments, recording writing activity, and for analysing recordings of writing activity are reviewed. Second, an overview of different lines of research is presented. Here, rather than attempting an exhaustive review of the state-of-art, we present selective illustrations from four areas of research where keystroke logging by means of the research tool ScriptLog was used as a basis for the analysis of writing: the contrastive study of speech and writing, the study of learning to write, the study of writing difficulties, and the experimental study of spelling. Also, the combination of keystroke logging with eye-tracking technology is illustrated. The paper ends with a discussion of future directions for research and applications, including test, diagnosis, evaluation, writing support, and a new generation of corpora of computer-logged writing and their use in research and education.*

**Keywords:** ScriptLog, keystroke logging, eye-tracking, online writing.

## 1 Methods and Tools

Analysing writing as it unfolds in real time presupposes three main components: a registration device, a representation of the registration which can be subjected to systematic

**Computer Key Stroke Logging and Writing: Methods and Applications**

**ISBN: 0-08-044934-4**

*Strömqvist, S., Holmqvist, K., Johansson, V., Karlsson, H., & Wengelin, Å. (with Ahlsén, E., Alves, R., Andersson, B., Bertram, R., Erskine, J., Grönqvist, L., Hagman, J., Hellstrand, Å., Hellum, I., Holsanova, J., Leiwo, M., Lyytinen, H., Malmsten, L., Nordqvist, Å., Solheim, O., Tufvesson, S., Uppstad, P. H, Wagner, Å.-K., & Wiktorsson, M.) (2006). What keystroke logging can reveal about writing. In G. Rijlaarsdam (Series Ed.) and K. P. H. Sullivan, & E. Lindgren. (Vol. Eds.), Studies in Writing, Vol. 18, Computer Keystroke Logging: Methods and Applications (pp. 45–71). Oxford: Elsevier.*

analysis, and a set of analysis procedures. The standards and requirements put on each of these three components depend, largely, on the types of analysis you want to perform. For example, Matsuhashi (1981, 1982, 1987) used video technique as a recording device to study text revision activities (handwritten text). This technique offers a time resolution of 25 pictures/frames per second, which amounts to one frame per 40 ms. That time resolution might be good enough for studying text revision activities, but it is far below the standards of reaction time experiments, which tend to require a time resolution accuracy better than 10 ms, preferably better than 2 ms.

One example of a computer tool, developed for the study of online writing, which provides the demanded time resolution accuracy is ScriptLog (Strömqvist & Karlsson, 2002; Strömqvist & Malmsten, 1998).[1] ScriptLog has been developed by the research group behind the present paper and will henceforth serve as a basis for illustrations of keystroke logging and what keystroke logging can say about writing.

ScriptLog has three main modules: a design module, where the conditions of the writing task are defined; a recording module, which produces a binfile containing a full representation of the events occurring during the writing activity together with their temporal distribution; and an analysis module, allowing the researcher to derive selected patterns from the binfile/recording. ScriptLog also allows you to play back a recording of a writing activity — or selected parts thereof — in real time.

Consider Example 1, for the purpose of illustration. The text fragment in Example 1 relates to a narrative writing task, where ScriptLog's design module was used to administer a wordless picture story as an elicitation instrument.[2] 1a shows the final edited version of the fragment, 1b a literal translation into English, and 1c shows the fragment of the logfile — a non-reduced representation of the recording — corresponding to the italicized part of 1a.

(1a) Efter ett ihärdigt lekande med hundvalpen och den lilla grodan föll Måns och hundvalpen *ihop på sängen.*

(1b) 'After an intense period of playing with the puppet and the little frog, Måns and the puppy *collapsed on the bed.*'

(1c)

| time | type | from | to | key |
|---|---|---|---|---|
| 3.01.034 | 7 | 00088 | 00088 | i |
| 3.01.333 | 7 | 00089 | 00089 | h |
| 3.01.473 | 7 | 00090 | 00090 | o |
| 3.01.601 | 7 | 00091 | 00091 | p |
| 3.02.635 | 7 | 00092 | 00092 | |
| 3.03.110 | 7 | 00093 | 00093 | p |
| 3.03.251 | 7 | 00094 | 00094 | å |
| 3.03.683 | 7 | 00095 | 00095 | |
| 3.04.105 | 7 | 00096 | 00096 | s |

[1]See www.ScriptLog.net for more information.

[2]In this particular task, the subject is retelling the picture story in writing — picture by picture — at his own pace. A screen shot from the same writing task — but with a different subject — is shown in Figure 6 in Section 5. The picture story, "Frog, where are you", was originally a wordless picture booklet by Mayer (1969).

(1c. contd.)

| | | | | |
|---|---|---|---|---|
| 3.04.246 | 7 | 00097 | 00097 | ä |
| 3.04.523 | 7 | 00098 | 00098 | n |
| 3.04.737 | 7 | 00099 | 00099 | g |
| 3.04.860 | 7 | 00100 | 00100 | e |
| 3.05.137 | 7 | 00101 | 00101 | n |
| 3.06.994 | 7 | 00102 | 00102 | |
| 3.07.943 | 7 | 00103 | 00103 | o |
| 3.08.082 | 7 | 00104 | 00104 | c |
| 3.08.226 | 7 | 00105 | 00105 | h |
| 3.08.761 | 7 | 00106 | 00106 | |
| 3.11.055 | 7 | 00107 | 00107 | <BACKSPACE> |
| 3.11.213 | 7 | 00106 | 00106 | <BACKSPACE> |
| 3.11.361 | 7 | 00105 | 00105 | <BACKSPACE> |
| 3.11.512 | 7 | 00104 | 00104 | <BACKSPACE> |
| 3.11.670 | 7 | 00103 | 00103 | <BACKSPACE> |
| 3.12.734 | 7 | 00102 | 00102 | . |

In the logfile, each event on the keyboard (or mouse event) during a writing activity is represented as a quintuple of arguments. The first argument is a point in time, more precisely, the number of minutes, seconds, and fragments of seconds (time resolution in 1/1000 s) that have elapsed since the beginning of the writing activity (in this case, when the subject pressed a start-button activating the first component picture of the elicitation instrument together with an editing window — see Figure 6 in Section 5). For example, the first event appearing in the example takes place 3 min and 1.034 s ("3.01.034") from the start of the writing activity and consists in that the subject strikes the key "i". The second argument is a figure representing the type of the event. Most events consist in writing lower case letters and those events are of the type "7", etc. The third and fourth arguments are figures representing the screen position(s) occupied by the event. The third argument is the source position and the fourth the goal position. Thus, if the event consists in using the mouse to mark/shade a piece of text from position 38 to 76, 38 will appear as the third argument and 76 as the fourth. In our present example, all events consist in typing one character and in the representation of such an event, the same number occurs in the third and fourth positions, since each of these events only occupies one single position on the screen. The fifth argument, finally, shows the identity of the key pressed or mouse operation performed.

At the sixth line from the end, at 3.11.055, the subject starts performing a revision, consisting in first the deletion of the five last characters written: the word *och* and the space bars immediately preceding and succeeding that word, and then the insertion of a full stop. In other words, the subject changed her mind: instead of expanding the sentence with a coordinated construction, she decides to close the sentence.

The logfile is generated by ScriptLog from the underlying recording/binfile. It offers a window on all information, which is actually stored during a ScriptLog recording. The logfile can be used as input to analysis scripts such as, for example, Awk or Perl, but it is never used as a basis for manual analysis. Instead, ScriptLog produces a variety of alternative output structures, all of them highlighting selective information patterns derived from the original binfile/recording. Some of these structures are pre-defined and offered as standard output from ScriptLog. Others can be interactively defined. For example, you can define a specific target string, such as a wordform or a particular phrase, and then ask ScriptLog to search for it in a recording and analyse all instances of it in terms of its production rate characteristics. This technique will be further illustrated in Section 3. Another possibility is to define a search string in terms of a type of micro-context with variables signifying objects such as letters and delimiters. ScriptLog will then search for instantiations of the type of micro-context(s) defined and provide an analysis output in terms of "transition time values", that is, production rate characteristics for the targeted micro-context. Micro-contexts are defined in more detail and their use for researching pause behavior in writing are discussed in Wengelin (this volume).

Keystroke logging generates a colossal amount of data. Yet, how can all these data from keystroke logging enhance our understanding of writing? In the following sections, we will discuss and illustrate the use of keystroke logging to shed light on a variety of research questions pertaining to written language, writing development, writing difficulties and spelling processes.

## 2 Speech and Writing

How can keystroke logging help us understand the nature of writing as distinct from speaking? When we engage in spoken communication, sender and receiver are almost always in the same place and at the same time. In written communication, by contrast, they tend to be located at different places and points in time. Further, when we are speaking, we have little time at our disposal and we therefore have to use our attention and cognitive resources with great discretion. When writing, some of these constraints can be lifted. The differences in communicative and cognitive constraints between spoken and written communication mean that we have to think in partly different ways when we speak and when we write. Therefore, it is only natural that we tend to find systematic differences between spoken and written "texts", differences which go beyond stylistics into content structure. Let us examine some of these differences in greater detail. (See also Strömqvist, Ahlsén, & Wengelin, 1999).

### *2.1 Product and Process*

Consider Example 2 below. It represents the beginning of a personal narrative by a Swedish 10-year-old. The original narration was spoken. Here, it is represented, word by word, in writing (a literal translation in English is rendered in the right-hand column).

| | |
|---|---|
| (2) *de va så här en gång efter skolan* | it was like this once after school |
| *så ja å min bästis Ane* | so I and my buddy Ane |
| *hon kommer från Norge då* | she's from Norway then |
| *vi va på en klätterställning* | we were climbing |

The original spoken narration was audio-recorded and written down word by word. Still, only a few of the properties of the original spoken version are captured in the written version in Example 2. Voice quality (indicating, e.g., degree of engagement, worry and certainty), tempo (hesitant, fast, staccato, etc.), intonation (falling, rising, etc.) and stress are all examples of properties which carry important communicative functions in speech but which are not rendered in writing. The only properties, which have been systematically rendered in the written version in Example 2 are words and word order. These are the linguistic properties, which our writing system handles in a systematic way and they are therefore easy to write down. In effect, the spoken narration has been reduced on the conditions of written language.

Now, consider Figure 1. It shows the fundamental frequency ($F_0$) of the speech signal corresponding to the beginning of the narration written down in Example 2 (Strömqvist, 2000). The fundamental frequency is the dimension in the speech signal, which we experience as the intonation or melody of speech. The curve in Figure 1 consists of dotted segments and lines. The dotted segments represent the presence and the lines the absence of $F_0$. Longer lines, that is, silence of a duration greater than 0.5 s, are perceived as pauses. The strings of words given in Example 2 have been roughly aligned with their corresponding parts of the speech curve in Figure 1.

As can be seen, there is a systematic interplay between content structure, intonation and pauses in the narration by the 10-year-old. The end of each larger content unit (sentence) is accompanied with a rising intonation contour, a "phrase final rise". The phrase final rise thus serves as an important cue to the listener that a larger information boundary in the discourse has been reached. In addition, the phrase final rises are followed by pauses. The pauses give the speaker an opportunity to plan how to continue the discourse. At the same time, they give the listener an opportunity to process the information just perceived and to give feedback to the speaker, if desired. There is only one instance of a pause which does not follow a larger information boundary, namely, the pause following the word *hon* 'she'. In this case, the speaker holds back all dynamic gestures from the intonation of the word immediately preceding the pause: *hon* is pronounced with a perfectly flat contour. Also, the speaker rests for a while, producing a "filled" pause, on the final, sonorant segment of the word, something we have marked with a double colon in Figure 1 (*hon:*). Through

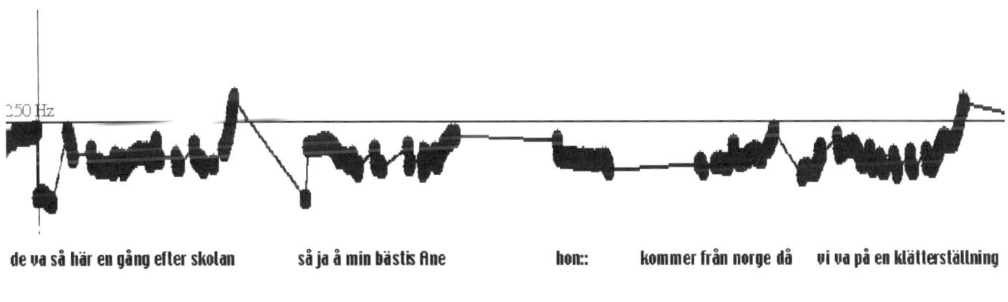


Figure 1: $F_0$-analysis of the first 12 sec of the personal narrative by a Swedish 10-year-old represented in Example 2.

Source: Adapted from Strömqvist, S. (2000). A note on pauses in speech and writing. In: M. Aparici, N. Argerich, J. Perera, E. Rosado, & L. Tolchinsky (Eds), *Working papers in Developing literacy across genres, modalities and languages* (pp. 211–224), Volume III. Barcelona, Spain: University of Barcelona. Copyright by Universitat de Barcelona. Reprinted with permission.

these measures the speaker informs the listener that she has not yet finished the information unit she has initiated, and the listener, accordingly, lets her go on, without interrupting, despite of the pause. As soon as the speaker has finished the information unit (*hon: kommer från norge då* 'she: is from Norway then'), something, which she, again, signals with a phrase final rise, the listener takes the opportunity to give feedback (*mm*). Another aspect of the dynamics of speech is that some words are foregrounded and others backgrounded. This dynamics serves as a guide to the listener's attention. If all words were made equally prominent, the listener would have a much harder time interpreting the utterance. Figure 1 also provides an illustration of the fact that speech is rapid. The whole sequence rendered in Figure 1 took just a little more than 12 s, yielding a production rate of 120 words per minute, including pauses.

Now, consider the written version (Example 3) by the same 10-year-old, produced shortly after the completion of the spoken narrative.

| | | |
|---|---|---|
| (3) | *Detta hände för ungefär* | This happened about |
| | *3 månader sen.* | 3 months ago. |
| | *jag och min bästis Ane* | I and my buddy Ane |
| | *(hon kommer från norge)* | (she's from Norway) |
| | *var på en klätterstälning* | we were climbing |
| | *det var efter skolan* | it was after school |
| | *så det var bara vi där.* | so only we were there. |

Content-wise, the beginning of the written version (Example 3) is somewhat richer than the beginning of the corresponding spoken version (Example 2). Did the narrator reflect more on lexical and grammatical choices in the writing condition? Where did the writer make pauses or edits during the writing process? What we see in Example 3 is the written *product*, not the *process*. A tape-recording of the spoken narration contains important information about the rhythm of the speech, about fluent and hesitant phases in the narration. How can we get a handle on these patterns in the written narration? This is where keystroke logging enters the scene.

The Swedish 10-year-old wrote her personal narrative on a computer and the writing activity was recorded by ScriptLog. Example 4, an analysis output from ScriptLog known as a "Linear file", shows the online patterning of keystrokes, pauses (>2 s) and edits during the writing activity which led to the final edited text fragment shown in Example 3.

(4) <START><105.48>det <3.06>var en <3.95>dag<DELETE14> Detta
hände <9.36>för unge fär 3 måm<DELETE>nader sen**<3.66>**.<CR>
**<4.48>**jag och min bästis an<DELETE2><2.15>Ane **<4.81>**(**<3.38>**
hon komer <2.45>från norge**<2.90>**) **<5.60>**var<12.16>på en <3.63>
klät<2.30>ter stälning **<12.06>**<LEFT22> <RIGHT22> **<2.83>**
det var efter <2.01>skolan så det var <2.78>bara<2.33> <CR>
<2.65>vi där**<4.35>**.

Among other things, we observe that the writer makes a long pause (105.48 s) after she activated the editor window ("START"), whereupon she writes *det var en dag* 'it was one day'. During the production of this first sentence, she makes two short pauses. Then she deletes the 14 characters (including spaces) just written ("DELETE14") and instead writes *Detta hände för unge fär 3 månader sen* 'This happened about 3 months ago'. When writing the new sentence, she makes a longer pause (9.36 s) after *Detta hände* 'This happened' and she corrects a misspelling (*mâm månader*). When, eventually, she has finished her second sentence (last word is *klätterstälning*), she makes a 12 s pause and then moves the cursor 22 characters back in the text so far produced ("LEFT22") — as if she was aiming at a revision — and then moves it back to its original position ("RIGHT22").

When speaking, the 10-year-old was pausing almost exclusively in large information boundaries (see Figure 1). When writing, in contrast, she is pausing mainly between words within syntactic phrases, whereas a minority of the pauses occur in larger information boundaries (these latter pauses are marked with boldface in Example 4). If she had produced this kind of pause pattern in speech, the listener would have had a hard time following what she was saying. Further, in comparison to speech, writing is very slow. The beginning of the written narrative (Example 4) took a little less than 5 min to complete. That makes less than 7 words per minute as compared to 120 words per minute in the corresponding spoken condition.

Why are the language processes in speech and writing so different? Let us examine in greater detail three important dimensions distinguishing speech from writing: the duration of the signal; the relationship between perception and production; and the linear versus simultaneous distribution of expressive features.

## 2.2 The Duration of the Signal

The acoustic signal in speech has a very short duration, whereas the graphical trace in writing has a potentially very long duration. This basic difference has several important consequences. For example, the written signal is easier to grasp, to reflect upon and to manipulate, than is the spoken signal. The initial editing by the 10-year-old (Example 4) or her shift of attention 22 characters back in the text (as reflected in her cursor movements) provide illustrations of things which can be done relatively easily in writing, whereas corresponding actions in speech are rare or non-existent.

A further illustration is provided in Figure 2 (from Strömqvist, Ahlsén, Wengelin, Grönqvist, & Hagman, 1999; see also Wengelin, 2002). Figure 2 shows the editing profile of the text-writing activity from an adult subject, writing a personal narrative. If there had been no edits during the writing activity, the graph in the figure would have reduced to a straight line. But the writer made several edits, and each edit is reflected as a slope. A slope downhill means that the writer is deleting text. A slope uphill means that the writer is adding text. A steep fall means that the writer is moving the cursor back in the text. Thus, we observe that, towards the end of the writing activity, the subject returns to the first half of the text and adds new text. This kind of fine-grained edits over long distances would be excessively memory demanding if the signal would have been of such a short duration as it is in speech; the whole text would have had to be kept in memory, word by word. This kind of edit is therefore rare or nonexistent in speech, but relatively frequent in writing.

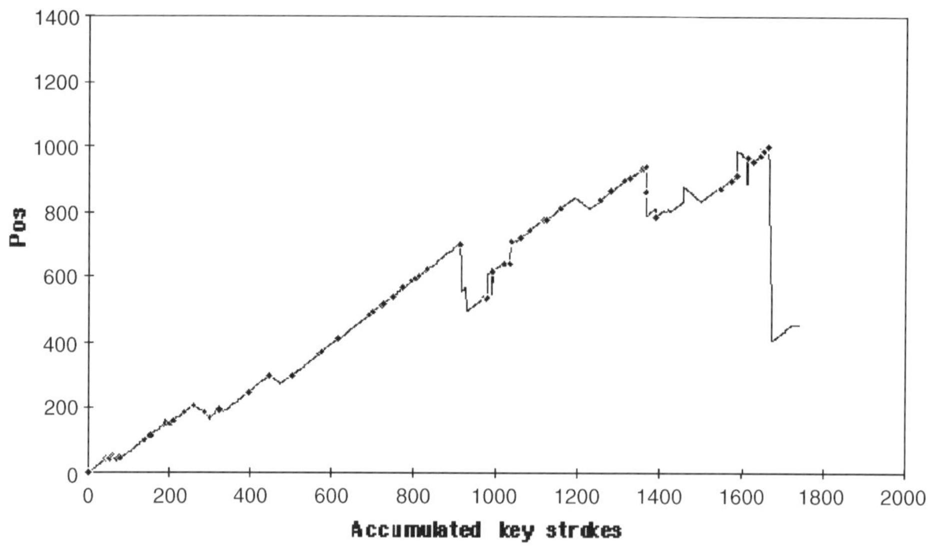


Figure 2: Editing profile during a text-writing activity.
Source: Adpated from Strömqvist, S., Ahlsén, E., Wengelin, Å., Grönqvist, L., & Hagman, J. (1999) Types of analysis. In: S. Strömqvist, & E. Ahlsén (Eds), *The process of writing — a progress report* (p. 48). Copyright by The Department of Linguistics, Gothenburg University. Reprinted with permission.

### *2.3 The Relationship between Perception and Production*

The relationship between perceiving and producing linguistic utterances is very different in speech and writing. In spoken communication, utterances must be perceived online (millisecond by millisecond in real time) just as they are (or were) produced online. In written communication, this online constraint is relaxed. It is only the final edited product which the writer intends to present to the reader. Therefore, the reader never gets in touch with the pauses and revisions made by the writer during the production process.

One consequence of these differences is that the language user has more freedom to distribute his attention, to plan and to revise, when he is writing as compared to speaking. When you produce a written text, you are free to put the text aside for a moment, to reflect on the content and the reader's pre-understanding, to return to the text and revise it.

Conversely, writing is a lonely form of communication. In spoken communication, there is ample opportunity for sender and receiver to interact, to give feedback and to adapt to each other. The receiver can inform the sender about how he perceives, understands or reacts to what the sender is saying. This feedback also serves as a support for the speaker's further discourse production; the sender's speech production is partly driven by the receiver's feedback and reactions to what the sender is saying. In contrast, the feedback process is delayed in written communication; the reader's feedback and reactions are contingent upon the delivery of the final edited text by the writer. As a consequence, it takes more empathy and imagination on the part of the writer to compose a written text than to produce a spoken one, in order to adapt it to the receiver. Similarly, it takes more empathy and imagination on the part of the receiver to interpret a written text in the absence of the sender, than to interpret what is said in spoken communication in the presence of the sender. Also, the reader of the text in Example 3 does not get any systematic guide to how he should distribute his attention. In distinction to the spoken version (Figure 1), where the speaker made certain words more prominent by means of stress and intonation, the words in the written version are all alike in terms of typographical prominence. The reader therefore has to use more knowledge in order to direct his attention, for the purpose of orientation and interpretation of the text.

### *2.4 Linearity and Simultaneity*

Speech and writing also differ with respect to how their respective expressive features tend to be distributed. A comparison between Figure 1 (speech) and Example 3 (writing) provides a couple of illustrations. In writing, when we want to signal that a large information unit (a sentence) is ended, we put a major delimiter immediately *after* the last letter of the last word of the sentence. When we want to signal the corresponding end point in spoken discourse, we use an intonational gesture, often in combination with a decrease in speech tempo, *simultaneously* with the last word or words of the sentence. And when the writer in Example 3 wants to signal that a sentence — (*hon kommer från Norge*) — contains more parenthetical background information in comparison to the surrounding plot-advancing utterances, she uses brackets *before* and *after* the sentence in question to mark the particular status of the sentence in question. In contrast, the marking of the parenthetical status of the corresponding sentence in the spoken version was accomplished by two features distributed *simultaneously* with the pronunciation of the words of the sentence: a reduced voice range and a clear increase in speech tempo. The decrease in voice range, that is, the decreased distance between the highest and lowest pitch points of the phrase, is seen as a compression in the vertical dimension of the intonation curve in Figure 1. The increased speech tempo is reflected in the failure to align the transcript of the phrase (*hon kommer från Norge då*) with the intonation curve in Figure 1: since this phrase is spoken faster than its surrounding phrases, it has a decreased extension in the horizontal dimension of Figure 1, but the transcript still needs a lot of space.

Spoken language thus tends to distribute its expressive features both linearly (one after the other) and simultaneously, whereas written language is more consistently linear. This is not to say that written language excludes a simultaneous distribution of expressive features. To mark a word or phrase with italics provides a case in point.

## 3 Learning to Write

The comparison of speech and writing in Section 2 has a host of implications for the study of the acquisition of writing skills (see, e.g., Nordqvist, 2001; Strömqvist, 1996). For example, written language requires different methods than spoken language for foregrounding and backgrounding of information, for expressing attitudinal information, and for marking information boundaries. Also, the fact that the online constraints of speech can be lifted in writing presents new ramifications for processing which the learner has to adapt to. We might add that certain genres are manifest only in written language (such as, e.g., a composition), and learning to write, therefore, also means learning new genres. Here, we shall briefly look at a few examples of how keystroke logging can help shed light on the development of writing skills.

### *3.1 The Distribution of Keystrokes, Pauses and Edits Across a Narrative*

Consider Figure 3 that presents profiles of writing activity — in terms of keystrokes — derived from ScriptLog recordings of subjects in a narrative task (Strömqvist, Nordqvist, & Wengelin, 2004). Sixteen 9- to 12-year-olds, fifteen 15-year-olds and ten adults were asked to retell a wordless picture story, "Frog, where are you?" by Mayer (1969), in writing. The altogether 24 pictures depict the story of a little boy and his dog as they go search for a frog that has disappeared. ScriptLog's design module was used to administer the picture story as an elicitation instrument, and the subjects were instructed to click their way through the picture story at their own pace. When the subject activates a new picture, a corresponding editor window is activated, where the subject writes his story. A screen shot from this writing task is shown in Figure 6 in Section 5.

Figure 3 shows how many keystrokes the subjects spent on the 1st through the 24th picture. Figure 3 consists of three diagrams, one for each age group. The upper, dashed graph in each diagram shows the number of keystrokes in the linear text, that is, the total number of keystrokes made. The lower, solid graph shows the number of keystrokes remaining in the edited version of the text. The distance between the graph then, indicates the amount of editing made in relation to a picture. The values in Figure 3 are means across all subjects for picture 1, 2...24. From the production profiles in Figure 3, it is clear that, on a group level, the youngest age-group, the 9- to 12-year-olds, write the least, the 15-year-olds a little more, and the adults the most. Further, the profiles indicate group differences in terms of the distribution of writing activity across the discourse. The 9- to 12-year-olds write a lot in the beginning, then less and less and they have a very meagre finish. It is reasonable to interpret this profile as indicative of effort and exhaustion. In contrast, the 15-year-olds show a much more smooth and balanced profile. Along the same line of interpretation, they seem to be able to better plan their discourse and to control their expenditure of effort. They also spend a little more on the finish. The adults, finally, describe a very dynamic overall profile: they spend a lot of their writing activity in the beginning and at the end of the story and vary themselves in between according to the richness and ramifications of the individual pictures.

In terms of editing activity, the amount of editing tends to decrease towards the last third of the story for all three age groups. The last picture/episode constitutes an exception in the two older age groups: the 15-year-olds and adults perform a relatively large amount of editing in relation to the last picture. The 9- to 12-year-olds, in contrast, perform very little editing in relation to the last picture. In terms of relative amounts, the 9- to 12-year-olds edit 23.3% of the keystrokes they spend on the initial picture of the story elicitation

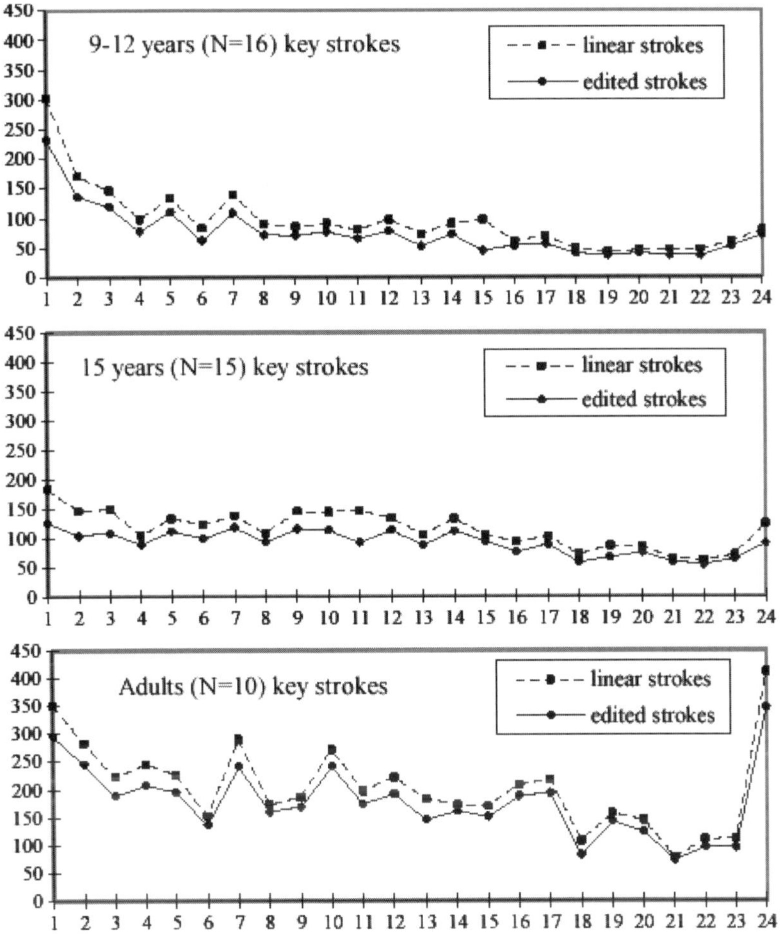


Figure 3: Production profiles for different age groups in terms of key strokes across the 24 pictures of the picture story "Frog, where are you?". The upper, dashed graph in each diagram shows the number of keystrokes in the linear text, that is, the total number of keystrokes made. The lower, solid graph shows the number of keystrokes remaining in the edited version of the text. The distance between the graphs indicates the amount of editing made. The values are means across all subjects.
Source: Adapted from Strömqvist, S., Nordqvist, Å., & Wengelin, Å. (2004). Writing the frog story — developmental and cross-modal perspectives. In: S. Strömqvist, & L. Verhoeven (Eds), *Relating events in narrative — typological and contextual perspectives* (p. 373), Mahwah, NJ: Lawrence Erlbaum. Copyright 2004 by Lawrence Erlbaum Associates, Inc. Reprinted with permission.

instrument, but only 10.1% on the final picture. The great majority of the edits concern spelling mistakes, and many spelling errors remain in the edited text. The 15-year-olds have a higher and more balanced proportion of edits: 30.6% for the initial and 26.6% for the final picture. Again, the great majority of the edits concern spelling mistakes, but very few errors remain in the edited text. The adults show a perfectly balanced editing rate, 15.5% for the initial and 15.6% for the final picture. The great majority of their edits concern content structure, and their texts are almost completely error free from the point of view of spelling. For a developmental study detailing types of editing operations, see Johansson (2000).

Strömqvist et al. (2004b) also analysed the distribution of pauses across the 24 pictures of the story task. A particular attention was given picture initial pauses, that is, the time elapsing between the pressing of the button by which the subject activates a new picture and the first keystroke made when starting to write in relation to the picture. It turned out that the picture initial pause made in relation to the first picture, that is, the discourse initial pause, was different for the three age groups. Thus, the 9- to 12-year-olds made a relatively short planning pause before they started writing in relation to the first picture of the frog story (on average, less than half a minute), the 15-year-olds made longer discourse intitial planning pauses (around 1 min), whereas the adults made very long planning pauses (on average, more than 2 min).

### 3.2 The Production Rate of Selected Strings

Consider, further, the examples provided in Examples 5 and 6. The sequence in 5a relates to a personal narrative by a Swedish 10-year-old (an English translation is given at the bottom of the figure). The sentence co-ordinating *och* 'and' marked by a ring in 5a was selectively subjected to ScriptLog analysis in terms of transition times between the keystrokes preceding, internal to, and succeeding the target string *och*, and the output is presented in 5b. The English translation is given in 5c.

As can be seen, "och" is preceded by a relatively long pause (1.683 s after the last word of the first sentence but before the space bar "_" before och, and 3.083 s after the space bar but before "och"), suggesting that the 10-year-old had not decided to produce a coordinated sentence structure at the point where she finished her first sentence (ending with the verb "träffas" 'meet'). The relatively long pause after "och" further suggests that, when the subject has decided to develop her simple sentence into a coordinated sentence structure and written "och", she has still not planned the second constituent sentence of that coordinated structure.

5a) *...och vi fyra började att träffas och jag*
*tror att jag och Patrik är bästa kompisar nu.*

5b) *...träffas* 1.683 _ 3.083 *o* 1.017 *h* 0.167 _ 2.667 *jag*
*tror att jag och Patrik är bästa kompisar nu.*

5c) '...and us four started to meet and I
think that I and Patrick are best friends now.'

In contrast, consider Example 6, taken from an expository textwriting activity by an adult subject. Here, the swift transition between the first and second constituents of the coordinated structure suggests that the adult subject had planned the whole coordinated structure in advance of writing it. Keystroke logging can thus help reveal differences in planning and production strategies behind sentences, which are structurally similar as products.

6a) *...att det finns alternativa synsätt på samma situation och att man kan spegla filmen i vårar egna liv.*

6b) *...situation* 0.217 _ 0.183 *o* 0.133 *c* 0.167 *h* 00.67 _ 0.117 *att man kan spegla filmen i vårar egna liv.*

6c) '...that there are alternative perspectives on the same situation and that you can project the film onto our own lives.'

### *3.3 The Production Rate of Assumedly Prefabricated Phrases*

The technique just illustrated was used by Wiktorsson (2000, 2003) in an investigation designed to validate the hypothesis that certain phrases, the so-called pre-fabricated phrases, are stored as ready-made units in memory and therefore are likely to have certain performance characteristics, such as being easily accessible or having an even production rate (since they are not built up analytically word by word during production). Wiktorsson, who studied the acquisition of English as a foreign language, further entertained the hypothesis that pre-fabricated phrases are characteristic of advanced learners, whereas beginners tend to treat the same phrases in an analytic fashion. Wiktorsson used ScriptLog to record free textwriting in two groups of students: students of English who had just started their university courses, and advanced learners with several semesters of university courses in English behind them. The analysis of the keystroke-logging data confirmed Wiktorsson's hypotheses. Pre-fabs were produced at a higher — and, above all — far more even production rate than other phrases, and this effect was more tangible in the advanced learners.

## 4 Writing Difficulties

Writing tends to be more effortful than speaking. In order successfully to encode and communicate thoughts through writing, the writer has to be able to keep focussed on higher level processes in writing, such as the management of content structure, style and communicative strategies. Unless the writer masters spelling, interpunctuation and the retrieval of words and grammatical schemata, he will have to expend an amount of cognitive resources on these low-level processes which typically causes him to have problems maintaining that focus. Also, successful textwriting requires models for textwriting, and reading is a main way to acquire such models (Olson, 2002). By implication, if a person has reading difficulties, that will typically lead to a deprivation of models for textwriting.

## 4.1 Speed and Amount of Pausing

Alves (2002) studied narrative writing in a group of young Portuguese adults ($N = 21$), exploring the cognitive cost of problems with low-level writing processes (see also Alves, Castro, de Sousa, & Strömqvist, in press). Among other things, Alves analysed the relation between speed of writing and amount of pausing, where speed of writing was operationalized as median transition time between letters within words.

On the basis of speed, Alves (2002) divided his subjects into two groups, those who had a median transition time value greater than 300 ms in this context (slow writers) and those who had a lower transition time value (fast writers). The median transition time for the fast writers was 210 ms, whereas the median transition time for the slow writers was 440 ms, a difference, which turned out to be significant ($p = .0001$). And it turned out that the difference in amount of pausing (>2 s) between the two groups was also significant (mean total pausing time during the writing activity was 615.8 s in the fast writers versus 1227.4 in the slow writers ($p = .005$). Alves interpreted this result in support of his hypothesis that slow writers need to expend so much cognitive effort on low-level processes during writing that they often loose track of the content structure they had planned to realize, and therefore need to pause more often than fast writers, in order to retrieve the thread.

## 4.2 Speed and Accuracy

Erskine (1999) compared a group of university students with an independently assessed dyslexic background ($N = 10$) to a group of controls ($N = 12$), using ScriptLog to assess their speed of writing during a textwriting task. She then statistically divided the control group into four areas of strengths and weaknesses based on speed (keystroke rate) and accuracy (number of errors) and thereafter sorted the dyslexic writers into these categories based on each subject's speed and accuracy. As expected, the controls were over represented in the category Fast and Accurate. The category Slow and Inaccurate, however, was almost empty and most of the dyslexics were either trading speed for accuracy or accuracy for speed.

## 4.3 Editing Activity

Wengelin and Strömqvist (2000) demonstrate how the word level problems in dyslexic writers also show up in editing activity. A fragment of the final product of a route description produced by a dyslexic subject is given in Example 7a below. A translation is given in Example 7b. The translation is intended to preserve the flavor of the original writing problems.

7a) Väg beskrivnig.
Om du skall gå **till Bodil som sitter på första våningen och du befiner dig på 3våningen i klass rumet för läs- skrivsvårheter.** Du går till ......

7b) Routedescriptio.
If you want to go **to Bodil who sits on first floor and you are on 3floor in the class rom for reading writing diffilties.** You go to ......

Consider in particular, the text in boldface. Notice that the description tells us how to go *to* Bodil from *the classroom for reading and writing difficulties*. In Example 8a below, a version of the same text, but with all edits included, is shown. The translation is given in 8b. The brackets show text, which is deleted, and the text to the right of the brackets shows in most of the cases what is produced directly after the deletion. Each bracketed editing is given a numerical index and the numbers show in which order the deletions are made. The revision notation in 8a was automatically generated by ScriptLog and is closely related to S-notation (Kollberg, 1998; Matsuhashi, 1987). To illustrate how the notation works, we will explain the first action of editing [0 s 0]. We first see how the subject has written the title of the text, namely "Väg beskrivnig" (Route Descriptio). She writes "Väg". Then she (incorrectly) makes a space. After that she continues to the other half of the word, writes a 'b', misses out the 'e', writes an 's' and then realises that she has missed a letter and deletes the 's' and continues. In the end the word still misses an 'n' ("Vägbeskrivning" is the correct word). The following three consecutive "<CR>" indicate three Carriage Returns made by the subject, in order spatially to delimit the title just written from the first paragraph of the text to be produced.

8a) Väg b[0 s 0]eskrivnig.<CR><CR><CR>Om du skall gå **[12 från[10 [1 dyslexi 1]dy[5 [4 s[3 [2 ele 2]e 3]x 4]silex 5]selexsi[6 6]s klass ru[8 n[7 n 7]m 8]m till B[9 idil 9]odil som sitter på första vånigen, 10] [11 klass rumet 11]3vånigen där 12]**till Bodil som sitter på första vånin[13 f 13]gen och du befiner dig på 3våningen[14 där 14] i klass rumet för läs- skrivsvårheter.

8b) Route d[0 s 0]escription.<CR><CR><CR>If you want to go **[12 from the[10 [1 dyslexia 1]dy[5 [4 s[3 [2 ele 2]e 3]x 4]silex 5]selexsia[6 6]s class roo[8 n[7 n 7]m 8]m to B[9 idil 9]odil whose room is on the first flor, 10][11 the classrom 11]3floor where 12]** to Bodil whose room is on the first fl[13 i13]oor and you are on the 3floor[14 where 14] in the class rom for reading writing diffilties.

The bold text within the brackets **[12...12]** shows the subject's subsequent attempts to write "from the dyslexia classroom" and her final attempt to avoid the difficult word "dyslexi" (dyslexia). Interestingly, she first produces the word correctly (brackets 1). But she is not certain that it is correct, so she tries several different variants (brackets 2–5) before she settles on the incorrect version "dyselexsi". Then she has some problems (brackets 7–8) with "rummet" (the room) before she goes on to describe the target of the route description, namely the office of Bodil (the teacher of the Dyslexia course), which is situated on the first floor. However, when she has finished the sentence, she is still not certain of the spellings and deletes the whole sequence all the way back to the preposition "från" (from) and ventures a new round. This time she appears determined to avoid the word "dyslexi" and starts with "klass rumet" (incorrectly spelled, changes her mind again, deletes what she has just written (brackets 11) and restarts by mentioning the floor in question ("3vånigen där"). However, here she gives up, deletes her last attempt, and, interestingly, also deletes the preposition "from" (brackets 12). She ends up with the text shown in Example 7a. In effect, she has changed the information structure of the route description from a first version where she mentions the source of the locomotion (classroom on the 3rd floor) before the goal (office on 1st floor) to a version where the goal is mentioned before the source. The first version thus honors what is often referred to as the "principle of natural order" (see, e.g., Levelt, 1981), whereas the second version violates the same principle. It is reasonable to assume that the violation is not a consequence of a stylistic decision, but, rather, that it is an unintended consequence of the struggling with word level spelling problems.

### 4.4 Frequency Effects

The time needed to arrive at and strike a particular key on the keyboard can easily be extracted from the log-file. By plotting the duration (time value) of the transition to a key against the frequency of occurrence of that key, we can test whether there are any frequency effects present. For example: are those letters that are used frequently also typed at a faster speed?

A first analysis of this kind is presented by Strömqvist (1999) and here summarized in Figures 4 and 5. Strömqvist (1999) analysed keystrokes from two groups of adults, a group of dyslexic subjects ($N = 10$) and a control group ($N = 10$), each in four different writing

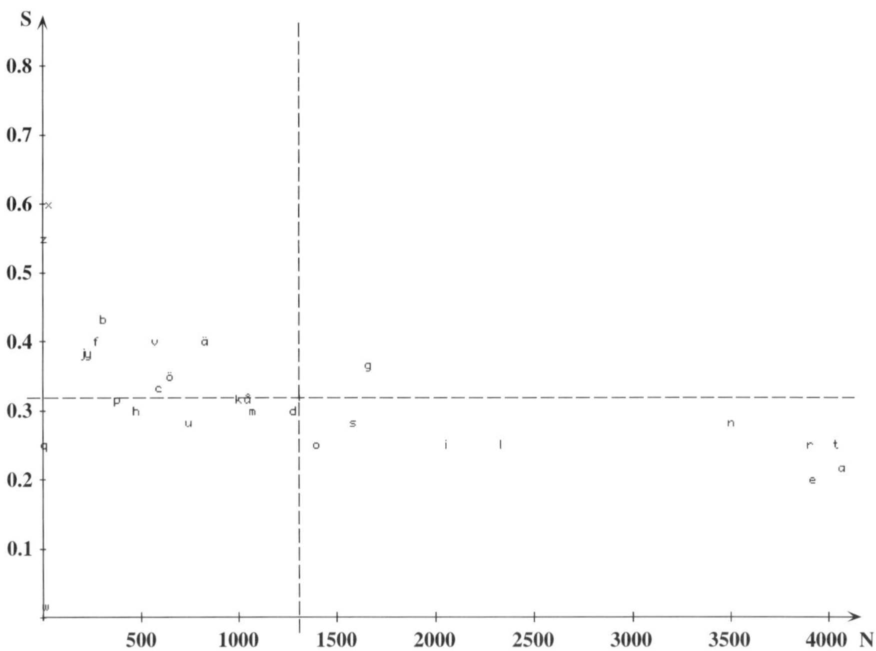


Figure 4: Frequency effects on typing speed in 10 control subjects with no reading or writing diffculties X 4 writing activities. The mean of medians of the transition duration (in sec) ($y$-axis) is plotted against frequency of occurrence ($N$) of the key ($x$-axis).
Source: Adapted from Strömqvist, S. (1999). Production rate profiles. In: S. Strömqvist, & E. Ahlsén (Eds), *The process of writing — a progress report* (p. 68). Copyright by The Department of Linguistics, Gothenburg University. Reprinted with permission.

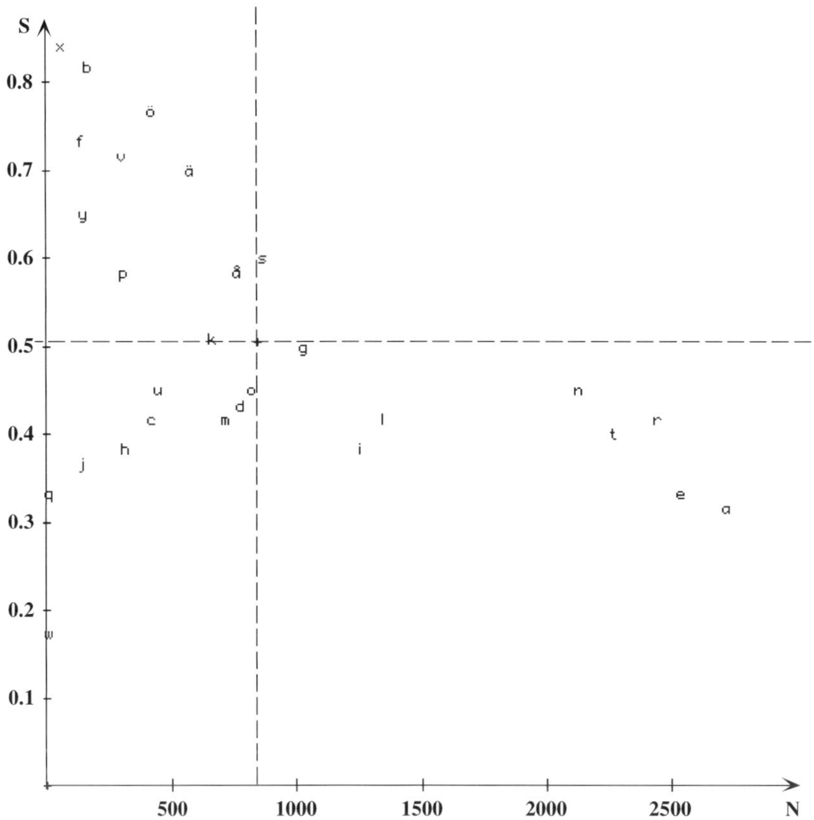


Figure 5: Frequency effects on typing speed in 10 dyslexic subjects X 4 writing activities. The mean of medians of the transition duration (in seconds) (*y*-axis) is plotted against frequency of occurrence (*N*) of the key (*x*-axis).
Source: Adapted from Strömqvist, S. (1999). Production rate profiles. In: S. Strömqvist, & E. Ahlsén (Eds), *The process of writing — a progress report* (p. 69). Copyright by The Department of Linguistics, Gothenburg University. Reprinted with permission.

activities (a route description, a personal narrative, a job-application letter, and a letter to the editor). In the figures, the mean of medians of the transition duration (in seconds) across the 10 subjects and 4 writing activities is plotted against frequency of occurrence (*N*) of the key.

The dashed horizontal line represents the mean duration and the dashed vertical line the mean frequency across all letter tokens. The two dashed lines partition the two-dimensional space in the figure into four fields. Roughly speaking, the upper left field represents infrequent letters which are typed at a slow speed, the lower left field infrequent letters which are typed at a high speed, the upper right field letters which are frequent and typed at a low speed, and the lower right field represents letters which are frequent and typed at a high speed.

A first observation is that the upper right field is empty in both figures (with the exception of a single letter close to the intersection of the dashed lines), whereas the other three fields are filled out with a similar number of letters. This distribution shows a frequency effect in that *if a letter is frequent, then it is typed at a high speed*. A comparison between Figures 4 and 5 indicates that this effect is stronger for the dyslexic group. A tentative conclusion, then, is that frequency of usage has a greater effect on non-proficient writers, and that this effect levels out as a writer is getting more proficient. Further, a comparison of the pictures shows that very similar topological relations hold between the distribution of letters in the two subject groups (compare, e.g., the most frequent letters, which are exactly the same). The figures reflect the fact that the dyslexic group writes less and at a slower speed than the control group, and this makes the impression of the strength of the frequency effect in this group slightly greater than it actually is.

Some of the distributions observed in Figures 4 and 5 can be interpreted as an effect of the interaction between letters and lexical items. For example, the fact that *c* and *h* are typed at a high speed although they are not so frequent, might be explained by the fact they are "overrepresented" in the Swedish function word *och* 'and'. Probably, this reflects the fact that the typing/construction of some very frequent words, notably function words, are automatized. A couple of letters are distributed at the extreme left of the lower left field in the figures. Those instances are most probably typos. For example, *w* (a very infrequent letter in the spelling of Swedish words) is adjacent to *e* (a very frequent letter in the spelling of Swedish words) on a Swedish keyboard, and so the extremely fast single *w* observed close to the lower left corner in both Figures 4 and 5 probably is the result of the writer's attempt to strike an *e*.

The analyses presented above can easily be extended to pairs, triples and n-tuples of letters, and to selected subsets of n-tuples, such as, for example, consonant clusters or function words. Also, this kind of analysis is well suited for the detection of crosslinguistic differences. For example, already given individual letters show a crosslinguistic variation in the extent to which they are used for the construction of words (*w* is used much more in English than in Swedish). Combinations of letters, such as consonant clusters are used to a very different degree in different languages (e.g., to a large extent in Swedish and to a minimal extent in Finnish). These differences can be expected to influence the topological landscape of letters for both dyslexic writers and those with no reading and writing difficulties as mapped out in the kind of plots illustrated in Figures 4 and 5.

## 5 Combining Keystroke Logging with Eye-Tracking

Producing a text involves an interplay between the main processes: Planning, Execution and Monitoring. Production-rate data derived from keystroke logging can, as we have seen, provide clues to fluent and hesitant phases during textwriting. Combining key logging with eye-tracking provides a powerful way of getting even closer to the textwriting subject, especially during his monitoring and revision activities, which necessitate visual feedback, that is, the reading of (relevant parts of) the emerging text. Further, data about eye movements can help refute hypotheses about what is going on in a pause, for example, is the subject (re)reading his text or not?

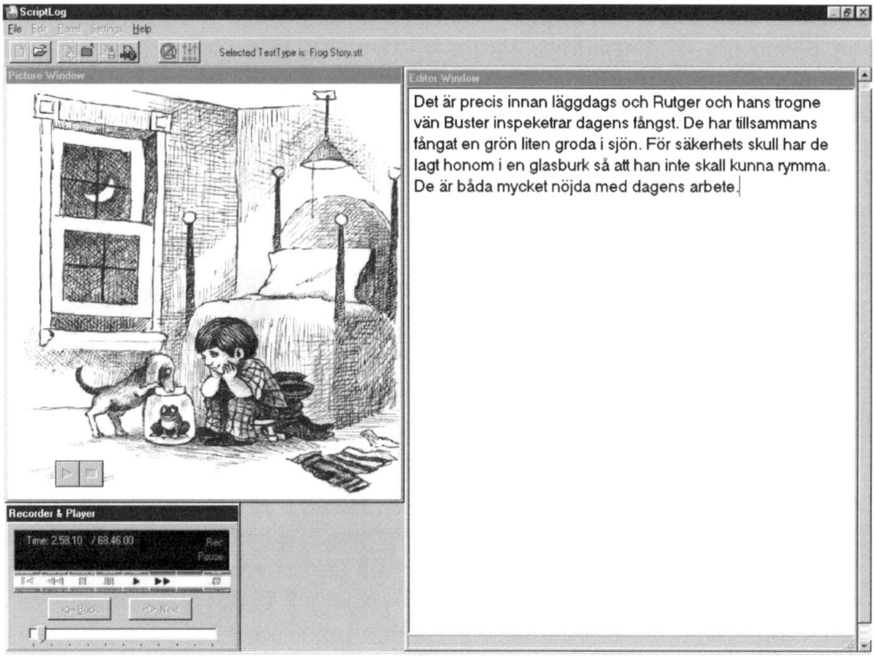


Figure 6: Screen-shot from a writing experiment with a 23-year-old Swedish university student. Stimulus picture (upper left), the resulting narrative text fragment in the editor window (right), and the recording panel (bottom left).
Source: Adapted from Holmqvist, K., Holsánová, J., Johansson, V., and Strömqvist, S. (2005). Perceiving and producing the frog story. In: D. Ravid, & H. Bat-Zeev Shyldkrot (Eds), *Perspectives on language and language development* (p. 290), Dordrecht: Kluwer. Copyright 2005 by Kluwer. Reprinted with permission.

Consider the screen-shot in Figure 6, taken from Holmqvist, Holsánová, Johansson, and Strömqvist (2005). It is derived from a recording of a computer-based narrative task, using the wordless picture story *Frog where are you?* (Mayer, 1969) as elicitation instrument (see also Berman & Slobin, 1994). The screen-shot was taken 2 min and 58 s into the recording. At that point, the subject, a 23-year-old Swedish university student, had just finished writing in relation to the first picture (out of 24) of the story.

How can we get a handle on the processes behind the product in Figure 6? How did the flow of writing interact with the distribution of visual attention? These are the main questions addressed in a study by Holmqvist, et al. (2005) (see also Holmqvist et al., 2002).[3]

[3]The combined technology ScriptLog—Eyetracking has been developed in the project "The dynamics of perception and production during text writing", sponsored by The Swedish Research Council and The Centre for Reading Research, University College of Stavanger. Project leaders are Sven Strömqvist, Department of Linguistics, and Kenneth Holmqvist, Department of Cognitive Science, University of Lund. Eyemovements are recorded with an iView X HED + HT eyetracking equipment.

Consider, to begin with, the linear file corresponding to the final edited text fragment shown in Figure 6. The linear file is shown in Example 9. Information about movements, such as using the backspace and delete keys, starting and ending the writing session, activating various elicitation stimuli, and pausing (shown in minutes, seconds and milliseconds) is indicated with angular brackets. The linear file differs from the final edited text in that the former contains elements that have been deleted from the final edited text. In the linear file, the insertions are thus found in the order in which they were produced during the writing session. The original Swedish linear text is followed by a facsimile in English.

9) <START><SECTION1><STIMULUS-ONSET><0.12.519>Det är precis innan läggdags och <0.06.980>Rutger och hans <0.06.810> trogne vän <0.14.495>Buster<0.07.341><0.09.760>inspeketrar dagens fångst. De har tillsammans fångat en grön liten groda i dammen.<BACKSPACE7>sjön. För säkerhetss<BACKSPACE> skull har de lagt honom i en glasburk så att han inte skall kunna rymma.<0.16.757> De är båda mycket nöjda med dagens arbete.

<START><SECTION1><STIMULUS-ONSET><0.12.519>It is just before bedtime and <0.06.980>Rutger and his <0.06.810>faithful friend <0.14.495>Buster<0.07.341> <0.09.760>are inspecting today's catch. They have together caught a green little frog in the pond.<BACKSPACE7>lake. For the sake<BACKSPACE> of security they have put him in a glass jar so that he won't be able to run away.<0.16.757> They are both very pleased with today's work.

The first item in the linear file shown in Example 9 is "<START>" which indicates that the subject pressed the start button to activate the editor window and the first stimulus picture. "<SECTION1>", then, indicates that the first elicitation picture was loaded and "<STIMULUS-ONSET>" that it was displayed on the screen. Pauses are indicated within angular brackets. In the linear file in Example 9, only pauses longer than 5 seconds are shown. Deletions are indicated by "<BACKSPACE>". In the first instance, "<BACKSPACE7>", the writer performs a lexical replacement. She strikes backspace seven times to delete the word *dammen* ('the pond') and a period, and then she writes the word *sjön* ('the lake') and a period. In the second instance, "<BACKSPACE>", the writer corrects a spelling/writing mistake by deleting an *s* in *säkerhetss* ('security'ss'). She replaces the *s* with a space and then writes *skull* ('sake'). In the final edited text, one spelling mistake remains uncorrected: the word *inspeketrar* (should be *inspekterar* 'inspect').

Further, we see that the writer had seven pauses longer than 5 s. The first pause of 12.5 s occurs in the beginning of the text. One can hypothesise that she looks at the picture, planning what to write next. Two of the pauses precede the naming of two story characters (the boy *Rutger* and the dog *Buster*), probably reflecting the writer's effort trying to find suitable names for these characters. One pause precedes the noun phrase *trogne vän* (*Buster*) ('faithful friend (Buster)'), and two consecutive pauses precede the verb phrase *inspekterar dagens fångst* ('are inspecting today's catch'). In both of these cases we assume that the pauses occur for planning reasons, such as composing the adjective phrases, selecting the appropriate verb (*inspektera*) etc. The longest pause (16.7 s) occurs in the sentence boundary before the last sentence. During that pause, the subject is probably reading through what she has written so far, in order to see if something is missing, or to get new ideas on how to continue the story. Before moving on to the next picture, she writes a final sentence, summing up and evaluating: *De är båda mycket nöjda med dagens arbete* ('They are both very pleased with today's work').

A detailed analysis example of the interplay between the writing behavior in Example 9 and the subject's visual behavior is presented in Figure 7. The example focuses on the first 90 s of the frog story narration, which amounts to the first sentence in Example 9. On the basis of eye-tracking and ScriptLog data, we have created a temporally ordered multimodal score-sheet (defined in Holsánová, 2001) which shows the visual behavior and writing behavior synchronised over time. Figure 7 shows the score-sheet for those first 90 s.

In Figure 7, the time line is projected downwards from the top to the bottom of the page. Objects present on the screen in the original writing condition (see Figure 6) are represented as columns in the score-sheet. The rightmost column represents the editor window and the second column from the right represents the picture (depicting the boy and his dog watching the frog). Then, in the order from right to left, follow columns representing details (sub-areas) of the picture: the boy, the frog, the dog, the window in the room, the lamp and bed. The left-most column in Figure 7, finally, represents the "Next" button (floating panel). When the subject is looking at a given object/sub-area of the screen for a certain period of time, this is indicated through a corresponding shading/blackening along the time line in the column representing the object/sub-area in question. For example, during the first few seconds, the subject is first looking at the lamp and bed in the stimulus picture, then at the frog and the boy, and then at the "Next" button. With the exception of the "Next" button, the viewing of these different objects is conflated in the Picture column. A grey stripe across all columns indicates that the subject is looking in another direction than that of the screen (e.g., at the keyboard, when typing). To the right of the picture, a layer with the writer's emerging text is added. Each letter has been placed at a height that indicates the point in time when it was typed. In effect, the decline of the row of letters mirrors the speed of writing: the decline is small when typing is fast and increases as typing gets slower. Consider, as an extreme case in point, the steep decline between "preci" and "s" as the subject writes the word "precis" ('just/precisely'), making a 2 s pause before the "s" at the end of the word. Pauses in writing which are longer than 5 s are marked with angular brackets.

From the temporally aligned eye-tracking and writing data in Figure 7, several patterns can be deduced and interpretations suggested. Thus, during the 12.5 s pause preceding the first keystroke of the writing activity, the eye-tracking data shows that the writer is looking at the picture. For the greater part of this time, she is looking back and forth between the three agents: the dog, the frog and the boy. This can be interpreted as time spent forming the first ideas for the narrative.

Further, typing activity in the subject always coincides with grey stripes across the columns in Figure 7, indicating that the subject is consistently looking at the keyboard when writing. When she redirects her visual attention to the screen, she very often looks directly at the text in the editor window (see rightmost column in Figure 7). We interpret these latter fixations as indicative of a need for visual feedback in the writing process.

The naming of the story characters is associated with very long pauses. During the almost 7 s long pause around 20 s into the writing activity, the writer first looks at the editor window, reading the text she has produced so far. She then alternates between looking

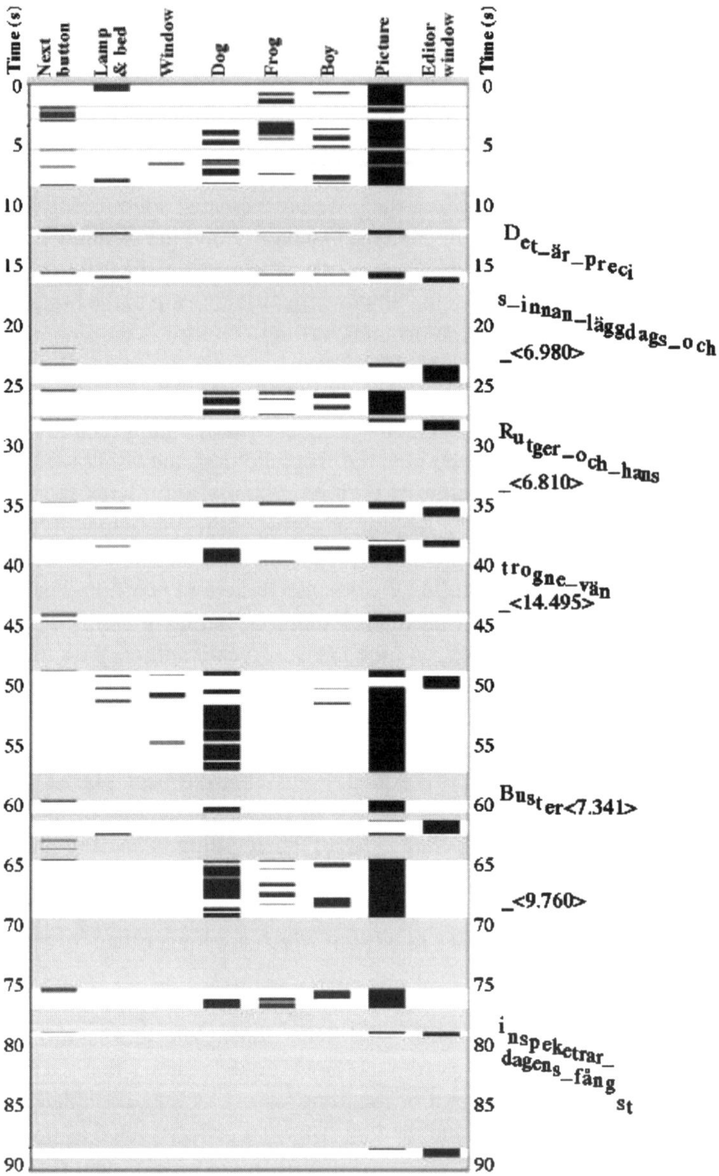


Figure 7: A multimodal score sheet representation of visual behavior and writing behavior during the first 90 s of a frog story narration.
Source: Adapted from Holmqvist, K., Holsánová, J., Johansson, V., and Strömqvist, S. (2005). Perceiving and producing the frog story. In: D. Ravid, & H. Bat-Zeev Shyldkrot (Eds), *Perspectives on language and language development* (p. 297), Dordrecht: Kluwer. Copyright 2005 by Kluwer. Reprinted with permission.

at the boy and the dog, before she looks back at the editor window and types a name referring to the boy, *Rutger*, together with the beginning of the noun phrase *och hans* ('and his'). Then, there follows a 6.8 s long pause, during which the subject divides her visual attention between first the dog, the boy and the frog, then the editor window, the keyboard, the editor window again, and ends with a long look at the dog. After the pause, she types the noun phrase *trogne vän* ('faithful friend'). In relation to both of these pauses the visual data indicates that she is searching the picture for information which might help her formulate the name and the descriptions.

The naming of the dog seems to be an even more effortful procedure. The writer spends the better part of an almost 14.5 s long typing pause looking at the dog. It is possible that the image of the dog helped her finding a suitable name, but it is more likely that the persistent looking at the dog helped her focus on the task of finding a name. After the pause, the subject types the name *Buster*. After *Buster*, the subject makes two consecutive pauses (7 and 9 s, respectively). She spends them looking back and forth between the dog, the frog and the boy, except for an almost 5 s long look down at the keyboard. Maybe she is looking down in order to start typing, but then changes her mind and decides to take a second look at the picture first. Again, this second look, around 75 s into the writing session, is directed towards the three main characters of the narrative. The subject then types *inspeketrar dagens fångst* ('inspecting today's catch'). Two very short glimpses at the text in the editor window are interleaved with this typing activity.

## 6 Experimental Research on Word-level Writing

The combination of a flexible module for designing writing experiments with very high standards of temporal resolution (1 ms) in the recording module makes ScriptLog adequate for real online experiments. Profiting from this resource, Nordqvist, Leiwo and Lyytinen (2003) used ScriptLog for implementing a dictation experiment. The experimental design is summarized in Figure 8. Figure 8 shows a series of events arranged along a time line and interconnected by the symbol "^", marking the transition interval between the events. ScriptLog keeps track of the events and measures the transition times between them. First, the subject presses a start button, and, in effect, ScriptLog displays an acoustic stimulus, in Figure 8 the nonsense word *tamppi*, two consecutive times. In response to the repeated stimulus, the subject writes the word, and ScriptLog registers the keystrokes. When the subject is done, (s)he pushes a stop button, marking the completion of the writing of the dictation word. ScriptLog then displays the button again, and when the subject pushes it, a new stimulus word is displayed, and so on.

Just like other computer administered response-time (RT) experiments, the time elapsing between stimulus onset or offset ($S_{ON}$ or $S_{OFF}$) and response onset or offset ($R_{ON}$ or $R_{OFF}$) can be measured. (In Figure 8, the part of the time line extending from the offset of the repeated stimulus, throughout the response, and up to the stop button has received an additional marking underlining that this part might be of particular interest.) But in distinction to standard RT-tools, ScriptLog also measures the internal production rate of the response, in the example shown in Figure 8 the keystroke sequence "t^a^m^p^p^i". This permits a more fine-grained analysis of spelling, and Nordqvist et al. (2003) used this

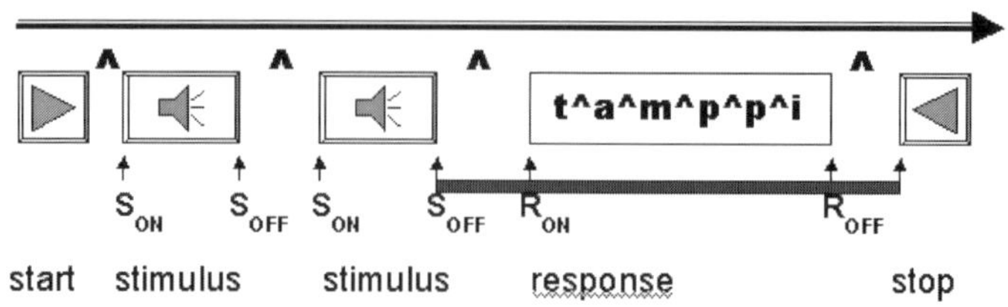


Figure 8: The design of a dictation experiment implemented in ScriptLog.
Source: From Nordqvist, Å., Leiwo, M., & Lyytinen, H. (2003). From nonsense words to space adventure: Developing a test battery to study and diagnose writing. Paper presented at the 13th European Conference on Reading, Reading-Writing-Thinking, Tallinn, Estonia.

technique for studying, among other things, the double-spelling of consonants to render quantity in Finnish. In a pilot experiment, Nordqvist et al. (2003) presented a set of nonsense words (including *tamppi*) to a group of Finnish 9-year-olds, divided into Poor readers ($N = 5$), Average readers ($N = 9$) and Good readers ($N = 5$). The results for *tamppi* — in terms of intra-word transitions — are summarized in Figure 9.

Figure 9 shows, by and large, a consistent pattern across the three subgroups. The interval immediately before the geminate consonant — that is, the transition "m^p" — is by far the slowest, and the transition "p^p" — that is, the transition internal to the geminate consonants — is by far the fastest. This difference is statistically significant when all 19 subjects are treated as one group. The difference suggests that the decision whether to double the consonant or not is taken before the first of the two geminate consonants is produced, and that the execution of the doubling of the consonant is then carried out without any hesitation. In slightly more interpretative terms, we might say that the former microcontext is a window towards cognitive processes (decision making), whereas the latter microcontext is a window towards keyboard motor skills. This interpretation is further bolstered by the fact that the poor readers take longer time than the average readers to reach the critical decision whether to double-spell or not, whereas the good readers take shorter time. These group differences are not statistically significant, however, something which is probably due to the very small number of subjects in each group. Further, the difference in production rate between the poor and good readers in the context "p^p" is marginal.

In a similar dictation experiment, Solheim and Uppstad (2003) studied the spelling of quantity in Norwegian 9-year-olds. In contrast to Nordqvist et al. (in press), Solheim and Uppstad used real words as stimuli. They replicated Nordqvist's et al. finding that the interval immediately before the spelling of the target geminate consonant was significantly longer than the transition within the geminate consonant sequence, and that this pre-geminate interval was longer for the poor than for the good readers. In contrast to Nordqvist's et al. (in press) finding, however, Solheim and Uppstad (2003) found different transition-time patterns in the two subgroups. In the strong writers, the pre-geminate interval was significantly longer and the inter-geminate interval significantly shorter than the average letter-to-letter transition "a^a". In the poor writers, there was no significant difference

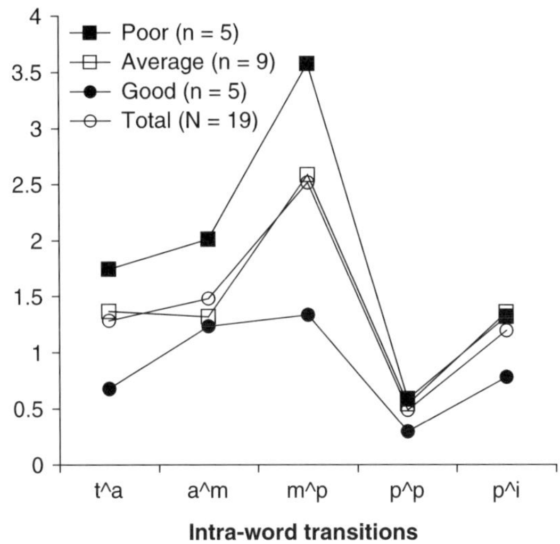


Figure 9: Intra-word transitions from a dictation experiment.
Source: From Nordqvist, Å., Leiwo, M., & Lyytinen, H. (2003). From nonsense words to space adventure: Developing a test battery to study and diagnose writing. Paper presented at the 13th European Conference on Reading, Reading-Writing-Thinking, Tallinn, Estonia.

between the pre-geminate interval and the average "a^a", whereas the inter-geminate interval was significantly shorter than the average "a^a". For a similar study of spelling in Swedish 9-year-olds, see Pelli and Sinimäki (2004).

Another type of online experiment, designed to explore word-level writing and using keystroke logging, was implemented by Bertram, Toennessen, Strömqvist, Hyönä, and Niemi (in preparation). Following Weingarten's work on sublexical features as a determinant to production rate (e.g., Will, Weingarten, Nottbusch, & Albes, 1992), Bertram et al. used ScriptLog to administer a naming task to a group of Finnish subjects. The technical design was similar to the one shown in Figure 8, except that the stimulus was visual and only shown once. The stimulus pictures were chosen to elicit lexical compounds. Bertram et al. (in preparation) was able to determine that sublexical features influence production rate very systematically. Thus, letter-to-letter transitions that coincided with morpheme boundary tended to have longer transition time values than transitions that coincided with syllable boundary, which in their turn, tended to have longer transition time values than transitions between letters within syllables. All these differences were statistically significant. For example, in the case of "lumiukko" 'snow man', the transition "i^u" coincides with the boundary between "lumi" 'snow' and "ukko" 'man' and resulted in an average transition time value of 383 ms. At the syllable boundary "u^m" an average transition time value of 276 ms was observed, whereas in the transitions "l^u", "m^i", "u^k" and "k^o" the value was 224 ms. The shortest average transition time value, 156 ms, was observed in the context "k^k".

Bertram et al. (in preparation) also analysed the transition time values between stimulus onset (the display of the picture) and response onset (the pressing of the key corresponding to the first letter of the word written in relation to the picture). The analysis revealed that the length of the response time was a function of the frequency of the target word. The higher the frequency, the faster the retrieval. Bertram's study amplifies the usefulness of keystroke logging for psycholinguistic research.

## 7 Research Directions

The behavioral flow of writing revealed by keystroke logging methodology takes the analyst closer to the processes brought to play when a word is written or a whole text is being produced. In the preceding sections, we have tried to give a bird's eye perspective on methods and procedures for studying aspects of writing by means of keystroke logging. Many questions and research problems remain to be solved, however, before a more fullfledged picture of textwriting emerges from the budding paradigm. And more research is needed to consolidate and refine the methods and observations reviewed in this paper.

One direction for future research is to combine keystroke logging with other online data. Here, eyetracking can play a key role. When eye-tracking data is added, an enhanced picture of attentional processes during writing emerges. The combination of computer logged writing with eyetracking offers a window on the dynamic interplay between perception and production during textwriting. In our further research, the subactivity of text revision will receive a special focus, since this is an activity that necessitates an interaction between reading and writing. It therefore provides a particularly fortuitous window on the dynamic interplay between perception and production during textwriting.

Another type of online data is ERP (event related potentials) data, registrations of the temporal patterning and amplitude of electrical activity in the cortex. This technology offers a registration with a very high time resolution, but a relatively small time window, which rules out its usage in connection with textwriting, at least at present. ERP-measurement would, however, present an interesting extension to the kind of word-level writing experiments reviewed in Section 6.

Further, extensive empirical research needs to be carried out, in order to determine developmental patterns and patterns characteristic of writers with reading and writing problems. Not the least, there is a need for large-scale studies and the standardisation of measures. Whereas there exist well-established standardised measures of reading skills in children of different age groups, there are, as yet, no corresponding standards for writing skills. Keystroke logging provides a basis for remedying that situation.

A firmer grasp of writing development in a first language — with its typical patterns as well as variability — also paves the way for comparative studies with writing development in a second or foreign language. See, for example, Hedbor (2003), Wagner, Hansen, and Uppstad (in press). See also Sullivan and Lindgren (2002).

Keystroke logging and the analysis of textwriting online has an important role to play for the enhancement of tests and diagnostic procedures, of language pedagogy and computer based writing support tailored to users with different needs and different abilities (*cf.* Ahlsén & Strömqvist, 1999).

Many pedagogical applications presuppose an awareness on the part of the student/writer. To what extent are writers consciously aware of the decisions they are making online as they are constructing and reconstructing their texts? An off-line method for tapping such information from writers is the Think Aloud Protocol (see, e.g., Bereiter & Scardamalia, 1987; Hayes & Flower, 1980). A disadvantage with this method is that the protocol intervention inevitably disturbs the production process (Janssen, Van Waes, & Van den Bergh, 1996). A post-writing debriefing interview supported by playback of a key-logged writing session may prove to be a way around that problem. For an interesting study exploring this method, see Sullivan and Lindgren (2002). For further ideas about the usage of keystroke logging and the analysis of online writing to support writing development in the classroom, see Hellum (2000).

Another line of research relates to the rapidly growing archives of recordings of writing activity. To date, we have some 3000 ScriptLog recordings from 10 different languages and from writers of different age-groups and abilities. The archive has already been used as a resource for the construction of a probabilistic tool for spelling support for dyslexic writers. In the near future, the archive will also serve as a testing ground for new types of crosslinguistic research questions. For example, do certain sequences of letters or certain grammatical constructions tend to be written faster or monitored more carefully in certain linguistic communities than in others? Again, we believe that the answer to this kind of questions can have important implications for applied areas, such as translation or second language learning. Also, a searchable, web-based archive of online writing data from writers of different languages, age-groups and abilities, would present a rich source not only for researchers, but also for teachers and students. Imagine a situation where, for example, a class of English pupils in upper secondary school engage in a process-oriented writing project as part of their studying French as a foreign language. The kind of web-based archive outlined above would make it possible for the students and their teacher to identify and download age-matched writing data from French school children writing compositions in French. The implications of this way of extending language pedagogy are huge. A truly integrated database of this kind, however, including data collected by the many different keystroke-logging programs available at the present time, poses important problems that call for an efficient solution. Most importantly, a consistent notation must be used for recorded writing sessions, regardless of the computer environment where they were generated (see Wittenburg, Johnson, Buchhorn, Brugman, & Broeder, 2004 for a related discussion). Also, a common metadata format is a prerequisite to the general searchability of the data (Strömqvist et al., 2004a).

It should be obvious from the examples and discussion in previous sections that any one scholar interested in the design of studies of online writing and the interpretation of the resultant data does well in making friends with scholars in adjacent fields of science. Thus, expertise and perspectives pertaining to linguistic and cognitive sciences, educational science, literary science and narratology — just to mention a few fields — are all relevant to the study of online writing. We end this article by cherishing keystroke logging and the analysis of online writing as a lure to crossdisciplinary cooperation.

Chapter 5

# Inputlog: New Perspectives on the Logging of On-Line Writing Processes in a Windows Environment

Mariëlle Leijten and Luuk Van Waes
*University of Antwerp, Antwerp, Prinsstraat, Belgium*

*The use of computers as writing instruments has not only had a profound effect on the writing practice and the attitudes towards writing, it has also created new possibilities for writing research. In the field of cognitive writing research especially, keystroke-logging programs have become very popular. In this paper we describe a new logging program, called Inputlog. The program consists of three modules: (1) a data collection module that registers on-line writing processes on a very detailed level; (2) a data analysis module that offers basic and more advanced statistical analyses (e.g., text and pause analysis); and (3) a play module that enables researchers to review the writing session. In this chapter we describe the technical and functional characteristics of Inputlog and we wind up the paper with a preview of the plans for further developments.*

**Keywords:** Inputlog, keystroke logging, registration tool, on-line writing processes, pauses, writing modes, text analysis, pause analysis, writing observation, cognitive processes.

## 1 Introduction

As most writers nowadays produce nearly all of their texts on a word processor, the computer has not only become the major writing instrument, its use as a research tool has also increased. The computer enables researchers to collect detailed information about the

---

**Computer Key Stroke Logging and Writing: Methods and Applications**

**ISBN: 0-08-044934-4**

*Leijten, M. and Van Waes, L. (2006). Inputlog: New perspectives on the logging of on-line writing processes in a windows environment.*
*In G. Rijlaarsdam (Series Ed.) and K. P. H. Sullivan, & E. Lindgren. (Vol. Eds.), Studies in Writing, Volume 18, Computer Keystroke Logging: Methods and Applications (pp. 73–93). Oxford: Elsevier.*

writing process that were hardly accessible before. Or, as Spelman Miller and Sullivan state in the introduction of this volume:

> As an observational tool, keystroke logging offers the opportunity to capture details of the activity of writing, not only for the purposes of the linguistic, textual and cognitive study of writing, but also for the broader applications concerning the development of language learning, literacy, and language pedagogy. (p. 1)

As we see throughout the book, nowadays, researchers make frequent use of keystroke logging tools to describe online writing processes in detail. These logging programs enable researchers to exactly register and accurately reconstruct the writing processes of writers that compose texts at the computer. The basic concept of the different logging tools that have been developed is more or less comparable. First, the keystroke logging tools register all keystrokes and mouse movements. During the writing process these basic data are stored for later processing. This continuous data storage does not interfere with the normal usage of the computer, creating an ecologically valid research context. At a later stage, the logged data can be made available for further analysis, either within the program environment itself or as exported data in statistical programs such as SPSS or SAS. Depending on the research question, researchers can choose to analyze different aspects of the writing process and the writing behavior by combining, for instance, temporal data (e.g., time stamps or pauses) with process data (keystrokes or mouse movements). The data collection (and processing) can be performed much faster and more accurately by means of the computer, than it could ever be done manually.

For the development of Inputlog we were able to fall back on the functionality of two existing programs: JEdit and Trace-it on the one hand (Kollberg, 1998; Severinson Eklundh, 1992, 1994; Severinson Eklundh & Kollberg, 1996b, 2003), and ScriptLog on the other (Strömqvist & Malmsten, 1998; Strömqvist, Holmqvist, Johansson, Karlsson, & Wengelin, this volume). As mentioned in the introductory chapter, JEdit and Trace-it are only suitable for Macintosh personal computers. JEdit only logs data in an in-house developed limited word processor. ScriptLog also mainly logs in a limited word processor that was developed for research purposes (i.e., mainly writing experiments with young children). Trace-it features an extended revision module, while ScriptLog combines logging data with recorded eye-tracking data.

### *1.1 JEdit*

JEdit is a logging word processor that has been developed for Macintosh. JEdit supports some of the most common text editing functions (e.g., cut, paste, undo, redo, text formatting). Furthermore, it provides basic statistics about writing sessions, such as information about pauses, commands used, input devices used, etc.

JEdit logs a writing session in an icon-based log file format (for example, see introductory chapter). This log can be exported to a file in the so-called MID-format. MID — an acronym for 'Movement, Insertion, and Deletion' — is an editor-independent format that

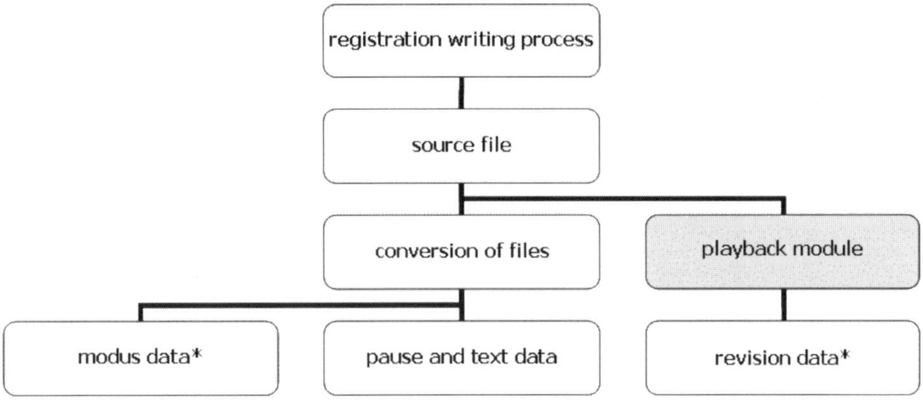


Figure 1: Basic flow of the logging and analysis conversion in Inputlog.

## 3 Technical Description

In this section we describe Inputlog from a more technical perspective. Technical terminology will be further explained in the glossary (see Appendix A). Inputlog captures input data at a level before they are converted to screen information. It captures

- scancodes of keystrokes;
- mouse activities (clicks, movements, location); and
- time stamps of all input events.

These data are stored in the so-called IDF-files (Inputlog Data Files) that are converted to different output files afterwards, preparing the rough data for qualitative and quantitative analyses (*cf.* functional description in Section 4).

### *3.1 Programming Language*

Inputlog is programmed in Visual C++ and the interface is programmed in Visual Basic. We have opted for C++ as a programming language because of its processing speed and its object-oriented feature. Each part of Inputlog is programmed in different classes (see Figure 2). This enables us to easily update and debug the current analyses, and to further extend the functionality of the program. It is important to note that the resident logging program does not interfere with the usage of the word processor, and consequently, that it does not hinder the writer during his or her writing process in any way. Inputlog runs on a PC with only one CPU and its use of system resources is quite limited, contrary to, e.g. Java.

For the logging of the writing process Inputlog uses two Windows Hooks: Journalrecord and Journalplayback. Journalrecord registers every keystroke and mouse operation (movement and click) together with the corresponding time stamps. The Journalplayback is the DLL-file that supports the playback module.

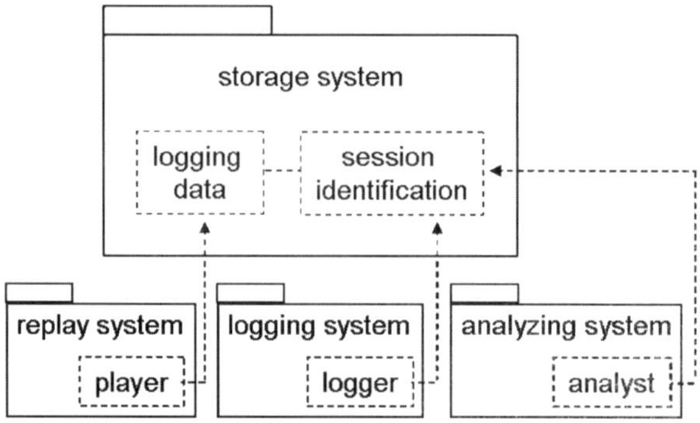


Figure 2: System topology of Inputlog.

### 3.2 Structure of Inputlog

Figure 2 shows the structure of Inputlog, or the so-called 'system topology'. Inputlog consists of four subsystems: storage, replay, logging, and analysis. The storage system activates the classes' session identification and processes the logging data. The session identification saves the relevant data to identify and name the session. The logging system saves all the logging data in a designed algorithm that is stored in an array list.

The storage system has three subordinated systems: replay, logging, and analysis. These three subsystems are all dependent on the storage system.

- The replay system needs logged data to replay a writing session.
- The logging system needs to provide information to the session information.
- The analysis system needs information about the session identification to confirm and name the correct writing session.

The session identification can run any type of analysis by initializing the right class (e.g., PauseAnalyst initializes the pause analysis). The classes' player and logger are the so-called 'singletons', *viz.* only one of them can be active in the system. Consequently, Inputlog always needs to perform a consecutive analysis to verify that only one of these two subsystems is active: the logger cannot log while playing and vice versa.

The three subsystems can function independently. The GUI interacts with the session identification to play, log, or analyze a logging session.

### 3.3 Structure of IDF-Files

Each IDF-file contains the data of one logging session. In this file the logging data are combined with the session identification data (see Section 4.1). The structure of the IDF-file is shown in Figure 3.

<table>
<tr><th>bytes</th><th>meaning</th></tr>
<tr><td>4</td><td>starting time of the log in milliseconds</td></tr>
<tr><td>14 * 4</td><td>14 digits that indicate the size (viz. number of signs) of the session variables<br>(6 values for the defined variables, 4 for the user defined variables and 4 for the undefined values)</td></tr>
<tr><td>14 * #</td><td>14 session variables * number of the size that has already been read</td></tr>
<tr><td># * 20</td><td>serial number of keyboard and/or mouse event (type Eventmsg)<br><br>Each event that is logged by Inputlog creates a log event of 20 bytes.<br>An Eventmsg is:
<table>
<tr><th>bytes</th><th>meaning</th></tr>
<tr><td>4</td><td>message type (key in, key out, mousemovement, left mouse button in, left mouse button out, etc.)</td></tr>
<tr><td>4</td><td>paramL<br>for keystrokes: virtual keycode<br>for mouse events: x-value of location of the mouse</td></tr>
<tr><td>4</td><td>paramH<br>for keystrokes: scancode<br>for mouse events: y-value of location of the mouse</td></tr>
<tr><td>4</td><td>timestamp in milliseconds starting from the beginning of the log<br>(time event – starting time of computer) * starting time of the log</td></tr>
<tr><td>4</td><td>handle to active window</td></tr>
</table></td></tr>
</table>

Figure 3: Structure of the IDF-file.

### *3.4 Conversion of Files*

The session identification information and the logging data are converted to a Microsoft Excel sheet or an HTML-file. The data files can also be converted to SPSS, or any other statistical program. Because the data are prestructured to facilitate further statistical analyses, it is important to define labels and variables before starting the writing session. Inputlog provides the possibility to attribute six predefined (participant, age, sex, session, group, experience) and four extra user-defined variables. Empty columns in the session identification, *viz.* undefined variables, are automatically assigned the missing code "99". This eases the process of filtering empty columns that are not needed for further analysis. Besides, in the Microsoft Excel output, the first column is automatically generated. This enables researchers to assign a unique number to every single variable or row.

### *3.5 Program Settings*

Inputlog is dependent on some basic settings that are particular to the computer configuration that is used to log the writing session. We shortly discuss three main configuration elements: screen settings, keyboard layout, and the memory allocation.

**3.5.1 Screen settings** As stated before, Inputlog replicates the writing session exactly as it is logged. Therefore, it is important that the computer settings — both screen and program settings (e.g., toolbars, language settings, personal dictionaries, etc.) — are exactly the

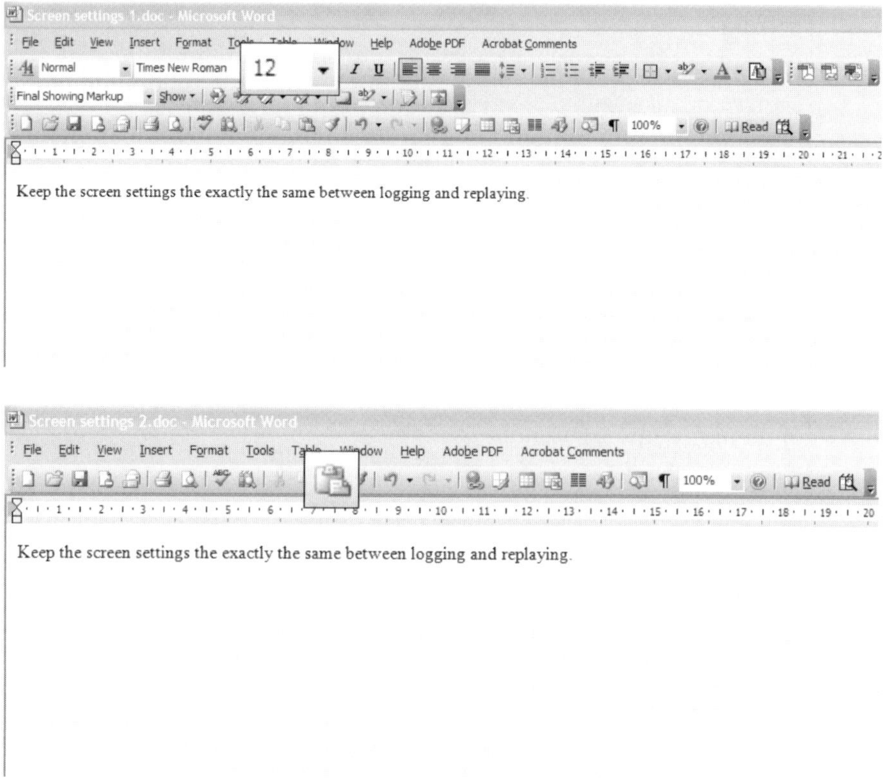


Figure 4: Illustration of a replay with different screen settings.

same when replaying a writing session as when the writing session was recorded. A short example is given to illustrate this issue. A writing session is recorded with only the standard toolbar active. However, between the logging session and the moment the observation session is replayed, the formatting and reviewing toolbar are added to the working environment which results in a different positioning of certain icons on the screen in comparison to the previous screen outline. Consequently, because the replay uses the graphic *xy*-position of mouse clicks, the cursor might select a different icon or item than it did at the time the session was recorded. Figure 4 shows, for instance, that during a replay with different screen settings, instead of changing the font into size 12, the paste-icon was selected. The result is that the continuity of the writing process reconstruction is severely disturbed. Therefore, researchers are recommended to keep the settings of the computer screen exactly the same between logging and replaying.

Note that this particular point of interest should only be taken into account when using the replay function of Inputlog. The generation of the different analyses[4] is not disturbed by different settings.

[4]Because the revision analysis is also based on the replay function, the settings should also be consistent for this analysis. However, in Inputlog 1.4 this function is not yet activated.

**3.5.2 Keyboard layout** A second configuration aspect that can influence the logging of a writing session are the keyboard layouts of the computer used during the logging session. As a result of the amount of different keyboard layouts, Inputlog has to detect the correct layout of the keyboard used. For instance, if a writing session is logged with QWERTY-settings and the actual layout of the keyboard is AZERTY, the following sentence will be represented incorrectly in the logging output:

Typed sentence: *This is a short writing session in Inputlog.*
Logged sentence: *This is **q** short zriting session in Inputlog.*

To avoid this problem Inputlog is programmed to detect the correct hard-coded keyboard layouts for the lowercase characters and reads the connected Windows settings for the uppercase characters. At this moment, 33 different keyboard layouts are predefined in Inputlog 1.4 (see the program's help-file for a detailed list).

# 4 Functional Description

The previous section described the technical background of Inputlog. In this section we shortly explain the basic functionality of the program and its interface. The interface of Inputlog consists of an entry screen and four different tab pages: record, generate, play, and help (see Figure 5). The help file is a standard html-file that can also be consulted without starting Inputlog itself. For more detailed information about the use of the program we refer to this file.

## *4.1 Entry Screen*

Inputlog starts with an entry screen that provides the user with a short overview of the pro gram. The user can opt to start a new logging session, he or she can generate files from an existing logging file or he or she can choose to replay a logged session. The different tabs give the user direct access to the different functions. By using the main menu items at the top of the screen — File, Settings, and Help — basic file operations can be activated, program settings can be changed and the help file can be accessed.

## *4.2 Record*

By selecting the record tab, users can start a new logging session. However, before a new session is started the researcher can first specify the file information and the identification data for a specific session. This information will be included in all the analysis files that will be generated based on the session source file, facilitating the identification of each writing session.

In the file information, users can indicate where they want to save the logging session on their computer hard or network drive, and they can enter the unique filename for the source file, e.g. FirstnameLastname1(=Firstname participant+Lastname participant+Number of

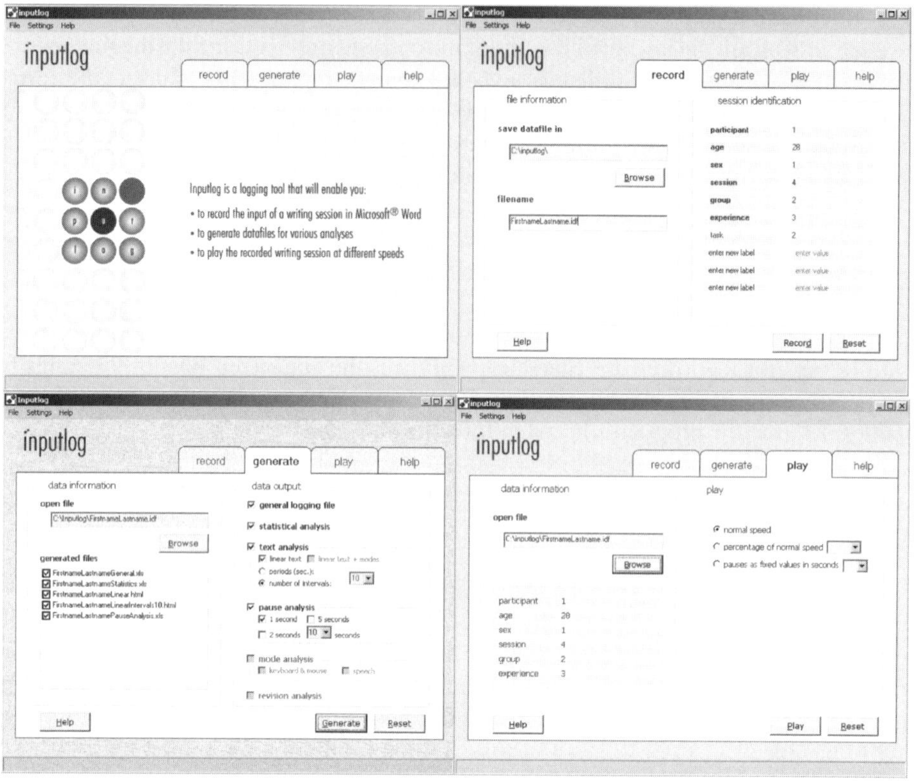


Figure 5: The four main tab pages of the Inputlog interface.

session). The file that will be generated in the recording session has the extension *.idf, which is added automatically. This file will be used as an input for the generate and play functions (*cf.* infra).

Each logging session can be identified by a maximum of ten variables (six predefined and four user-defined variables). These variables should enable the researcher to identify a writing session in detail.

### *4.3 Generate*

The generate tab opens a window showing the different analysis options. In this part of the program, analysis files can be generated on the basis of a source file that was recorded in a previous logging session. In other words, any IDF-file can be opened at any time to generate data output files for specific analyses. The generate window exists of three sections. In the data information section, users can specify the IDF-file from which they would like to generate the analyses. In the data output section the researcher can specify which output needs to be generated. In the section below the data information, a list of all the files to be generated is displayed.

Inputlog 1.4 offers four different data analyses:

(1) *General logging file*: a spreadsheet with a basic log file of the writing session in which every line represents an input action (letter, function, mouse click, or movement); for every input action the session information is stored together with an identification of the input, the time stamp, the pausing time that followed it, and — for a mouse operation — the *xy*-value of the screen position (for an overview see Appendix B).
(2) *Statistical analysis*: a spreadsheet with basic statistical information on the writing session such as the session information, some basic data about the written text (product and process), pausing behavior and the use of the different writing modes.
(3) *Text analysis*: a plain linear text in HTML format with the complete linear production of the text including mouse movements and other activities; extra options allow for the production of a linear output in which the writing activities are divided into periods (fixed time periods of × sec, free to choose) or intervals (fixed number of intervals in which the writing process is to be divided, free to choose).
(4) *Pause analysis*: a spreadsheet with analyses of every non-scribal period; the threshold for the pauses can be set to 1, 2, or 5 sec as a standard or to any user defined level.

Two other analyses are under construction at this moment:

(1) *Mode analysis*: a spreadsheet with information about the distribution of the writing modes (keyboard, mouse, speech technology) that were used as an input device during the writing session.
(2) *Revision analysis*: a spreadsheet with a basic analysis of the number, the level and the kind of revision that has taken place during the writing session.

Inputlog takes some time to generate the requested files; the progress is shown in the 'generated file' section. The different files are all placed in the same folder as the source file of the selected writing session (*cf.* 4.2 Record). This allows users to keep track of the recordings and analyses per writing session. The Excel files of the statistical and pause analysis consist of two parts (worksheets): a full analysis and an overview or summary of the writing session. The full analyses enable researchers to merge different files in a statistical program and to run further statistical analyses on the data. The overview on the other hand provides a short summary of the data. In addition, Inputlog creates for each level of pause analysis another worksheet in Microsoft Excel (e.g., pause-analysis-1-second and pause-analysis-5-seconds; see Appendix C for further information).

### 4.4 Play

A recorded writing session can be replayed using Inputlog. Again, the IDF-file is used as a source file for the replay. To verify the information labels of the file that is selected for a play back session, all defined variables of the session identification appear in the dialog box on the left side of the screen. The writing session can be replayed at different speeds. It can be played back exactly as it was recorded (in real time): this is an exact reproduction of the recording of the session. Another option is that users select a percentage of the real time speed. However, we would like to restrict this option to a maximum of 120% of the original speed. Otherwise the program may have difficulties in processing and performing certain actions that require extensive memory access. The final option 'pauses at a fixed value' enables researchers to assign a fixed value, e.g. 0.1 s, to every pause (non-scribal activity). This allows users to view a writing session without long interruptions or pauses.

### 4.5 Help File

The help tab contains a structured manual of the program. The help tab is a combination of a short instruction of Inputlog functionality and a program description. The main part of the help file consists of three chapters, each corresponding to the three basic functions of the software tool: record, generate, and play. The help on each of these functions is also directly available via the help button on the associated tabs.

## 5 Further Development

To facilitate a broad usage of Inputlog, the program is put at the disposal of the research community for free on www.inputlog.net, provided that reference is made to this publication. The users' feedback is very important for the evaluation and further development of Inputlog.

We have identified four important niches that may increase the applicability of Inputlog, especially in the domain of writing process research. In the near future we would like to further develop the following (in order of priority):

(1) a module for logging speech recognition events;
(2) a module for revision analysis;
(3) a module for progression analyses (basic and extended); and
(4) a module for integration with Morae (a macro oriented observation tool developed by Techsmith[5])

In addition to these developments, we will pay special attention to the further development and optimization of the existing modules. Furthermore, the compatibility with different versions of the Windows operating systems and the Office environment will require constant attention. Finally, the integration of our logging data with data from eye tracking observations is also on the agenda.

### 5.1 Speech Recognition

In our current research we are studying the influence of speech recognition on the writing process (Leijten & Van Waes, 2005). For this study we observed the writing processes of

[5]For more information about Morae we refer to the Techsmith's website: www.techsmith.com.

twenty participants who used speech recognition software during their day-to-day work in their professional business contexts (five observations of approximately half an hour per participant). The main research question is how writers adapt their writing process to the possibilities and limitations of this new writing mode, i.e. using continuous speech recognition as a writing device: How do they adapt their writing style to the dictation mode? How do they interact with the 'text produced so far' (=spoken text made visible on the screen)? How do they combine the different writing modes (speech, keyboard, and mouse) in their writing process? Does their writing strategy and their organization of the writing process change over time?

To answer these questions, we had to develop a research method that enabled us to describe the writing processes of persons using speech technology in their writing activities, taking into account the specific characteristics of this writing mode. In a previous research project we collected data of writing process data using QuickRecord (capturing the oral input of the dictators in a WAV format) and Camtasia (capturing the screen activity in an AVI format, i.e. representing the dictated text as it evolves during the writing session; see also Degenhardt, 2005). However, the analyses of the data collected in this way are extremely laborious. Therefore, computer assisted logging would be very helpful to facilitate the recording and analyses of writing sessions in which speech technology is used. Because Inputlog version 1.4 only logs keystrokes and mouse movements, we would also like to log the input produced by speech technology in the next release. More specifically, we would like to log the input of the most widely used speech recognition software, i.e. Dragon Naturally Speaking. To facilitate this integration, a new API was added to the professional version of Dragon Naturally Speaking 8.1,[6] which enables us to integrate the dictated text with the data logged by Inputlog. The new API makes it possible to generate an XML file of a recorded speech session, including time stamps for every event.

The general logging file generated by Inputlog also relies on time stamps as a basis for the data analysis. In Inputlog 1.4 this file is converted to Excel files for further analyses. For the new release of Inputlog we opted to convert this source file to XML files, because this format is more flexible to implement. The XML format also enables us to combine and integrate the speech recognition data into one general logging file based on the convergence of time stamps (see Figure 6). The result is a single file that can be used for further analysis of multi modal writing sessions in which speech input is combined with keyboard and mouse.

Figure 6 shows a short excerpt of a logged writing process in which three writing modes were used (column one): keyboard (1), mouse (2), and speech (3). When typing the word 'citation', the letters are each represented in one row, together with the time stamps of the key presses (in and out). The words that are dictated with the DNS software are each represented as tokens (of which also a WAV recording is logged). These logging data enable us to study the hybrid character of this kind of writing processes, e.g. by analyzing mode switches, repairs or productivity rate. In this example, for instance, we notice that it took the participant about 3 s to type the first word; the dictation of the eight words that followed the typing, took also about 3 s. This shows the potential productivity rate of speech recognition.

[6]We would like to thank Stijn van Even, Guido Gallopyn, and Neil Grant of Scansoft for all their efforts in making the logging facility at Dragon Naturally Speaking available to us.

| writing mode | output | input in_sec | input out_sec |
|---|---|---|---|
| 2 | Movement | 0,010 | 0,911 |
| 1 | C | 3,315 | 3,385 |
| 1 | i | 4,006 | 4,066 |
| 1 | t | 5,197 | 5,267 |
| 1 | a | 5,367 | 5,408 |
| 1 | t | 5,658 | 5,718 |
| 1 | i | 6,149 | 6,219 |
| 1 | o | 6,349 | 6,409 |
| 1 | n | 6,649 | 6,719 |
| 1 | SPACE | 8,352 | 8,412 |
| 1 | ENTER | 8,903 | 8,963 |
| 1 | ENTER | 9,053 | 9,133 |
| 3 | I | 9,974 | 10,133 |
| 3 | was | 10,133 | 10,393 |
| 3 | just | 10,393 | 10,732 |
| 3 | guessing | 10,732 | 11,291 |
| 3 | at | 11,291 | 11,410 |
| 3 | numbers | 11,410 | 12,009 |
| 3 | and | 12,009 | 12,168 |
| 3 | figures | 12,168 | 13,027 |
| 2 | Movement | 42,761 | 43,633 |
| 2 | Left Button | 43,893 | 43,893 |
| 2 | Left Button | 44,113 | 44,113 |
| 3 | evolution | 46,427 | 46,982 |

Figure 6: Example of integrated logging file combining three writing modes: keyboard (1), mouse (2), and speech (3) input.

The implementation of speech recognition in Inputlog will stimulate research on the effect of this new technology on the writing process (of both professional writers and writers with learning disabilities). Moreover, we would also like to explore the logging possibilities of speech recognition to simultaneously transcribe thinking-aloud protocols and/or retrospective interviews.

### *5.2 Revision Analysis*

Work on the revision analysis for Inputlog has already been started, but because of its complexity it is very time-consuming to further stabilize and extend the analysis. In the revision analysis we would like to produce an output analysis in which different characteristics of in-process revisions are described, e.g. the number of revisions, type of revisions, level of revisions, number of words and characters involved in the revision operation, as well as the location of the revisions in relation to the point of utterance. To define revisions we have developed an algorithm and a set of rules. The revision analysis first of all defines critical events in the writing process that might be linked to a revision and then evaluates these instances by comparing the operations in the isolated writing episode to the revision

| | begin (movement) | selection/positioning | deletion | end (movement) |
|---|---|---|---|---|
| **1** | - | - | backspace | - |
| **2** | mouse movement left | left click | delete | arrow right |
| **n** | … | … | … | … |

Figure 7: Example of rules to define revisions.

rules in the algorithm. Inputlog successively analyses the beginning of the revision, the selection of the text to revise or the positioning of the cursor, the (possible) deletion of the text and the end of the revision. In Figure 7 we describe two (technical) revision operations to change the last word of the sentence 'Questions of science, science and progress.' into 'evolution'.

Questions of science, science and [progress.]$^{1}|^{1}$ {evolution.}

The first operation is a very basic one: the writer simply uses the backspace key at the point of utterance to delete the full stop and the word 'progression' and then types the new word 'evolution' (see rule 1). This is a rather minimal operation, because the writer does not have to move nor position the cursor in the text produced so far. However, the writer could also opt for another sequence to realize this substitution: he can move the mouse to the left, position the cursor by clicking on the left button on the mouse, use the delete key to delete the word, change the text and move to the point of utterance by using arrow keys to the right (see rule 2).

At the moment we have predefined about 50 sets of rules to test the algorithm for deletions and substitutions. However, after the testing phase, the rules will have to be extended and further tested to cover a more complete range of revisions.

### *5.3 Progression Analyses*

At this moment the development of the text is represented in the linear text analysis. To visualize this textual development we would like to extend Inputlog with two graphical representations of the text progression, a basic and a more extended one. In the basic progression analysis we would like to visually represent the number of characters that are produced at each moment during the writing process taking into account the characters that are deleted at that stage. This basic progression analysis is based on writing strategies research by Perrin (2003).

Because this basic analysis is a static reproduction of the writing process, we would also like to develop a more interactive representation inspired by Lindgren (2005). She uses a Geographical Information System (GIS) to visualize and summarize the writing process. GIS enables researchers to analyze different subprocesses of the writing process by selecting representative variables. The graphical representations are not static, but they allow a researcher to interact with the data at different levels and to move back and forward between the data and their representation. Consequently, as well as being a tool for visualization and data-mining, this technique can support a dynamic analysis of the cognitive processes during

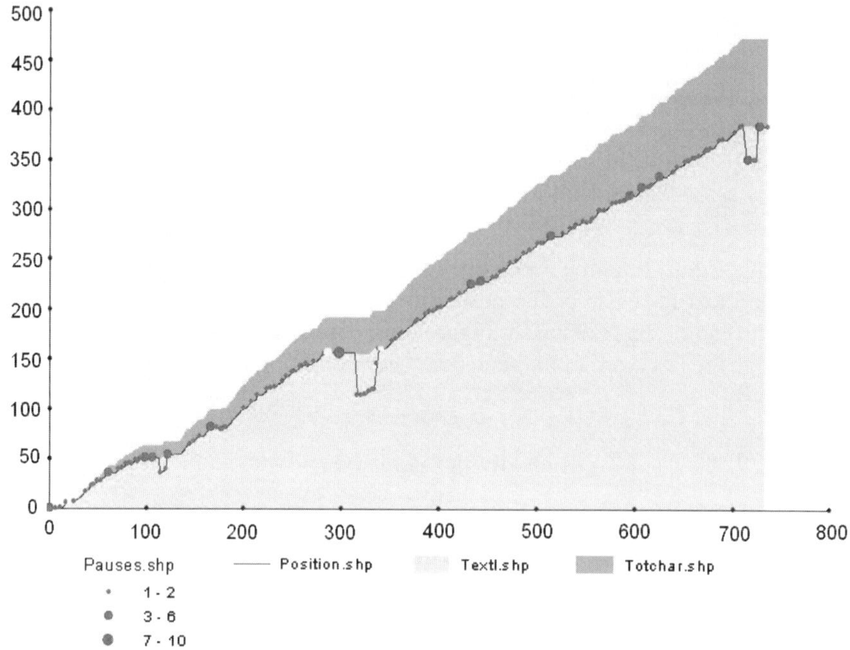


Figure 8: Graphic representation of text progression logged in Inputlog and visualized in a GIS application.

writing due to the interactive nature of the data-mining approach on which GIS is based. Figure 8 shows an example of a GIS graph that is based on a manually adapted dataset of Inputlog.[7] To generate these kind of progression analyses automatically, we first need to further optimize the revision analysis because these are based on the revision output.

On the *x*-axes the time (in seconds) is represented; on the *y*-axes the number of characters that are produced cq. realized effectively in the text produced so far are indicated. The top line indicates the total character production including deleted characters at each point in time; the bottom line indicates the characters retained after deletions at each point in time. The dotted line shows all the points in time at which the writer is working on the text, representing both pauses and deletions. The size of the circles refers to the length of the pause. When the line drops, a number of characters is deleted.

### *5.4 Integration with Morae*

Inputlog is designed for micro analytic research on writing processes. However, these very detailed data can easily be combined with more macro analytic research tools. Therefore,

[7]We would like to thank Eva Lindgren (Umeå University, Sweden) who generated this graph for us with Arc–GIS (ESRI).

we would like to complement the data of Inputlog with another observation tool, for example, Morae. This program is mainly developed for usability testing and uses an online screencam (Camtasia) to register every action on the screen. However, next to some lower level analyses, Morae also captures changes between programs on a higher level and registers, for instance, the url-addresses of websites that are accessed during a writing session. Just like Inputlog it also logs very detailed time stamps, which should enable us to integrate the additional data registered by Morae into the output of Inputlog. For the observation of writing processes during which the participants combine Word with other programs, this integration opens new perspectives for further analyses.

## 6 Conclusion

In this chapter we have briefly described the main characteristics and the functionality of Inputlog. The program differs from other keystroke logging programs in a way that it is not limited in its usage to a self-designed word processor. It is primarily developed to log writing processes in MSWord (Windows environment).

Inputlog offers three main functions — record, generate, and play — enabling the researchers to collect very detailed data about a writing process and to prepare some basic analyses for further study. The replay function allows for a review of the writing process and it can be also be used as a stimulus for a retrospective thinking aloud protocol. For more detailed information about the use of the program we refer to the help file and the detailed description on the program's website: www.inputlog.net.

To increase the applicability of Inputlog we would like to further develop the program by adding new modules. Four new components are planned: a module to log speech recognition events, a module for revision analysis, a module for progression analyses and a module to integrate macro-level data recorded by Morae. We hope to report about these further developments soon.

## Acknowledgment

We would like to thank Wesley Cabus, Ahmed Essahli and Bart Van de Velde for their excellent work in programming Inputlog. Thanks also to Tom Van Hout for editing and proofreading an earlier version of this chapter. We thank Eva Lindgren for producing Figure 8.

## Appendix A: Glossary

| | |
|---|---|
| **Scancodes** | The data from a keyboard comes mainly in the form of scancodes, produced by key presses or used in the protocol with the computer. The PC keyboard interface is designed so the system software has maximum flexibility in defining certain keyboard operations. This is accomplished by having the keyboard return scancodes rather than ASCII codes. Each key generates a 'make' scancode when pressed and a 'break' scancode when released. The computer system interprets the scancodes to determine what operation it is to perform. (http://www.barcodeman.com/altek/mule/scandoc.php) |
| **Windows Hook** | A hook is a point in the system message-handling mechanism where an application can install a subroutine to monitor the message traffic in the system and process certain types of messages before they reach the target window procedure. |
| **journalrecord** | Public static final Hook.Descriptor JOURNALRECORD Records input messages posted to the system message queue. (http://www.jniwrapper.com/docs/javadoc/winpack/com/jniwrapper/win32/hook/Hook.html) |
| **journalplayback** | Public static final Hook.Descriptor JOURNALPLAYBACK Posts messages previously recorded by a JOURNALRECORD hook procedure. |
| **Event** | Every action on the computer |
| **EVENTMSG** | The EVENTMSG structure contains information about a hardware message sent to the system message queue. (This structure is used to store message information for the JournalPlaybackProc callback function.) |
| **GUI** | Graphical User Interface |
| **CPU** | Central Processing Unit: It reads instructions from your software and tells your computer what to do. |
| **DLL** | Dynamic Link Library: A Windows library that can be shared by multiple applications |
| **Array List** | Implements the IList interface using an array whose size is dynamically increased as required |
| **Virtual Keycode** | Unique number that identifies one key |

## Appendix B: General Logging File

| Column | Labels | Variables |
|---|---|---|
| **a** | number | Set value: 1, 2, 3, 4, .... 998, etc. Every row is defined by a unique number |
| **b** | participant | Number assigned to the participant |
| **c** | sex | Sex of the participant (e.g., 0 = male, 1 = female) |
| **d** | session | Number of the experimental session (e.g., 1 = task 1, mode 1, 2 = task 1, mode 2...) |
| **e** | group | Type of profession (e.g., 1 = academic, 2 = lawyer) |
| **f** | experience | Experience with writing modes (e.g., 1 = speech, 2 = dictating, 3 = keyboard&mouse) |
| **g** | age | Age of the participant |
| **h** | ... | Optional user defined variables: maximum 4 |
| **i** | writing mode | Input mode (1 = keyboard, 2 = mouse, 3 = speech) |
| **j** | output | Text that appears on the screen |
| **k** | input in | Time of key in: hours:minutes.seconds,100th of a second |
| **l** | input in_sec | Time of key in: in seconds |
| **m** | input out | Time of key up: hours:minutes.seconds,100th of a second |
| **n** | input out_sec | Time of key up: in seconds |
| **o** | action time | Time between key down and key up: hours:minutes.seconds,100th of a second |
| **p** | action time_sec | Time between key down and key up: in seconds |
| **q** | pause time | Time between consecutive key ins hours:minutes.seconds,100th of a second |
| **r** | pause time_sec | Time between consecutive key ins in seconds |
| **s** | x value | Location of mouse on *x*-axis |
| **t** | y value | Location of mouse on *y*-axis |

N.B. Only the last two columns contain the values of the mouse. The location of the keystrokes are not detailed.

## Appendix C: Analyses (see also help file)

| Analyses | Output | Explanation |
|---|---|---|
| *General logging file* | Microsoft Excel spreadsheet | Basic log file of the writing session |
| *Statistical analysis* | Microsoft Excel spreadsheet | Basic statistical information on the writing session |
| *Text analysis* | Text file with the final text at the end of a writing session (without layout, font, etc.) This file is generated automatically | Final text |
| *Linear text* | Text file with the complete linear production of the text including mouse movements and other activities | Linear text |
| *Linear text + modes* | Same text file as the linear text, but now the different writing modes are included | Linear text and writing modes |
| *Linear text (periods)* | Text file with the complete linear production of the text including mouse movements and other activities of the writing process divided into periods (free to choose) | Linear text in periods |
| *Linear text (intervals)* | Text file with the complete linear production of the text including mouse movements and other activities of the writing process divided into intervals (free to choose) | Linear text in intervals |
| *Pause analysis* | Microsoft Excel spreadsheet with analyses of every non-scribal period of 1 second and longer | 1 s |
| | Microsoft Excel spreadsheet with analyses of every non-scribal period of 2 seconds and longer | 2 s |
| | Microsoft Excel spreadsheet with analyses of every non-scribal period of 5 seconds and longer | 5 s |

Appendix C: (*Continued*)

| | | |
|---|---|---|
| | Microsoft Excel spreadsheet with analyses of every non-scribal period of any – user-specified - pause length | Number of seconds free to choose |
| *Mode analysis** | Microsoft Excel spreadsheet | Basic writing mode information on the writing session |
| *Revision analysis** | Microsoft Excel spreadsheet | Information on different levels about the revisions in the writing session |

*Not active in Inputlog version 1.4.

Chapter 6

# Research Methods in Translation — Translog

Arnt Lykke Jakobsen
*Copenhagen Business School, Frederiksberg, Denmark*

*The process of translating a text from one language into another language is complex. Using the computer to record a translator's keystrokes provides a window onto the process. The chapter presents the computer keystroke-logging tool, Translog, which was specifically developed for researching the translation process. The motivation and development of Translog is outlined, the research undertaken is overviewed and the future research and development directions are presented.*

**Keywords:** keystroke logging, translation, Translog.

## 1 Empirical, Process-Oriented Translation Research

### *1.1 Introspective Methods*

In the 1980s, interest developed in studying the process of translation in addition to studying translation products, and increasingly research efforts aimed at studying the process of translation from an empirical and cognitive perspective. This line of inquiry, as represented, e.g. by Krings (1986, 2001), was based primarily on the methods of introspection, retrospection and think-aloud. Most of the data elicited and collected by means of these empirical methods derived from self-observation, interviews or more or less spontaneous think-aloud vocalizations. The standard method for eliciting, evaluating and analysing such subjective or qualitative verbal data was formulated by Ericsson and Simon (1980) and comprehensively in *Protocol Analysis* (1984/1993) by the same authors. Their book laid down a standard procedure for working with the think-aloud method and carried a strong vindication of verbal data, both in the form of concurrent verbal reports and in the form of retrospective reports. Ericsson and Simon systematically addressed and refuted the three main objections frequently raised against the quality of think-aloud data — their alleged incompleteness, their alleged irrelevance to the

**Computer Key Stroke Logging and Writing: Methods and Applications**

**ISBN: 0-08-044934-4**



*Jakobsen, A. L. (2006). Research methods in translation — Translog.*
*In G. Rijlaarsdam (Series Ed.) and K. P. H. Sullivan, & E. Lindgren. (Vol. Eds.), Studies in Writing, Vol. 18, Computer Keystroke Logging: Methods and Applications (pp. 95–105). Oxford: Elsevier.*

processes being studied and their alleged distortionary effect on these processes — and laid the first foundation of the methodology used in process-oriented translation research.

### *1.2 Keystroke-Logging Methods*

The original purpose for which *Translog* was created was to be an automatic, subject-independent tool for collecting hard, supplementary process data to the softer data collected by means of introspection, retrospection and think-aloud. The fundamental idea was that if the process by which a translation was typed on a computer keyboard could be saved, the researcher would have access both to all the various stages a target text passed through before reaching its final state, and to information about the timing of this process, reflecting underlying cognitive processes. The rhythm and speed with which a target text was produced could then be studied as a kind of prosody of writing reflecting the cognitive rhythm of meaning construction.

The idea that sparked the creation of *Translog* was a small model experiment carried out by J. Tommola and reported by Wollin and Lindqvist (1986). Tommola had used keyboard logging on a mainframe computer and subsequently generated a report which contained both the sequence of keystrokes and some indication of the lengths of pauses occurring between words. The pauses measured by the logging operation were related to linguistic features of the source text and accounted for in terms of cognitive psycholinguistics. It was immediately clear that the method suggested by Tommola had research potential far beyond the scope of his small experiment if a more generically designed research tool such as *Translog* could be developed.

The main methodological source of inspiration for the research method that developed from the invention of *Translog* was J. Schilperoord's *It's About Time. Temporal Aspects of Cognitive Processes in Text Production*, which appeared in 1996. Building on psycholinguistic research carried out in particular by Goldman-Eisler and Butterworth, his study investigated the temporal course of text production processes in a corpus of audio-recorded routine legal texts produced by dictation. In its current version, *Translog* does not include an audio component and can therefore only be used to record the temporal course of the typing process in text production across a computer keyboard, but the underlying idea in Schilperoord's study is also one of the pillars on which most *Translog*-based translation research rests, viz. that the temporal course of the typing process is an observable and recordable reflection of underlying cognitive processes. One key assumption is that by analysing recordings of this process, in particular of its temporal patterning by pauses, it is possible to arrive at a clearer understanding of the dynamic, real-time interaction of cognitive processes, not only in translation, but also more generally in language comprehension and production in monolingual as well as in multilingual contexts.

## 2 Translog History

The first version of *Translog* was developed in 1995 by Arnt Lykke Jakobsen and was programmed by his son, Lasse Schou (Jakobsen and Schou, 1999). From the start, the program had two separate components, originally called Writelog and Translog. The Writelog component (now *Translog* User) was designed to display a text in one window, to allow text to be written in another window and to log information about all keyboard activity while a text (the source text) was being displayed and another text (the target text) was being typed and edited. At the end of a session, this information, all of which was timed, could be saved in a logfile.

The function of the Translog component was, first, to allow source texts to be created and set up for subsequent display in Writelog. A text could be displayed in full, paragraph by paragraph, sentence by sentence or unit by unit (defined by the experimenter), and each screen display could be automatically timed. The second main function of the Translog component was to take the information in a logfile as input and represent it on the screen, either in the form of a dynamic replay of the original typing process or in the form of a linear representation of keystrokes and pauses. This linear representation used a combination of α-numerical keys and symbols (Wingdings), such as ↓←→↑, to represent all keystrokes. From the start, pause duration was represented either by asterisks, whose time value could be defined by the user or absolutely by minutes:seconds:centiseconds (*cf.* below).

The immediate research purpose for which *Translog* was developed was to 'log' or record process data about translation — hence the name (Jakobsen, 1998, 1999). Jakobsen was interested in studying cognitive aspects of the translation process and came upon the idea of logging keystrokes as a means of automatically recording process data that could supplement more subjective process data elicited by the think-aloud method and make triangulation possible (Alves, 2003). As more and more researchers started using the program, including in particular the members of the translation process research group at Copenhagen Business School, it soon became clear that *Translog* was capable of serving additional purposes. As a research tool, it could be used not only to study translation, but also to study most kinds of writing including, e.g. post-editing of machine-translated text. It could also be used in a variety of psycholinguistic and cognitive experiments, and from the response that came back from several subjects in the early experiments, it also became clear that the general concept underlying the program could be applied in learning and teaching scenarios.

With these additional applications of the program and with more and more people using the program, it became relevant to develop a more up-to-date interface, and a version for *Windows* labelled *Translog2000* was developed towards the end of 1999, a version that included several additional features suggested either by research colleagues or by the new purposes for which the program was being used.

In 2002, *Translog* acquired its own web domain http://translog.dk that features information about the program and has a forum where registered users of the program can exchange ideas. The version currently available is *Translog2004*.

## 3 Translog's Five Main Functions

*Translog* has two interdependent components, a Supervisor and a User component. The User component requires files created in the Supervisor component to run, and some of the main functions of Supervisor component can only be performed on logfiles created by the User component. Between them, they perform five main functions: (1) preparing projects (Supervisor), (2) displaying source texts and receiving textual input (User),

(3) logging keystrokes and 'time-of-day' information (User), (4) displaying logfile content (Supervisor), and (5) analysing logfile content (Supervisor option).

### *3.1 Preparing Translog Projects*

Projects are prepared in the Translog Supervisor component. A Translog project consists of a source text together with a number of parameters that control the way in which the source text will be displayed to subjects as part of a writing or translation experiment. 'Source text' is the term traditionally used in translation research about the text from which a translation (the 'target text') is made, but in Translog a source text is merely a text with instructions that serve as input to a subject in an experiment. Therefore, a source text can be anything from an empty document to a set of instructions or other stimuli, or a source text in the traditional sense of a text to be translated.

Source texts or other instructions can either be typed in the Translog source text editor or copied from an external source into the editor across the clipboard. Once a text has been typed, copied or selected, it has to be set up so that it will be displayed in the manner required by the experiment it will be part of. The main options for setting up source texts are to have them appear on the screen either in full or in segments. Segments can be paragraphs, sentences or pre-defined units. Segments can either be timed automatically and remain on display for the specified number of seconds, or they can remain on display until the subject chooses to have the next segment shown (Figure 1). Once a selection from these options has been made, a *Translog* project has been defined, and the *Translog* User component will be able to use the information in the saved file to display the source text as specified.

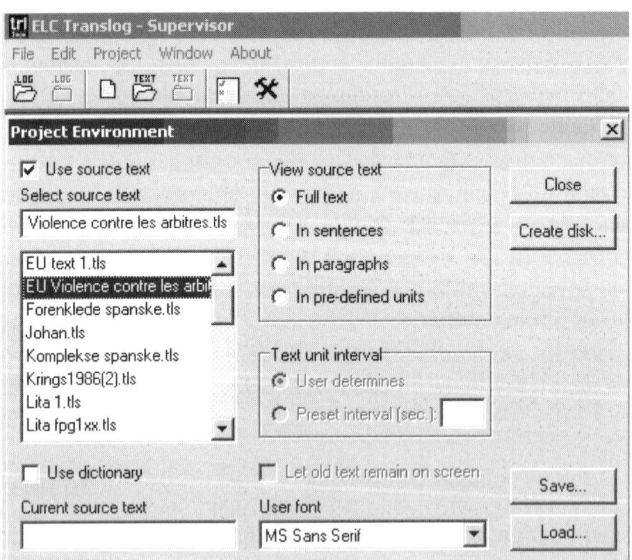


Figure 1: Translog Supervisor Project Environment options.

### *3.2 Displaying Source Texts and Receiving Textual Input*

The *Translog* User component displays a source text in the manner specified in the project prepared in the Supervisor component. As soon as a project has been loaded into the *Translog* User component, and the start icon has been pressed, the source text or a segment of it appears in a window in the top half of the screen (by default). If the source text to be displayed is too long to be contained within the source text window, it can be scrolled.

In the bottom half of the screen another window opens. This is the window in which the target text can be edited. Since text editing takes place in a standard *Windows* environment, subjects used to working on a computer will be familiar with the value of the various keystrokes. For most writing or translation research purposes, the set-up with a source text window and a target text window is sufficiently realistic for data to be experimentally valid. Nevertheless, the environment is necessarily somewhat more controlled than the real-life environment of writers and translators. For instance, there is full access to editing text material in the target text window, but no access to editing text in the source text window, as any accidental alteration of the source text would invalidate data from the experiment. *Translog* User is a controlled environment with considerable likeness to the environments in which texts and translations are normally made, but it cannot claim, and does not aim at, complete verisimilitude.

### *3.3 Logging Keystrokes and Time-of-Day Information*

The data logged by *Translog* User are a simple alternation of keystrokes and indications of time. Each time a key is pressed, *Translog* records the number of the key and at the same time records the exact time ('time-of-day') that the key was pressed. Thus the behaviour isolated for observation by this method is the activity across the computer keyboard. This behaviour may seem far removed from the thinking that underlies text production, but the advantage of such focussing is that hard, machine-recorded data are made available about an aspect of the total behaviour in text production, which our theorizing about text production in translation cannot ignore. It may not be possible to make detailed inferences about mental language processes from these data alone, but any attempt to account for these processes should take evidence from every aspect of the total situation into account.

When performed from a hard disk installation, the logging function does not interfere perceptibly with a subject's text-editing activity. However, at the end of an experiment a dialogue window appears asking the user for a file name so that the logfile can be saved. Apart from reminding users not to lose valuable data, this dialogue also serves as an overt reminder to a subject of the experimental context in which a writing task has been performed. In all experiments involving *Translog* that have been reported, the program has been used as a fully overt experimental tool, and subjects have been fully informed about the context in which their efforts would be used.

By being dedicated to logging keystrokes and time-of-day information and to re-using logged data for re-representation and analysis, *Translog* is a very different program from screen capture programs (such as ScreenCam or Camtasia) that create a video of all activity across a computer screen. By focussing attention on the two key features of the typing process (what key? at what time?), and by automatically discriminating among five types of keystrokes, *Translog* generates a highly relevant data set that can be analysed quantitatively, and the Replay function produces a calculated replay which functions in nearly every respect as an adequate visualization of the process. However, *Translog* is currently unable to reproduce, e.g. Internet searches. In research designs where such information needs to be recorded, a screen capture program can be run in combination with *Translog* (as has been done by Fabio Alves at UFMG in Belo Horizonte and by Ida Rambæk at the University of Oslo). The flexibility and speed with which the *Translog* linear representation can be re-calculated and re-represented for maximum relevance to a given research purpose is another great advantage not offered by a screen capture program.

### *3.4 Displaying Logfile Content*

**3.4.1 Process replay function** Taking a logfile containing information about the entire sequence of keystrokes by which a text was created as input, the Translog Supervisor component can replay the entire typing process any number of times and at the speed (accelerated or decelerated) that gives the researcher the best opportunity for making relevant observations, e.g. of production rhythm, pauses or editorial changes. By observing the typing process repeatedly, the translation researcher can get a rough view of the typical length of a translator's production segments, can examine the textual environments that appear to either facilitate or delay text production, and make detailed observation of all the changes in terms of additions, deletions and corrections that result from the translator's attempt to improve the target text.

The source text available to a subject can be displayed along with the dynamic replay of the typing process, and at any moment the replay can be paused (Figure 2). This means that at any point the current (unfinished) version of a target text can be printed. From Translog's point of view, the final version of a target text is merely the last of thousands of current versions along the process path from start to finish. When the replay stops, the final text version will be displayed.

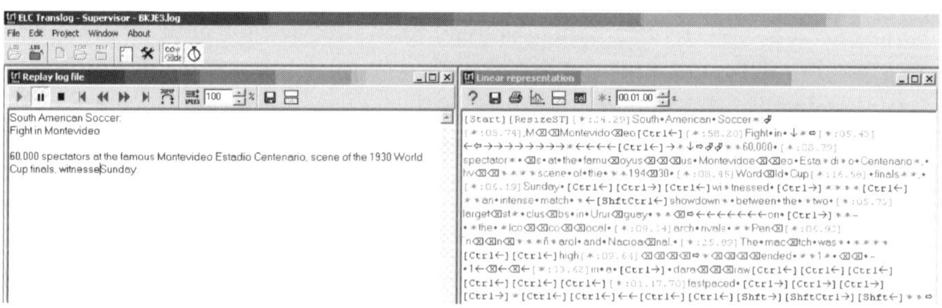


Figure 2: Replay logfile window (paused) alongside linear representation window (Translog Supervisor default setting).

**3.4.2 Linear representation of the typing process** Translog Supervisor's linear representation of the typing process displays the complete sequence of keystrokes used to produce a text. By default this is done in a window alongside the window in which the replay occurs (Figure 2). Keystrokes such as Space, Backspace, Arrows, End and Enter are represented by Wingdings, and a mouse icon is used to represent mouse clicks. Each keystroke is counted as an 'action', and is assigned an index number by the program. For each keystroke action the program creates a small record. In addition to assigning an index number to each keystroke action, the program also records the exact moment in time that the key was struck (with an accuracy of one-hundredth of a second) and assigns the keystroke to one of the five categories: (1) a text production keystroke, (2) a text elimination keystroke, (3) a cursor navigation keystroke, (4) a mouse click, or (5) a miscellaneous action. This information can be accessed by right-clicking the mouse on the relevant keystroke symbol in the linear representation.

In the replay window, original speed variations and production pauses are indicated dynamically by matching speed variations and pauses during the replay. In the linear representation, temporal information is represented very differently. A pause, as interpreted in *Translog*, is any distance in time, long or short, between two keystrokes. Even in very fast typing the distance in time between two keystrokes is generally greater than 0.05 s (50 m s). A computer has no difficulty in recording and reproducing such activity very accurately, but for many research purposes such detailed temporal information is redundant. Therefore, temporal information can be reported flexibly. The distance in time between two keystrokes can be represented as an absolute figure. For instance, a pause occurring between two keystrokes (*a*, *b*) and lasting 1.12 s can be indicated as *a[*:01.12]b*. If only pauses lasting 2 s or more are deemed interesting in a research project, information about shorter pauses can be suppressed, and the linear representation would simply be *ab*. If a rough indication of the duration of pauses is found to be relevant, pause duration can be represented by asterisks, to which a variable time value can be assigned. Thus, if the value assigned to one asterisk is 1 s, the linear representation will be *a*b*, indicating a pause lasting at least 1 s, but less than 2 s. With a value of 0.20 s for each asterisk, the representation will be *a*****b*, indicating a pause lasting at least 1 s, but less than 1.20 s. Thus, the researcher can decide on the accuracy with which the temporal information contained in a logfile needs to be represented. If the main interest is in text revision, temporal information can be reduced to a minimum. If the main interest is in pauses and speed variation, temporal information can be maximised.

A linear representation, with minimal temporal information (a 'blue' representation) is shown in Example 1, where an asterisk has been assigned the time value 5 s.

(1) all♦the♦players♦and♦officials♦ended♦up♦in♦a♦gigancti⌫
⌫⌫tic♦*Westernlike♦fight

A linear representation of a portion of the same data ('players and officials'), but maximizing the temporal information (a 'red' representation) would look like this:

(2) p[*:00.19]l**********a[*:00.14]y[*:00.30]e**********
r[*:00.21]s*********♦[*:00.13]a*********n[*:00.12]d*
*******♦[*:01.18]o*********f[*:00.12]f[*:00.11]i[*:00.64]
c[*:00.12]i[*:00.16]a[*:00.12]l[*:00.20]s

Here the value of one asterisk equals 0.01 s, and *Translog* has been set up to print up to ten asterisks and to return absolute time values for pauses longer than 0.1 s between keystrokes.

A linear representation of the data with one asterisk representing a 0.20 s duration (a 'mixed' representation) would look like this:

(3) all♦the♦play*er*s♦and♦*****offi***cial*s♦[*:04.83]ended
♦*u*p♦in♦a♦gi*ganc*ti**⌫⌫⌫*tic*♦[:06.98]W*ester*n
*****lik*e♦[*:04.08]fi**ght*******

Different representations help visualize different information points and therefore serve different purposes, and *Translog* can quickly calculate the representation that is most suitable for a particular purpose.

Any linear representation of a text can be saved as an .rtf file. This makes it possible to edit the representation, e.g. for presentation purposes or in order to interlace the representation with other concurrent data, perhaps from a think-aloud protocol, an eye-tracker device or from an audio or video recording, in a label file.

# 4 Using Translog in Translation Experiments

## *4.1 Translog Solo*

*Translog* can be used as a stand-alone instrument for recording the typing process in a translation event. In the simplest experimental design, a subject reads the source text displayed by *Translog* according to the specification in the project environment and types a translation. *Translog* keeps track of all keystrokes and the points in time at which they occur, and also performs a number of simple counts. Each time a key is pressed, this behaviour is counted as an action. Since different keys have different purposes, *Translog* distinguishes between text production keys (characters, punctuation marks, spaces), text elimination keys (delete and backspace), cursor navigation keys (e.g. arrow-left, ctrl-arrow-left, page-up, end), mouse clicks and miscellaneous actions. For each category, *Translog* counts the number of actions. Since the overall duration of a writing session is also calculated, a rough measure of overall typing speed can be calculated by finding the total number of actions per minute. A more accurate indication of text production efficiency is given by the figure for text production keystrokes per minute. The different measures and counts permit more refined calculation, e.g. of the overall number of segments, of segment duration and segment length (in terms of the number of keystrokes), of the duration of initial orientation and of the drafting and revision phases, some of which could be calculated automatically. The information recorded in a logfile also makes it possible to replay the process and to represent the full sequence of keystrokes.

The data about which key was struck at what time can be used by the researcher to underpin conclusions not only about typing speed and typing skill, but also more importantly about such phenomena as text production speed and rhythm, segmentation patterns (Dragsted, 2004) or patterns of text production and revision. Process data provide a much richer reflection of the activities that constitute text production than the finished target text product. This appears particularly to be the case with subjects used to producing electronic text and who have excellent typing and editing skills. Their typing is sometimes so fast and their keyboard skills so routinized that they tend to immediately type any idea that suggests itself. One striking effect of this manner of typing is that a linear representation of such a subject's typing process carries information similar to that elicited by means of concurrent think-aloud (a 'type-along think-aloud protocol').

### *4.2 Translog in Combination with Other Data Elicitation Methods*

In many of the experiments that have been reported, *Translog* has been used in research designs combining keystroke logging with other data collection methods so that it is possible to triangulate from two (or more) synchronized data sets deriving from the same event.

**4.2.1 Translog and retrospective interview** One approach has been to combine keystroke logging with retrospective interviewing, and retrospective interviews have typically been done with concurrent, interrupted replay in Translog of the subject's typing process. This replay or re-visualization of the process has been found to provide very strong support for subjects' recollection of what ideas they had in mind at specific points in the process. This was the method used, e.g. in Hansen (2005).

**4.2.2 Translog and concurrent think-aloud** Though Translog does not have an integrated audio component, Translog data can easily be combined and synchronized either with the transcribed think-aloud data or with a digital audio recording of think-aloud data. Jakobsen (2003) compared data from log sessions with think-aloud with those without think-aloud and found that the think-aloud constraint delayed translation speed by an average of more than 20% and forced translators to work in smaller segments than when working without the think-aloud constraint.

**4.2.3 Translog and video/audio recording** Translog in combination with video (and audio) recording permits the researcher to study, e.g. facial expression and gestures or to document a subject's dictionary search or other behaviour. Video can also be used to document screen activity outside Translog, such as Internet searches, but less efficiently than by means of a screen monitor.

**4.2.4 Translog and screen logging** Translog only records data retrieved from external sources to the extent that they are imported across the Windows clipboard. For research where it is important, e.g. to track information retrieval procedures from the Internet or from other electronic resources, Translog can be combined with screen capture programs such as ScreenCam and Camtasia.

**4.2.5 Translog and eye tracking** The text production pauses recorded in Translog can be interpreted as pauses reflecting both comprehension and production, but the data logged by Translog are primarily data related to production only and therefore only of limited value for researchers primarily interested in cognitive aspects of translation. The advent of powerful and flexible methods of eye tracking offers new possibilities for combining keystroke logging with eye tracking and for getting better separation of comprehension and production data. The eye tracker can supply data on what words were in focus at any given point in time and on whether the source text or the target text was in focus, and by synchronizing data from the two sources it is possible to study the extent to which language comprehension and production processes overlap and interact.

## 5 Analysing Translog Data

From the point of view of writing and translation research, the most obvious advantage of the data stored in a *Translog* logfile is that the data constitute a complete record of all the keys struck in a text production event. Some of the data recorded, such as accidental typos, may not be highly relevant, but in general a logfile contains very little noise. The keystroke data can be interpreted quantitatively and unambiguously in terms of either text production, text elimination or cursor navigation (including mouse click) actions. (The overwrite function, which combines text production with text elimination, has been disabled in the *Translog* editor.) This means that the keystroke record is also immediately interpretable in terms of linguistic units (letters, words, clauses, etc.) giving the researcher full access to studying the typing process by which a text is produced.

The complete record of first solutions, false starts, corrections and editorial changes is a treasure of accurate information. It makes it possible for the researcher to track and analyse a writer's entire text production path reflecting a wide range (but not necessarily all) of the language decisions made along the way. From this information detailed analyses can be made of decision-making processes and of the strategies employed in editing and/or revising a translation, or any other text. It is also possible to identify production phases very accurately, e.g. in terms of initial orientation, drafting and revision (Jakobsen, 2002), and to study text production strategies employed by writers working in different conditions, e.g. time pressure (Jensen, 1999, 2001; Jensen and Jakobsen, 2000).

Second, since in addition to recording language data, *Translog* also records the exact time at which any key was struck, and generates a dynamic visualization of the typing process, it is possible to study text production in time. *Translog* does a simple calculation of the total number of keystrokes and the number of text production keystrokes, and when combined with information about the duration of a typing event, information is returned on the speed with which a writer typed a text.

From a cognitive point of view, a much more interesting phenomenon than mere speed can be studied on the basis of language-in-time data, viz. segmentation or 'chunking'. Text production has a 'pulse' or rhythm arising from the alternation of key tapping and pausing, which is a reflection of 'cognitive rhythm' (Schilperoord, 1996). What constitutes a segment and a segment boundary pause must be determined both theoretically and experimentally in each case. From the point of view of *Translog*, a segment is one keystroke, and *Translog* records a pause before and after each keystroke, but from a cognitive point of view it is much more relevant to study higher level segments bounded by pauses longer than most of the ones occurring between individual keystrokes. Exactly how long a pause must be in order to qualify as a segment boundary, however, is a matter to be determined by the researcher. So far, no pause values have been found that indicate universal or even clear cross-individual threshold levels of segmentation.

Segmentation analysis of Translog data can be performed automatically. Utility software that automatically segments a logfile by a given pause value and automatically counts both the duration of each segment and the number of keystrokes per segment (segment length) can be created. Such utility programs can be helpful, e.g. if a researcher proposes to test the facilitation hypothesis according to which segment length can be predicted to be greater in the second half of the drafting phase than in the first half.

Other methods of data analysis that have been used (Lorenzo, 1999, 2001 are acute critical discussions of *Translog* data analysis) include analysis of latency in responses to semantically ambiguous anaphoric expressions (Lundquist, 2002, 2003), analysis of inverse (L1 to L2) translation as opposed to L2 to L1 translation (Lorenzo, 2002), analysis of the effects of experimental conditions on text production, e.g. of think-aloud on translation speed, revision and segmentation (Jakobsen, 2003), and analysis of the influence of working memory constraints on translation performance (Rothe-Neves, 2003).

## 6 Conclusion

This chapter has overviewed Translog, a keystroke logging program that was developed specifically to study the translation process and has demonstrated how various aspects of the translation process can be researched using Translog. The research presented by Englund Dimitrova (this volume), although undertaken using ScriptLog (Strömqvist & Malmsten, 1998; Strömqvist & Karlsson, 2002) further demonstrates how keystroke logging provides a window onto the translation process, and Lindgren and Sullivan (this volume, Chapter 12), who have worked primarily with JEdit (Cederlund & Severinson Eklundh, nd.), show how keystroke logging programs such as Translog can be used in teaching translation. Translog provides the research and the educator a tool to work with and research the process of translation.

Chapter 7

# Examining Pauses in Writing: Theory, Methods and Empirical Data

Åsa Wengelin
*Lund University, Lund*

*This chapter will address both theoretical and methodological issues in pause analysis. First, the theoretical assumptions concerning how pause analysis can contribute towards our understanding of written language production are discussed. Subsequently, some measures, methods and tools for automatic pause analysis are presented and some empirical analyses are given. Most of the analyses and tools presented will be based on the concept of a "micro-context". A micro-context is defined here as the context around a certain transition between two keystrokes. By categorising micro-contexts in terms of categories such as "within word", "between words", "between letter and punctuation mark", pause frequencies and durations in certain types of micro-contexts can easily be analysed automatically and we can quickly gain an impression of how writers use their pauses. Finally, the complexity of pause definitions and operationalisations of the same are addressed. In typing, each letter is produced as a discrete unit and each transition between two keystrokes is a possible candidate for a pause because there will always be a short inactivity between keystrokes. However, obviously not every transition should be defined as a pause. Intuitively, a pause is a transition time between two keystrokes, which is longer than what can be expected for the time needed to merely find the next key. To make a pause writers have to "interrupt" their typing considerably longer than the "normal" transition time between two keystrokes. The problem is how to define a good pause criterion, taking into account the different typing speeds of individual writers.*

**Keywords:** keystroke logging, corpus linguistics, concordance, pause, language production, writing, reading and writing difficulties, language development.

**Computer Key Stroke Logging and Writing: Methods and Applications**

**ISBN: 0-08-044934-4**

*Wengelin, Å. (2006). Examining pauses in writing: theory, methods and empirical data. In G. Rijlaarsdam (Series Ed.) and K. P. H. Sullivan, & E. Lindgren. (Vol. Eds.), Studies in Writing, Vol. 18, Computer Keystroke Logging: Methods and Applications (pp. 107–130). Oxford: Elsevier.*

## 1 Introduction

Pauses in language production are assumed to provide us with a window to the cognitive processes underlying language production. In typical written communication there is no trace left of these pauses. They have to be traced during the actual production process of the message. One way of doing this is through keystroke logging. However, keystroke logging quickly provides the researcher with a vast amount of data, which is very time-consuming to analyse. In this chapter, I will discuss the usefulness of pause analysis and specifically focus on some methodological questions in pause analysis, such as how to automatically analyse large bodies of pause data, the problem of how to define a pause criterion and the consequences of different pause definitions. The chapter will start with a discussion of how pause studies can contribute to our knowledge about writing and how automatic corpus-based analyses could be used for pause analyses. Then, I will present some examples of empirical analyses of pauses based on automatic corpus analysis. Some of these results have also been published in Wengelin and Strömqvist (2000) and in Wengelin (2001, 2002). Finally, I will discuss the complexity of pause studies, especially regarding the definition of pauses. Throughout this chapter examples from authentic data will be given. These data belong to two corpora.The first corpus was collected in the research program "Reading and Writing Difficulties of Disabled Groups", which was funded by the Swedish Council for Social Research (Sociala Forskningsrådet, SFR). In the rest of this paper this corpus will be called the R&W corpus. It consists of data from three groups: ten university students with no known history of disorders or reading and writing difficulties, eleven adults, diagnosed with dyslexia and nine congenitally deaf adults with Swedish Sign Language (SSL) as their first language. All participants wrote five texts on five preset topics: a picture elicited narrative (*The boy and the frog*, Mayer [1969]), a personal narrative (I was never so afraid), an argumentative text (A letter to the editor), a route direction and a job application.

The second corpus was collected within the cross-linguistic project "Developing literacy in different languages and different contexts" funded by the Spencer Foundation. Only the Swedish part of this corpus will be used. In the rest of this paper it will be called the "Swedish Spencer corpus". It consists of data from 20 4th-graders, 20 7th-graders, 20 10th-graders and 20 university students, with no known history of reading and writing difficulties or other disorders. These subjects each wrote two texts: a personal narrative and an expository text, both elicited by a short video clip about school situations involving cheating and bullying.

Most of the examples given are taken from university students who are assumed to have developed "normal writing skills" for a Swedish adult. However, these writers will also be contrasted with some of the other groups in order to illustrate how pause patterns — and hence the production process — can vary according to level of development and also according to writing problems of different kinds. The writing process can no doubt also vary with social factors in the writing situation, such as who the receiver is, the aim of writing the text and the mood of the writer. However, such factors are not discussed in this chapter.

## 2 How Studies of Pausing can Contribute to our Understanding of Writing

In the study of spoken language, pauses and other types of *disfluencies* (e.g. speech repairs, repetitions, false starts and hesitations) have long been viewed as being indicative of the mental processes underlying speech production. As early as 1968 Goldman-Eisler showed that the majority of the people in her study were silent (paused) as much as 40–50% of speaking time. Several other studies have shown that about 5% of all vocalized items in spontaneous speech are disfluencies (e.g. Swerts, 1998). The term *pause* in spoken language research is often used to include both silent pauses and so called filled pauses (i.e., hesitation sounds such as 'eh', and 'um').

Pauses in language production have been argued to enable the speaker to gain time for processes related to ongoing choices concerning content and expression (i.e., planning) (see, for example Allwood, Nivre, & Ahlsén, 1990); the execution of utterances; and the monitoring of utterances (e.g. Brotherton, 1979; Goldman-Eisler, 1968). Of these three kinds of processes "planning" appears to be the one that has received most attention. According to Levelt (1989), language producers have to plan both *what* they want to say and *how* to present their message. The latter form of planning includes choosing the type of utterance to be used, ordering constituents within the utterance and selecting appropriate lexical items. For example, Swerts (1998), investigated "filled pauses" and suggested that these may signal difficulties in word finding and conceptualisation at major discourse boundaries.

However, it has also been argued that most pauses in spoken language production do not signal problems, but are used to coordinate speakers with their addressees (e.g. Clark, 1999). Several researchers have presented evidence that "filled pauses" in spoken communication have communicative import (e.g. Allwood et al., 1990; Chafe, 1994; Stenström, 1994), for instance, in relation to turn holding. In most spoken-language situations, speakers are constrained by time and cannot be silent for too long, if they want to keep the floor.

The claim that pauses can tell us something about the spoken language production process is based on the assumption that language production is subject to real-time constraints and the presence of a receiver. Indeed, this assumption applies to most speech situations. However, although online written communications such as computer chats and text telephone conversations, which are rapidly increasing in frequency, the typical writing situation is still an "off-line" one in which a monologue is produced with no addressee present. In such a situation, the sender has plenty of time to plan, encode and revise the message before sending it, something that is rarely the case in speaking, even if the communicative setting is in that aspect monologic. Studies of disfluencies in spoken monologues, for example, Swerts (1998), have shown that there is a system underlying how speakers produce filled pauses in monologues. These studies have shown that the pauses often carry information about larger-scale topical units. Similar patterns — but involving silent pauses — can also be expected to occur in writing; even if filled pauses such as 'eh' and 'um' are normally not expected to occur in messages written "off-line", it goes without saying that, just as in spoken production situations, planning and monitoring as well as production problems also occur in the written production situations. Another feature that generally distinguishes writing from speaking and that probably influences the production process — and thereby the pause patterns — is that writing typically gives the language producer access to an external store of the language produced so far. In other words, writers can look at their papers or their screens and read through what they have written so far. This access also gives them opportunities to change their message at any time, as long as the text has not yet been sent to the receiver.

## 3 Tracing Pauses in the Written Language Production Process

The study of written language production from a cognitive point of view is still quite a new phenomenon. Before 1980, when Hayes and Flower published their model of written language production, most studies of writing focused on pedagogical issues of revision and its effects on writing quality (e.g. Bridwell, 1980; Faigley & Witte 1981). The "off-line" communicative setting in the typical writing situation discussed above is probably an important reason for this focus. Real-time processing phenomena such as pauses, repetitions and repairs have mainly been associated with the spontaneous production of spoken language.

Another reason why disfluencies have not been investigated to any large extent in writing is that until recently there have been no tools for 'recording' writing, and therefore only the finally edited products of the language production have been available. Recordings of spoken language on the other hand are always "online". The use of computers has afforded substantial new opportunities for the study of written language production. The written language production process can now be recorded by means of keystroke logging. Pauses can now be measured, the context extracted and edits can be traced automatically. Compared to, for example, think-aloud-protocols, planning notes and retrospective reports, keystroke logging makes possible "more natural" studies of spontaneous writing, without any interference from the researcher. Keystroke logging also provides more exact temporal data. Consequently, it can add some new information about pauses to important knowledge already gained from previous studies. In this chapter I use the keystroke logging program ScriptLog which is described in detail in Strömqvist, Holmqvist, Johansson, Karlsson, and Wengelin (this volume).

## 4 Paused Definition Used in the Empirical Studies

In this chapter, I am mainly interested in *pauses*, that is, only a subset of the possible disfluencies in writing. However, although the pause is a basic concept in the study of temporal aspects of language production, a great problem is how to define a pause. Very few studies of spoken or written language address this question. Clark and Clark (1977) claimed that speed of talking is almost entirely determined by pausing. They argued that people increase their rate of words not by shortening words but by eliminating hesitation pauses. If this were true, the rate at which individual words are produced should not influence what ought to be counted as a pause. Indeed, according to this interpretation, all silences are pauses, independently of how fast a speaker produces individual words. The most common way of counting silent pauses in spoken language is to count all silences that are longer than 200 milliseconds.

In contrast, in typing, each letter is produced as a discrete unit and each transition between two keystrokes is a possible candidate for a pause since there will always be a short inactivity. These transitions can be used to investigate how the subjects distribute their time over different linguistics units. However, it should be obvious that it is not very meaningful to interpret every transition as a pause. A working definition is that a *pause* is a transition time[1] between two keystrokes, which is longer than what can be expected to be necessary for the time needed to merely find the next key. Thus, in order for a transition to be considered as a pause, a writer has to "interrupt" her typing considerably longer than that "normal" transition time between two keystrokes.

As in spoken language research, the most commonly used method to operationalise a pause is to stipulate a pause criterion that suits the aims of the research. For example, if the focus of the research were on the planning of the sentence, it would perhaps be a good idea to exclude very short pauses that are more frequent within words. This method has been used in several studies. Jansen, Van Waes, and Van den Bergh (1996) studied pauses in order to investigate whether the think-aloud method is reactive. They used a minimum pause length of 3 sec "for practical reasons" (p. 240). Several studies, including the ones upon which the discussion in this chapter is based, have used a set 2-sec criterion (e.g., Chanquoy, Foulin, & Fayol, 1996; Spelman Miller, 2000a; Sullivan & Lindgren, 2002; Wengelin, 2001, 2002). This is also the strategy used in the studies presented in this paper. Hence a *pause*, which is longer than what can be expected to be necessary merely for finding the next key was operationalised as a transition between two keystrokes that was longer than 2 s. There were two reasons for this. First, this pause criterion is about twice as long as a "normal transition" even for the slowest writer. A "normal" transition time was defined as the *median transition time between lower-case letters within words* for each writer. This is discussed in further detail in Section 10. In the R&W corpus the mean (standard deviations within brackets) median intra-word transition time was for the university students, who were the fastest writers in that corpus, 0.247 s (0.06) and for the writers with reading and writing difficulties, who were the slowest writers in that corpus, 0.488 (0.186). In the Swedish Spencer corpus the correspondent numbers were 0.568 (0.232) for the 4th-graders, who were the slowest writers in that corpus, and 0.181 (0.032) for the university students, who were the fastest. The maximum median intra-word transition times, i.e. the maximum "normal transition time", in the two corpora were 0.796 (produced by a writer with dyslexia) in the R&W corpus and 1.083 (produced by a 4th-grader) in the Swedish Spencer corpus. Second, several earlier studies of typing have used a 2-s criterion (e.g. Chanquoy et al, 1996; Spelman Miller, 2000a) and using the same criterion increases comparability between studies. However, setting a pre-determined pause length for all writers, independent of their writing speed is a strategy that should be treated with caution since individual writing speeds are not taken into account. See Section 10 for a more thorough discussion on the complexity of pause criteria.

[1]"Transition times" between two keystrokes has also been called interkey intervals in some research. See for example Weingarten, Nottbush, and Will (2004).

## 5 Earlier Research

Many studies of pauses in written language production have focused on *durations* (e.g. Jansen et al., 1996; Matsuhashi, 1981; Spelman Miller, 2000a). Other important aspects of pausing are the distribution of pauses across different locations in the texts and the frequency of pauses. Turning briefly to spoken language again, Goldman-Eisler (1968) showed that in spoken language, pauses often occur at clause boundaries, sometimes between words within sentences but almost never within words. Furthermore Swerts (1998) found that discourse boundaries between larger units, such as sentences, were more predictive of pauses than smaller units, such as words. Similar results have been found for written language. For example, Wengelin (2001, 2002) showed that discourse boundaries between larger units were more predictive of pausing than between smaller units, that is pauses are more likely to occur at sentence boundaries than at word boundaries, which are, in turn, more predictive of pausing than locations within words. This result holds for both writers with reading and writing difficulties and writers with no known history of reading and writing difficulties. Moreover, Zesiger, Orliaguet, and Monoud (1994) found that transitions at syllable boundaries were longer than other intra-word transitions and Spelman Miller (2000a) found that the pause duration increases as the text unit level increases.

Pauses in speaking are often associated with forward planning. However, as the access to an "external store" in written-language production gives the producer ample opportunity to edit the text, we could expect that more time would be spent on monitoring the discourse already produced than in spoken-language production. It is, of course, impossible to tell whether a pause is used for planning, for monitoring, or both, but it could be expected that people with reading and writing difficulties spend more time monitoring their texts, if they do indeed manage to re-read their texts at all. It could moreover be the case that it takes too much effort to monitor larger units. In this chapter, an attempt will be made to distinguish pauses before from pauses after linguistic units, and the question of whether pauses that occur *after* linguistic units, could be pauses for monitoring, rather than for planning only, will be discussed.

## 6 Corpus-Based Analysis of Pauses

In corpus linguistics large bodies of text are used to find out how frequent certain words or expressions are and in what types of contexts they occur. This is usually done by creating a concordance. A concordance lists every occurrence of a chosen string within its closest context. Thus, if we are interested in how the word "pauses" was used in Section 5 (Earlier Research), a concordance program asked to search for all instances of the string "pauses" (with lower-case 'p') in any context would produce the following concordance:

| | |
|---|---|
| 1) Many studies of | **pauses** in written language |
| 2) are the distribution of | **pauses** across different locations in |
| 3) and the frequency of | **pauses**. Turning briefly to |
| 4) in spoken language, | **pauses** often occur at clause |
| 5) more predictive of | **pauses** than smaller units, such as |

| | |
|---|---|
| 6) more predictive of | **pauses** than word boundaries which |
| 7) made to distinguish | **pauses** before from pauses after |
| 8) pauses before from | **pauses** after linguistic units, and |
| 9) units, and whether | **pauses** which occur *after* linguistic |
| 10) units could be | **pauses** for monitoring rather than |

This concordance shows that the string "pauses" was used ten times. If we instead had made a more general search for the string "paus" we would have found that the singular form "pause" had also been used twice and the string "pausing" three times.

We can treat keystroke logged data in a similar way. Let us take a linear file from ScriptLog, such as example 1 below (for more details on ScriptLog output, see also Strömqvist et al. this volume):

(1) <START><95.92>ALDRIG HAR GA<2.93>G <DELETE4>JAG VARIT SÅ RÄDD<4.82>2<DELETE>2<DELETE><4.25>" <4.98><MOUSE(29,0)><2.18>"<5.73><MOUSE(1,30)><3.20> <CR><CR><154.22> Aldrig har jag varit så rädd<15.07> <DELETE20> r jag varit s rädd som när jag rökte i min fars bil sist<5.20><DELETE4><6.53><DELETE21> senaste gången rökte i min fars bil<2.47>.<CR>

Searching for all pauses that are longer than 2 s would results in the following concordance:

| | |
|---|---|
| <START> | **<95.92>**ALDRIG HAR GA<2.93>G |
| ...,30))><3.20><CR><CR> | **<154.22>** Aldrig har jag varit så |
| ...5.92>ALDRIG HAR GA | **<2.93>**G <DELETE4>JAG VARIT SÅ |
| ...2<DELETE>2<DELETE | **<4.25>**"<4.98><MOUSE(29,0)><2.18>" <5 |
| ...<4.98><MOUSE(29,0)> | **<2.18>**" <5.73> <MOUSE(1,30)><3 |
| rökte i min fars bil | **<2.47>**.<CR> |
| <5.73> <MOUSE(1,30)> | **<3.20>**<CR><CR><154.22> Aldrig har |
| har jag varit så rädd | **<15.07>**<DELETE20> r jag varit s rädd |
| sist<5.20> <DELETE4> | **<6.53>**<DELETE21> senaste gången |
| i min fars bil sist | **<5.20>**<DELETE4> <6.53><DELETE21> |
| VARIT SÅ RÄDD | **<4.82>**2<DELETE>2<DELETE><4.25>"<4 |
| ...TE>2<DELETE><4.25>" | **<4.98>**<MOUSE(29,0)><2.18>" <5.73> |

We could then narrow down the search and say that we want to see only those pauses that precede a deletion. This would give us the following concordance:

| | |
|---|---|
| har jag varit så rädd | **<15.07><DELETE20>** r jag varit s rädd |
| sist<5.20> <DELETE4> | **<6.53><DELETE21>** senaste gången |
| i min fars bil sist | **<5.20><DELETE4>** <6.53><DELETE21> |

We can now easily calculate the average time this person pauses before making a deletion. However, it would be hard to find any general patterns if we had to analyse concordances like these manually. If we, for example, were interested in finding out if a certain subject frequently makes pauses before words, we would prefer not to list all pauses and manually count how many of these are followed immediately by a new word. Instead, we want to be able to describe general contexts for these patterns. To do this, we proposed the concept of the *micro-context* (see, for example Strömqvist, Ahlsén, & Wengelin, 1999; Wengelin 2001, 2002; Wengelin & Strömqvist, 2000). A micro-context is defined as the type of characters surrounding the transition in which we are interested.

Table 1 provides an overview of a subset of the types of micro-contexts that can be defined with ScriptLog. The symbol "^" marks the transition (the transition time value of which ScriptLog provides a calculation) targeted in the micro-context. In the rest of this chapter it will always denote a location of a pause. "a" is a letter which could be either upper case or lower case, "." denotes a major delimiter, i.e. a full stop, a question mark or an exclamation mark, "," denotes a minor delimiter, i.e. a comma, a colon or a semicolon, "_" denotes a space and "D" denotes delete/backspace keystroke.

Let us take two examples: (1) the micro-context "a_^a" shows that the transition we are interested in — i.e. the potential pause location — is located between a space which follows a letter and another letter. In practise this is almost always a space just before the start

Table 1: A subset of the types of micro-contexts definable in ScriptLog: their description and notation.

| **Micro-context** | **Notation/ symbols** |
|---|---|
| Inactivity after a minor delimiter (that is, any of the delimiters belonging to the set {,;:-}) and before a space bar followed by a letter | ,^_a |
| Inactivity after a minor delimiter followed by a space bar and before a letter | ,^a |
| Inactivity after a major delimiter (that is, any of the delimiters belonging to the set {.?!}) and before a space followed by a letter (In less technical terms: after finishing a sentence by typing a full stop, a question mark or an exclamation mark) | .^_a |
| Inactivity after a major delimiter followed by space and a letter (In less technical terms: before starting the first word of a new sentence) | ._^a |
| Inactivity after a minor delimiter followed by space and a letter | ,_^a |
| Inactivity after a letter and before a minor delimiter | a^, |
| Inactivity after a letter and before a major delimiter (In less technical terms: after the last word of a sentence and before typing a full stop, a question mark or an exclamation mark) | a^. |
| Inactivity after the last letter of a word and before a space followed by a letter (In less technical terms: after finishing a word within a phrase) | a^_a |
| Inactivity between two subsequent letters (In less technical terms: within a word) | a^a |
| Inactivity before a letter and after a space bar preceded by a letter (In less technical terms: before starting a new word within a phrase) | a_^a |
| Inactivity between a letter and a deletion | a^D |
| Inactivity between two delete/backstrokes | D^D |
| Inactivity between a deletion and a letter | D^a |

of a new word. (2) The micro-context ".^_a" describes a transition, which occurs just after a major delimiter and before a space which is followed by a letter. In most cases this transition occurs just after a sentence has been concluded. This micro-context can also occur after an abbreviation, which could be anywhere in the sentence. This ambiguity could be removed, if necessary, by specifying a difference between lower- and upper-case letters in the analysis.

In the analysis of a corpus of texts produced by ten university students presented in Table 2, the cases of abbreviation marked by punctuation were so rare that in this corpus all major delimiters in micro-contexts were counted as sentence delimiters.

Table 2 shows the types of micro-contexts that occurred at least 180 times in the corpus, how many of each occurred in the whole corpus, the mean number per text for each writer and the mean of the median times each transition took for each writer in each text.

Table 2 shows us that the most frequent micro-context in the corpus is the transition between two letters in a word; this result suggests that this is a good candidate for "a normal transition", which could be used for example to determine a person's typing speed, as was mentioned in section 4 and will be discussed further in Section 10. See also Section 10 for a more detailed discussion on what a "normal transition is". This concurs with the findings and conclusions of Strömqvist et al. (1999). They analysed the writing of one Swedish adult writer during the composition of the task "I was never so afraid".

They found that the most frequently instantiated micro-context in this text was "a^a" and that its distribution peaked around 0.5 s. Strömqvist et al. (1999) suggested that the high speed of "a^a" probably reflects a minimum of planning and monitoring processes and concluded that the combination of the properties high frequency and relatively high speed makes "a^a" a good context, for the reliable measurement of a subject's keyboard

Table 2: The number of times each micro-context occurred in a corpus of texts produced by ten university students in the R&W corpus, the mean number per text for each writer and the mean of the median times each transition took for each writer.

| Micro-context | Total *n* | Mean *N*/text | Mean–median transition time (s) |
|---|---|---|---|
| a_^a | 8649 | 216.2 | 0.49 |
| a^a | 36,799 | 920.0 | 0.25 |
| a^_a | 8649 | 216.2 | 0.23 |
| ._^a | 412 | 10.6 | 2.72 |
| a^. | 550 | 13.8 | 1.84 |
| .^_a | 412 | 10.6 | 0.52 |
| ,_^a | 317 | 8.1 | 0.95 |
| a^, | 189 | 7.3 | 1.85 |
| ,^_a | 226 | 8.1 | 0.27 |
| a^D | 884 | 22.1 | 1.44 |
| D^D | 6030 | 150.8 | 0.20 |
| D^a | 884 | 23.8 | 0.86 |

proficiency. That is, it is a good candidate for measuring typing speed in terms of "normal transition" times.

This section has shown how corpus linguistics approaches can be applied to the study of keystroke transitions and how it can provide data for detailed pause analysis. In the following sections empirical analyses of pause behaviour of the writing of adults with and without reading and writing difficulties are used to illustrate how micro-context analysis can contribute to our understanding of written language production.

## 7 Pause Frequencies, and Durations in Different Microcontexts in the Writing of Adults with no Reading or Writing Difficulties

Pause frequencies will always be affected by the pause criterion chosen by the investigator. The lower the pause criterion the more frequent pauses will appear. This means that comparing pause frequencies between groups and individuals can be a hazardous task if the writers have very different typing speeds. A similar problem occurs for durations. Let us assume that we are interested in comparing adults with children. We happen to have very skilled secretaries in our group of adults and beginner typists among them are children. Is then a pause of 3 s a long pause for the children and a pause of 1 s a short pause for the skilled secretaries or are they equal, or can they be compared at all? It would probably not be a good idea to compare the mean durations or the general frequencies of the pauses of two such different groups.

However, what we *can* do is to investigate how pauses are distributed within the writing process of a certain individual and compare the relative distributions across individuals or groups. In other words, is it, for example, generally the case that pauses are longer or occur more frequently between sentences than between words within sentences both for adults and children?

It is worth noticing that pause frequency can also be affected by variables other than the typing speed. One such variable is the writing task. As was mentioned earlier the subjects in the R&W corpus were given five writing tasks representing four different genres, namely two narratives, one argumentative task, one route direction and one job application. One of the narratives was picture elicited (The frog story [Mayer, 1969]) and the other was a personal narrative on the topic "I have never been so afraid". The genre, *per se*, did not make a difference, but the picture-elicited narrative generated significantly more pauses than the other tasks (see Wengelin, 2002), something that is explained by the writer's looking at the picture. Table 3 shows the mean number of pauses per keystroke in the five different tasks for ten university students.

In this chapter, pause frequency is measured as pauses per keystroke rather than pauses per word. The reason for this is that pause frequency is a process measure rather than a

Table 3: Pause frequency in ten university students in the R&W corpus.

| The frog story | I was never | Route directions | Argumentative | Job application |
|---|---|---|---|---|
| 0.091 | 0.040 | 0.045 | 0.035 | 0.042 |

product measure and "number of words" is a product measure — counted in the final edited texts. The writer could easily — especially in computer typing — have changed his or her text many times and deleted many of the words in which the pauses occurred. Pause/keystroke, therefore, more adequately measures how often pauses occur in the writing process.

As was mentioned earlier, in both spoken and written language, discourse boundaries of larger units are more predictive of pauses and associated with longer pauses than smaller units. Table 4 shows the distributions of pauses in four written tasks produced by 10 university students in the R&W corpus. The first column shows the total number of pauses in the corpus, the second, the mean number per writer, the third, the relative pause frequency in that context and the fourth the mean of the mean duration per writer. The relative pause frequency is calculated as the number of transitions that are longer than 2 s as a percentage of the total number of transitions in a certain micro-context. The duration is calculated in seconds as the mean of the mean duration of all pauses longer than 2 s produced by each writer.

Table 4 shows for example that 31.3% of the micro-contexts just before the start of a new sentence ("._^a", i.e., the transition between a space which follows a major delimiter and a letter) are pauses longer than two seconds and that these pauses are on average 6.9 s long. Pauses within words on the other hand are rare. Only 0.3% of the micro-context "a^a" are longer than 2 s and these few are on average 3.3 s long. Considering that the R&W corpus includes 36,799 intra-word transitions and only 412 sentence-beginning transitions altogether, there is no doubt that pauses in discourse boundaries between larger units are relatively more frequent than pauses in boundaries between smaller units. In other

Table 4: The distribution, the mean number per writer, the pause frequency and the mean of the mean duration per writer for pauses in four written tasks produced by the 10 university students in the R&W corpus.

| **Micro-context** | **Total number of occurrence** | **Mean number per writer** | **Pause frequency (%)** | **Mean of the mean duration per writer (s)** |
|---|---|---|---|---|
| a_^a | 506 | 50.6 | 7.1 | 5.2 |
| a^a | 101 | 10.1 | 0.3 | 3.3 |
| a^_a | 252 | 25.2 | 2.8 | 5.6 |
| ._^a | 169 | 16.9 | 31.3 | 6.9 |
| a^. | 191 | 19.1 | 22.3 | 5.8 |
| .^_a | 65 | 6.5 | 12.4 | 6.7 |
| ,_^a | 35 | 3.5 | 11.1 | 6.7 |
| a^, | 119 | 11.9 | 36.6 | 4.3 |
| ,^_a | 5 | 0.5 | 2.5 | 7.1 |
| a^D | 259 | 25.9 | 26.4 | 7.5 |
| D^D | 122 | 12.2 | 2.0 | 9.9 |
| D^a | 98 | 9.8 | 11.3 | 6.1 |

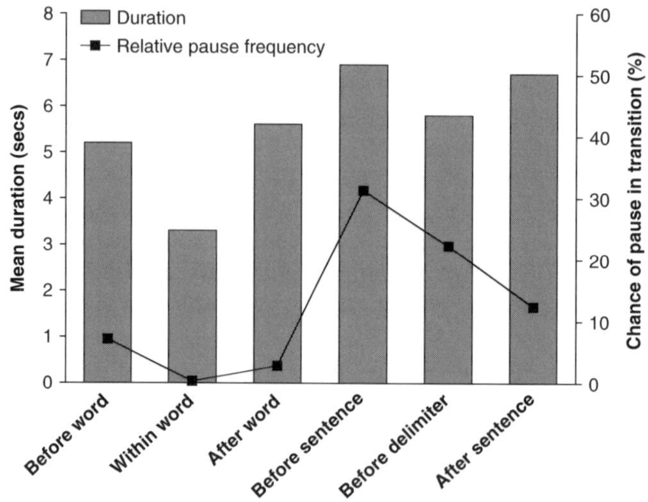


Figure 1: Relative pause frequency and mean pause duration in six different microcontexts for four written tasks produced by the ten university students in the R&W corpus. The bars show the mean pause duration in seconds. The durations are shown on the left *Y*-axis. The dots on the line show the relative frequency of a pause occurring in these contexts. These are shown on the right *Y*-axis.
Source: From Wengelin, Å., & Strömqvist, S. (2004). Text-writing development viewed through on-line pausing in Swedish. In: R. Berman (Ed.), *Language Development across Childhood and Adolescence*, John Benjamins, Philadelphia, (pp. 177–190). Reprinted with permission from John Benjamins publishing company.

words, pauses are more likely to occur between larger units than between smaller units. Table 4 also gives the impression that sentence related pauses ("._^a", "a^." and ".^_a") are slightly longer than the word related pauses. However, this is not a statistically reliable effect. The results are illustrated in Figure 1.

Figure 1 shows that while the relative pause frequency clearly differs across the different micro-contexts, the durations are relatively similar. This is surprising and does not agree with, for example, Spelman Miller (2000a). One reason for this non-effect could be the pause criterion. Perhaps for these writers a lower pause criterion would have showed different mean durations while for Spelman Miller's subjects' 2 s was an appropriate criterion. Another possible explanation could be that the automatic micro-context analysis is not fine grained enough. Spelman Miller's analysis was conducted manually and she included not only word and sentence boundaries but also phrase boundaries. In the automatic analysis there is no possibility to distinguish between word boundaries and phrase boundaries since the phrase boundary is not marked in any special way. This means that some of the word boundaries included in my automatic analysis are also phrase boundaries; this may raise the mean duration of the word boundary micro-contexts. Although, this is a shortcoming of the automatic corpus-based micro-context analysis, the automatic approach facilitates rapid analysis of large amounts of data.

## 8 Using Microcontexts to Analyse Pauses in the Writing of Young Writers and Writers with Writing Difficulties

So far I have shown how micro-contexts can assist in the analysis of the writing of adults without reading and writing difficulties. In this section we will look at some young writers from the Swedish Spencer corpus, and from the R&W corpus some adult writers with well-documented reading and writing difficulties and some congenitally deaf writers with written Swedish as their second language (Swedish Sign Language as their first). Let us start with the young writers. They were all participants in the Spencer project, "Developing literacy across genres, modalities and languages". Looking at the same micro-contexts as the ones we examined for the adults without reading and writing difficulties, i.e. the word-related and the sentence-related ones, we find that not all children include these micro-contexts in their writing. Nine of the 20 4th-graders neither include the micro-context "._^a" nor the micro-context ".^_a" in their writing. The same situation is repeated for six of the twenty 7th-graders. The 11th-graders and the university students from the Swedish Spencer corpus, on the other hand, all used these micro-contexts. Further three 4th-graders and one 7th-grader did not include the micro-context "a^." in their writing. This does not mean that they do not use punctuation marks in their writing. It means that they do not write them immediately after a letter or that they do not press the space bar immediately after the punctuation. In some cases they make a space before the punctuation and in some cases they delete something immediately after the space. This could also be the case for some of the older writers. The micro-contexts we have analysed do not tell us anything about this. In other words, we may not jump to conclusions on the basis of automatic analyses of micro-contexts. However, it appears possible that the punctuation behaviour changes across ages and that the more skilled writer you are, the better the chance is that your punctuation marks will occur immediately after the last letter of your sentence and be followed by a space and a capital letter. For all writers, but especially for young writers, we may want to investigate other possible micro-contexts around the delimiters than the few we have chosen here, but that is outside the scope of the current paper. Keeping in mind that some of the writers would not be included, an analysis of the relative pause frequency in the word- and sentence-related micro-contexts, we have discussed so far, was conducted. The result of this is shown in Figure 2. Notice how similar the curves for the fourth, seventh and tenth-graders are and how similar they also are to the curve for the university students. The patterns are surprisingly stable.

This shows us that sentence related micro-contexts are predictive of pauses across groups of different ages and different typing speeds. The profiles of the four age groups differ on two crucial points. The 4th-graders appear to make many more pauses before words compared to the others and both the 4th- and 7th-graders appear to make more pauses before the major delimiter than before the sentence or after the delimiter. This is more marked for the 4th-graders. One possible explanation is that these subjects are hesitant because their knowledge about punctuation is still quite unstable (see, e.g. Ledin, 1998). It could also be the case that they spend more time reading the sentence they have just written before they close it with a punctuation mark.

Turning to the adults with reading and writing difficulties whose writing form a part of the R&W corpus we find that all of the subjects used all the six micro-contexts which have

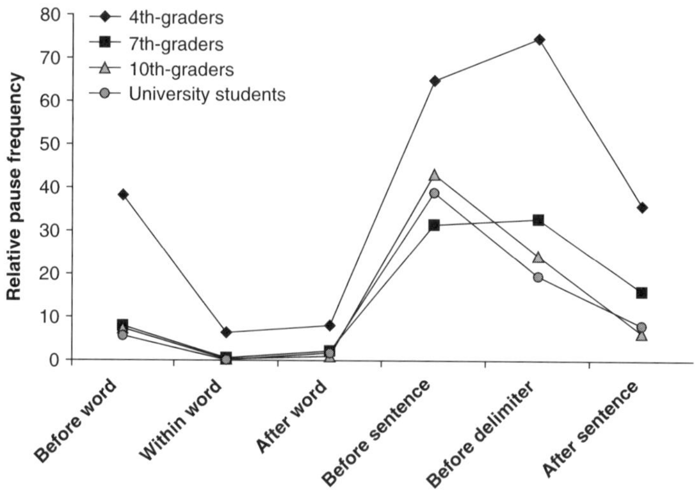


Figure 2: Relative pause frequency in six micro-contexts across four age groups in the Swedish Spencer corpus.
Source: From Wengelin, Å., & Strömqvist, S. (2004). Text-writing development viewed through on-line pausing in Swedish. In: R. Berman (Ed.), *Language Development across Childhood and Adolescence*, John Benjamins, Philadelphia, (pp. 177–190). Reprinted with permission from John Benjamins publishing company.

been under discussion so far. As mentioned above, concerning pause *durations*, no differences were found between sentence and word-related pauses for the university students in the R&W corpus. Surprisingly, however, the subjects with reading and writing difficulties made a difference here ($p = 0.0001$). There are several possible explanations. It could be the case that the subjects with reading and writing difficulties need more time to read through and perhaps plan their sentences. However, it could also be due to the pause criterion. If shorter pauses had been included, the means would have looked different. Another explanation could be high individual variation. Finally, as was also mentioned above, categories need to be more fine-grained. It could be the case that we would see another pattern if we marked phrase boundaries as well in the texts.

Concerning pause *frequency* in the different micro-contexts, the frequency profiles of the subjects with reading and writing difficulties (R&W corpus) is shown in Figure 3 along with the university students (with no reading and writing difficulties) from the R&W corpus.

Once again the pause frequency profiles of the two groups are surprisingly similar to each other and to the four age groups in the Swedish Spencer corpus. Thus, although, the 4th- and 7th-graders differed marginally from the 11th-graders and the university students, and the profile of the writers with reading and writing difficulties resembles a combination of the 4th- and 7th-graders above, the general patterns are clear:

1) Micro-contexts around sentence boundaries are more predictive of pauses than micro-contexts around words.
2) Micro-contexts before words are generally more predictive of pauses than micro-contexts within and after words.

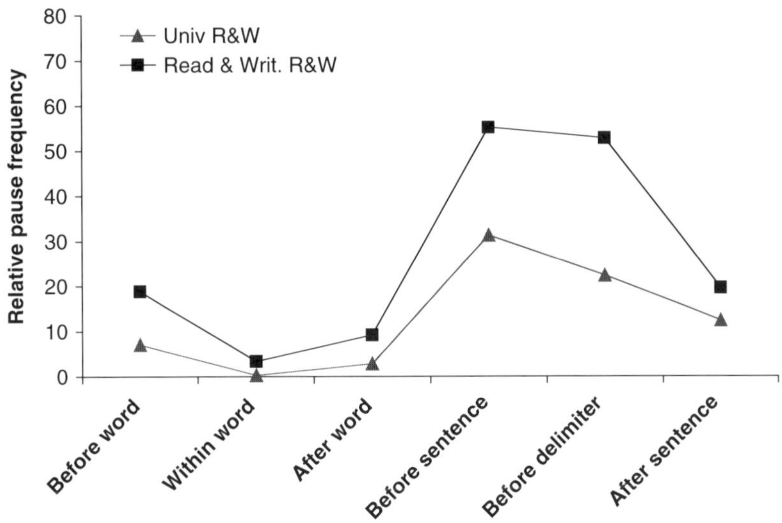


Figure 3: Relative pause frequency in six micro-contexts across two groups of writers: the adults with reading and writing and the university students from the R&W corpus.

3) Micro-contexts before sentences are more predictive of pauses than micro-contexts after sentences.
4) Micro-contexts just before a major delimiter change systematically with age or perhaps writing development — if we assume that our R&W writers are still in the process of developing their fundamental writing skills.

It is thus clear that the analysis of micro-contexts is a useful methodology for revealing general aspects of pause behaviour in the writing process. It is, however, also a methodology that is able to reveal differences between individuals and groups of writers. Wengelin and Strömqvist (2000) found for example that the pause distribution around words distinguishes the groups from each other. The adults with reading and writing difficulties made relatively more pauses within words than the university students in the R&W corpus. Table 5 shows that the university students made few (101) pauses within words, the adults with reading and writing difficulties made 736 such pauses and that the relative pause frequency in micro-contexts within words is 3.4% for the group with reading and writing difficulties, yet only 0.2% for the controls (see also Wengelin (2001). Thus the writers with reading and writing difficulties are less fluent than the control writers when writing individual words. This could be due to spelling difficulties, to an awareness of spelling difficulties or a combination of both (see Wengelin, 2002). A writer with no known reading or writing difficulty, who makes a spelling error without knowing it, probably makes no pause within the word to consider the spelling, as the writer's focus is not concentrated at the level of spelling. On the other hand writers, who know that they are poor spellers, may interrupt the writing of individual words to consider a spelling even if they have spelt it correctly. See Wengelin (in press) for an analysis of the relation between spelling problems and pause behaviour.

The writers' production rates in these micro-contexts further illustrate how the group with reading and writing difficulties and the control group focus differently when writing. Table 6 summarises Wengelin and Strömqvist's (2000) findings concerning the times (means over median transition time values) spent before, after and within words, and before, in the end of, and after sentences for all three groups in the R&W corpus. The third group of writers ($N = 9$), the group of deaf writers will be included in the remainder of the discussion in this section.

Three patterns in Table 6 are particularly striking. First, taken together, the transitions between units (words and sentences) are longer than the transitions within units, for university students and adults with reading and writing difficulties alike. Further these inter-unit-transitions are longer for the larger units (sentences) than for the words. It appears reasonable to assume that this temporal distribution is an effect of planning and/or monitoring activity; there is more planning and monitoring going on between than within units.

Second, the writers with reading and writing difficulties are about twice as slow as the other two groups in all contexts associated with the construction of a word, and considerably slower than the other two groups in the contexts associated with the construction of a sentence, except in the context immediately after a major delimiter (.^_), where the deaf subjects are almost as slow. Part of the explanation may be the fact that the subjects

Table 5: Absolute number and relative pause frequency of pauses in word-related micro-contexts for university students and the adults with reading and writing difficulties in the R&W corpus.

| | University students | | Adult with reading and writing difficulties | |
|---|---|---|---|---|
| **Micro-context** | **Number** | **Predictability (%)** | **Number** | **Predictability (%)** |
| a_^a | 506 | 7.1 | 1152 | 18.9 |
| a^a | 101 | 0.3 | 736 | 3.4 |
| A^_a | 252 | 2.8 | 579 | 9.2 |

Table 6: Transition times in seconds for six micro-contexts associated with the construction of words and sentences (after Wengelin & Strömqvist, 2000) in the R&W corpus.

| Micro-context | Control group | R&W group | Deaf group |
|---|---|---|---|
| a_^a | 0.491 | 1.024 | 0.316 |
| a^a | 0.247 | 0.491 | 0.210 |
| a^_a | 0.229 | 0.478 | 0.226 |
| ._^a | 2.726 | 3.387 | 1.083 |
| a^. | 1.837 | 4.926 | 1.131 |
| .^_ | 0.516 | 1.218 | 1.087 |

with reading and writing difficulties are about twice as slow typists as the university students in the same corpus (consult, in particular, "a^a", as a control measure). However, an additional explanation could be that the subjects with reading and writing difficulties are slow readers and have severe spelling difficulties. If you read slowly and know that your spelling is poor you will need extra time both for constructing and for reading your sentences.

Third, for the group with reading and writing difficulties and the control group alike, the transition time associated with opening a sentence (._^a) is much longer than the transition time associated with closing a sentence (.^_). But while the control subjects tend to spend less time in the context immediately before a major delimiter (a^.) than in the context immediately before a new sentence (._^a), the group with reading and writing difficulties appears to go the other way round. They spend considerably more time in the end of than before the sentence (a^.). A possible explanation is that the writers with reading and writing difficulties need more time to read their sentences before they close them, than the control group.

The deaf group shows a totally different pattern from both the other groups. They spend almost the same time before, in the end of, and after the sentence and all these transition times are relatively short. This is so, despite the fact that the deaf subjects make several errors in their sentences. One possible explanation could be that they are not aware of their mistakes. Considering that the deaf community in Sweden, on several occasions, have asked for better computer aids to improve their writing, we do not expect this to be the whole explanation. Rather, the observed production rate patterns may be a consequence of the frequent use of the text telephone and other online communications systems in this group. The use of text telephones and computer chat systems means that they normally use written language in a communication situation that resembles a spoken or signed dialogue, that is, they have to produce their messages fast with few or short pauses. Indeed, under those circumstances, it might be more disturbing for the receiver if the sender tried to correct the message. In short, an explanation for the writing behaviour observed needs to make reference both to cognitive factors and to socio-communicative factors.

## 9 Macro-Level Pause Distribution

So far we have considered pauses at the micro-level of the writing session. However, another aspect of pausing is how the pauses are distributed across the writing session from a macro perspective, i.e. *when* in the writing session do pauses occur? Are, for example, pauses longer or more frequent in the beginning of the process or are pauses evenly distributed across the writing session?

Figure 4 shows how the pauses are distributed over the writing session for one adult writer with no reading and writing difficulties. The left *y*-axis shows the position in the text and the *x*-axis shows the number of keystrokes the writer has made. The solid line, text flow, shows how the writer moves in the text. As long as the graph is growing in a linear way the writer is moving forward by writing letters. If, however, it drops vertically the writer has used the mouse to move backwards in the text. The right *y*-axis shows pause duration in seconds. The vertical bars with diamonds on top show where in the

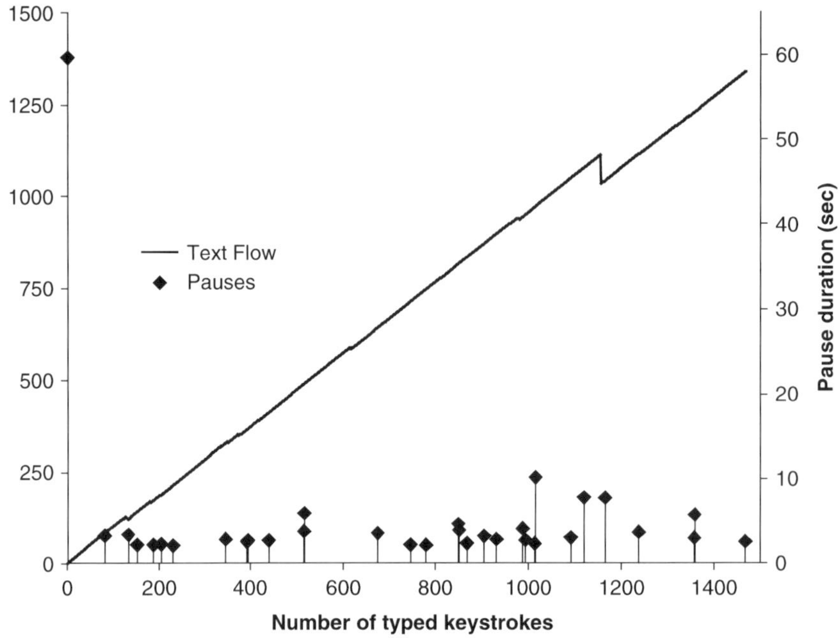


Figure 4: Text flow, pause position and duration in the production of one narrative. Source: From Wengelin, Å. (2002). Text production in adults with reading and writing difficulties. *Gothenburg Monographs in Linguistics, 20*, 208, Copyright by Å. Wengelin. Reprinted with permission.

text flow the pauses occur and the length of the bar indicates duration of the pause. The first vertical bar shows that this particular writer started her writing session with a long pause — perhaps thinking about what to write and/or how to start her story. She then wrote her text with small clusters of shorter pauses and made almost no changes to her text. The most obvious action in her text flow is that at about 1200 keystrokes she moved backwards within her text. This writer can be described as having a linear writing profile.

Her pause pattern is typical for an adult writer who is writing a narrative. Most writers appear to either make one long pause or several "semi-long" pauses in the initial phase of their writing (see Wengelin, 2002). This pause, or these pauses occurs either before the first keystroke, immediately after the main heading of the story or one or a few words in to the story if there is no heading. Figure 4 also shows how this writer pauses across the entire writing process. How writers use their pauses across different discourse units is a topic worth investigating that would complement the pause distribution data presented in Figure 4 (see Spelman Miller, this volume). As an initial stage to investigate discourse units Johansson (forthcoming), using automatically generated pause data, divided each text in the Swedish Spencer corpus into five equally long time segments and compared how the writers in the four age groups distributed their pauses across a writing session. She found a genre difference between the first sections in narrative and expository writing. In the first section of the narrative texts, the writers devoted a significantly higher percentage of the time to pausing than in the expository texts. A developmental pattern was also seen, in that the 4th-graders showed no difference between the genres, while the 7th- and 10th-graders did. The university students, again, showed no difference between the genres. The results indicate that writing an expository text requires different planning (and thus pausing) strategies than writing a narrative text. While the 4th-graders were not yet aware of the genre differences (and consequently do not differ in their pausing behaviour), the 7th- and 10th-graders were. The adults do not only know the genre difference, but are also so skilled in writing, that they put an equal amount of effort into the beginning of both genres. Thus, no genre differences were found in the beginning of the adults' texts.

An example of the sort of data that can be derived by combining automatically generated data and hand-marked aspect of topic structure is shown in Figure 5. Figure 5 (see also Wengelin, 2002) shows the mean pause duration for the first T-unit and the rest of the text for the adult controls (10 pieces of writing "I have never been so afraid") and adult R&W writers (11 pieces of writing "I have never been so afraid") from the R&W-corpus. The control group's mean pause durations confirm the impression we got from the example in Figure 4. That is, in writing narratives skilled writers appear to spend a lot of time pausing — most probably planning — at the beginning of the writing session. For writers with reading and writing difficulties no such effect was found (Wengelin, 2002). In this aspect the adults with reading and writing difficulties resemble the inexperienced 4th-graders in Johansson's (forthcoming) study.

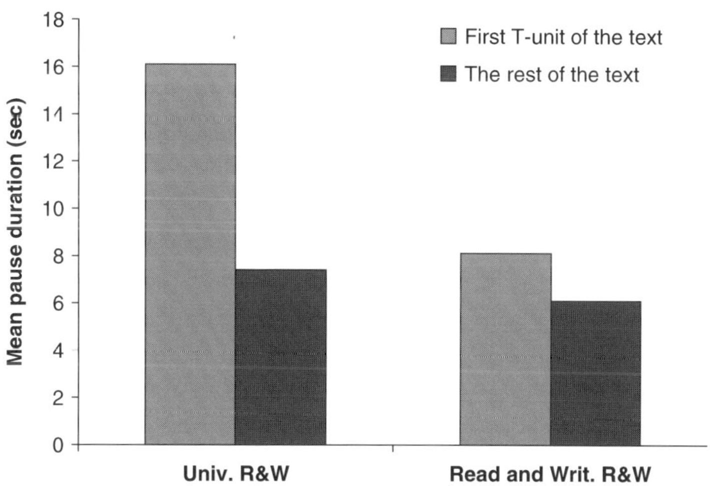


Figure 5: Pause durations in the beginning and the rest of the text production. Data from the R&W subcorpus I have never been so afraid.
Source: From Wengelin, Å. (2002). *Text production in adults with reading and writing difficulties*. Gothenburgh Monographs in Linguistics, Vol. 20, p. 208. Copyright by Å. Wengelin. Reprinted with permission.

## 10 The Complexity of Pause Studies

The pause studies referred to in this paper — my own as well as others — have been conducted and reported without any deeper analysis of what a pause is. This issue is rarely addressed in studies of pauses in writing — or speaking. The most common way of defining pauses in written as well as in spoken language is to stipulate a pause criterion that suits the aim of the research and this pause criterion is then used for all writers included in the research.

As was mentioned earlier, in my studies I have defined a *pause* as a transition time between two keystrokes that is longer than what can be expected to be necessary for the time needed to merely find the next key. Thus, in order for a transition to be considered as a pause, a writer has to "interrupt" her typing considerably longer than that "normal" transition time between two keystrokes. However, in most cases this probably means that each typist would need her own pause criterion, depending on her typing speed. An interruption in typing that may seem very long for a fast typist may be quite short for a slower one. This is illustrated by the empirical data below.

Table 7 shows how transitions between keystrokes registered during a writing session can vary in duration for the ten university students in the R&W corpus. The data is from the personal narrative on the topic "I have never been so afraid". For each person the total number of keystroke transitions (from one keystroke to the next) they have made during the writing session, the shortest and longest transitions they have made (Min and Max), the median, the mean and the standard deviations for each writer's transition times.

Table 7: The total number of keystroke transitions between characters (i.e. letters, numbers, punctuation marks, spaces, and line breaks), the duration of the shortest and longest transition (Min and Max, respectively, in seconds), made by each writer along with the median, mean and standard deviation for each writer's transition times and the group mean and standard deviation for these values. The ten writers undertook the personal narrative writing task "I have never been so afraid" and had no known writing difficulty.

| Subject | Number | Min | Max | Median | Mean | St. dev |
|---|---|---|---|---|---|---|
| AH | 1188 | 0.03 | 68.62 | 0.267 | 0.638 | 2.539 |
| CF | 3051 | <0.01 | 55.18 | 0.217 | 0.408 | 1.378 |
| CO | 1460 | <0.01 | 20.50 | 0.233 | 0.442 | 1.012 |
| DM | 1127 | <0.01 | 15.97 | 0.233 | 0.455 | 0.944 |
| HS | 4193 | <0.01 | 75.87 | 0.267 | 0.482 | 1.482 |
| JN | 975 | <0.01 | 513.08 | 0.283 | 1.345 | 17.134 |
| JM | 8447 | <0.01 | 161.52 | 0.433 | 0.825 | 3.930 |
| KP | 2510 | 0.02 | 39.23 | 0.200 | 0.476 | 1.725 |
| LJ | 600 | 0.07 | 65.85 | 0.317 | 1.174 | 4.430 |
| MM | 1363 | <0.01 | 59.60 | 0.300 | 0.493 | 1.709 |
| MEAN | 2491.4 | <0.01 | 107.54 | 0.275 | 0.674 | 3.628 |
| SD | 2475.8 | <0.01 | 256.02 | 0.070 | 0.348 | 5.138 |

From this data the limitations of setting a pre-determined universal pause cut-off duration are clear. Let us take a closer look at AH. She has made 1188 keystroke transitions between characters (i.e. letters, numbers, punctuation marks, spaces, and line breaks) in total, the shortest of which was 0.03 s and the longest 68.62 s. Her mean transition time is 0.638 s. LJ on the other hand has similar minimal and maximum transition times but his mean transition time is 1.174 s. The question of where the cut-off point between normal variation in typing speed and "actual interruptions of the writing" is arises immediately.

The insensitivity of a pre-determined minimum length of keystroke transition as the criterion for a pause could possibly be solved by setting individual pause criterion for each subject. This could be based on individual typing speeds according to some general principle, say, three times a writer's "normal transition times" between two keystrokes. Using individual pause criteria is a good solution for the *counting* of pauses, but it would make comparison of pause *durations* and the categorisation of pauses more difficult. Moreover, this solution, demands a definition of a *normal transition* time and a definition of *how much* longer than an individual's normal transition time a transition has to be in order to be considered a pause.

A possible "normal transition time" candidate is the average time it takes a writer to make the transition from one lower-case letter *within a word* to another. The reason for only including intra-word transitions and for not including transitions to and from capital letters and punctuation marks is that they are quite rare compared to lower-case transitions and that a transition from a lower-case letter to, for example, a major delimiter often takes extra time, both because a shift may be needed (for an exclamation mark or a question mark) and because major delimiters occur mainly at the end of sentences, where the writer can be expected to spend extra time monitoring, e.g. the sentence just produced and/or thinking about whether to continue or close the sentence. These longer pauses, that skew the mean, and to a lesser degree the median, should not form part of the calculation of the normal transition time. Thus, in order to get as little "noise" as possible in the measure, only transitions within words should be used. Table 8 shows the same information as Table 7, including *only the intra-word transitions.*

However, the question still remains which measure that best represents "a normal transition". The *mean* of all lower-case intra-word transitions may not be a suitable candidate as long pauses that are made owing to reasons other than poor typing skills impact upon the value of the mean. This sort of word-internal pause should not be included when determining the normal transition time for a composition. A better choice may be the *median* transition time of each subject, since medians are not affected by extreme values in the same way as means. Notice JN in Table 7, this writer's mean is clearly increased by a few very long pauses, with the result that the mean transition time is much longer, and less representative of the norm, than the median.

The need for the development of an individually tailored transition criterion for the pause is even more clearly demonstrated from Table 9. The table shows the correspondent data to Table 8 for the group of adults with reading and writing difficulties from the R&W corpus, i.e. the descriptive statistics of the intra-word transitions in the personal narrative "I have never been so afraid". These statistics show a greater degree of individual variation (sd = 0.186, subjects with reading and writing difficulties, *cf.* 0.070, no known writing difficulty group) and a higher mean median transition time (0.488 s *cf.* 0.275 s). Thus, unlike, the median column of Table 8 which indicates that the individual differences in typing speed

Table 8: The number of intra-word transitions, the duration of the shortest and longest (Min and Max, respectively, in seconds) such transition, made by each writer along with the median, mean and standard deviation for each writer's transition times and the group mean and standard deviation for these values. The ten writers were university students from the R&W corpus undertook the personal narrative writing task "I have never been so afraid". They had no known writing difficulty.

| Subject | Number | Min | Max | Median | Mean | St. dev |
|---|---|---|---|---|---|---|
| AH | 734 | 0.08 | 3.30 | 0.233 | 0.301 | 0.227 |
| CF | 1870 | 0.00 | 4.25 | 0.217 | 0.265 | 0.185 |
| CO | 869 | 0.00 | 6.57 | 0.233 | 0.281 | 0.276 |
| DM | 655 | 0.00 | 2.90 | 0.200 | 0.256 | 0.198 |
| HS | 2513 | 0.00 | 3.03 | 0.250 | 0.335 | 0.238 |
| JN | 600 | 0.00 | 3.77 | 0.267 | 0.349 | 0.300 |
| JM | 5291 | 0.00 | 20.850 | 0.417 | 0.469 | 0.480 |
| KP | 1484 | 0.02 | 2.22 | 0.200 | 0.237 | 0.167 |
| LJ | 374 | 0.07 | 3.25 | 0.217 | 0.390 | 0.386 |
| MM | 882 | 0.00 | 4.07 | 0.267 | 0.316 | 0.217 |
| MEAN | 1527.20 | 0.02 | 5.420 | 0.250 | 0.32 | 0.270 |
| SD | 1478.98 | 0.03 | 5.550 | 0.060 | 0.07 | 0.100 |

Table 9: The number of intra-word transitions, the duration of the shortest and longest transition (Min and Max, respectively, in m s), made by each writer along with the median, mean and standard deviation for each writer's transition times and the group mean and standard deviation for these values. The ten writers were adults with reading and writing difficulties in the R&W corpus who undertook the personal narrative writing task "I have never been so afraid".

| Subj | Number | Min | Max | Median | Mean | Std. dev |
|---|---|---|---|---|---|---|
| JW | 906 | 0.15 | 3.10 | 0.317 | 0.405 | 0.332 |
| KS | 335 | 0.15 | 5.60 | 0.750 | 0.858 | 0.614 |
| LO | 665 | 0.12 | 4.50 | 0.467 | 0.579 | 0.500 |
| LD | 811 | 0.17 | 7.85 | 0.500 | 0.655 | 0.513 |
| LB | 331 | <0.01 | 3.50 | 0.283 | 0.473 | 0.465 |
| MM | 509 | 0.02 | 5.13 | 0.333 | 0.590 | 0.687 |
| RH | 883 | <0.01 | 13.28 | 0.350 | 0.470 | 0.582 |
| RR | 368 | 0.15 | 11.38 | 0.783 | 0.986 | 0.980 |
| RL | 501 | 0.08 | 4.13 | 0.417 | 0.512 | 0.396 |
| TP | 803 | 0.12 | 8.13 | 0.683 | 0.896 | 0.828 |
| MEAN | 611.2 | 0.10 | 6.66 | 0.488 | 0.642 | 0.590 |
| ST.DEV | 230.2 | 0.06 | 3.45 | 0.186 | 0.202 | 0.198 |

may not be too worrying for the researcher who adopts a pre-determined universal pause criterion, the median column of Table 9 indicates that when working with writers or comparing different groups of writers a pre-determined universal pause criterion places limitations upon the comparisons that can be made and the conclusions the researcher can draw.

The importance of considering differences in keystroke transition speeds when setting pause criterion in writing research is further illustrated in Figure 6 with data from the Swedish Spencer corpus and from the R&W corpus.

Figure 6 shows the mean median transition times for six groups of writers. The error bars indicate standard deviations. Figure 6 clearly demonstrates how both the speed and the individual variation vary with the groups. As was mentioned earlier the slowest groups are the 4th-graders in the Swedish Spencer corpus and the writers with reading and writing difficulties in the R&W corpus. These groups are also the groups with the highest standard deviations. Setting a pause criterion that enables us to compare these groups with for example the university students in the Swedish Spencer corpus is obviously a tricky business. It is thus clear that we should control for typing speed and that ideally we should define individual pause criteria for each subject depending upon each subject's personal typing speed. However, so far there is no accepted method for accomplishing this task and it is therefore suggested as a very important question for further work — especially for any researcher who is interested in the written language production processes of writers with different typing skills.

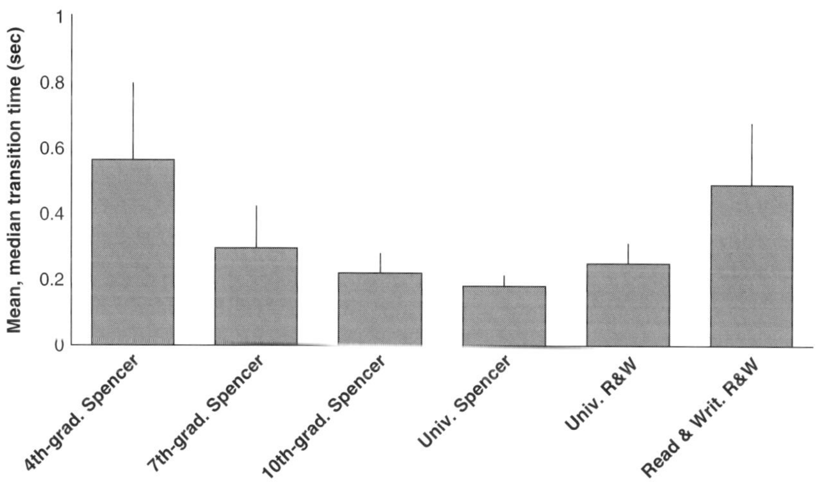


Figure 6: Median transition times within words four groups from the Swedish Spencer corpus: (4th-graders, 7th-graders, 10th-graders, and university students) and two groups from the R&W corpus (the university students with no history of reading and writing difficulties and the adult writers with reading and writing difficulties (Read and Writ.). All writers undertook a personal narrative. The 4th–10th grade students and the university students in the Spencer corpus wrote about an occasion in which they helped someone in trouble or someone else hade helped them getting out of trouble. The university students and the adults in the R&W corpus wrote the "I have never been so afraid" task. The error bars indicate one standard deviation.

## 11 Summary and Future Research Directions

In this chapter, I have demonstrated how pause studies can contribute to our knowledge of written language production. Pause studies tell us something about the language production process in general and about writing development and writing difficulties. I have also shown how pauses in writing can be investigated automatically by means of corpus-based studies using micro-contexts. Micro-contexts are useful for finding general pause patterns over large bodies of data as long as the pause locations we are interested in can be formalised in unambiguous expressions. However, two things should be remembered when using micro-contexts. The first is that some interesting discourse boundaries, like for example phrase boundaries, cannot be uniquely defined by means of micro-contexts. The second is that some writers, especially young inexperienced writers and writers with reading and writing difficulties may not use the writing conventions in expected ways. For example, the fact that we find no instances of the micro-context ".^a" in a young persons written production, does not mean that the young person has not used any delimiters. It could, for example, mean that this writer has the habit of making a space before delimiter. It is, therefore, important to explore the final edited texts visually before defining the micro-contexts that will be used for analysing the text(s). However, even with these two limitations micro-contexts are a powerful approach for analysing pause patterns in large corpora in a stringent way.

Three important aspects of pausing in writing need further investigation. As was mentioned above, the first and most important is the question of what a pause is in writing. How could it best be defined to suit different aims of research and what would be the best way of setting individual pause criteria, taking individual typing speeds into account?

The second is how does pause behaviour interact with the genre of the writing task? Among others, Hadenius (1992), Severinson Eklundh and Kollberg (1999), Andersson, Lindgren, Spelman Miller, and Sullivan (2001), Lindgren and Sullivan (2002) and Johansson (forthcoming), have, explicitly or otherwise, suggested an interaction between genre, pausing and revision. However, none of these have addressed pausing and genre using the microcontext and corpus-based techniques presented in this chapter.

The third aspect of pausing that is in need of further investigation is, what is the writer doing during a pause? A disadvantage with keystroke logging is that although it can tell us exactly when something is happening (e.g. when a pause occurs) it does not provide any information about what cognitive activity it signals. Does the writer, plan what to write next, monitor her text produced so far, look for a key on the keyboard or drink coffee? Owing to the complexity of this issue, multiple modes of investigation are needed. Strict experimental approaches, think-aloud protocols, retrospective reports, eye movement studies (see Strömqvist et al., this volume) and ERP measures are all possible approaches which could contribute towards a better knowledge of what writers are doing when they make a pause when writing texts.

## Acknowledgement

Thanks to Victoria Johansson and Sven Strömqvist for providing the Spencer data and for commenting the results of the analyses of the same.

Chapter 8

# Pausing, Productivity and the Processing of Topic in OnLine Writing

Kristyan Spelman Miller
*The University of Reading, Whiteknights, Reading, UK*

*In this chapter we present an approach to the analysis of online writing, which focuses on temporal aspects of composing, pausing and productivity. The pausological data underpinning this study provide valuable insights into the nature of planning, formulating and revising processes in the cases of the L1 and L2 writers whose writing behaviour was recorded. Underlying any such analysis of written text production is the selection of a valid unit for describing and measuring language produced online, and it is the purpose of this chapter to offer such a framework for analysis which draws not only on traditional grammatical notions of word, phrase and clause, but also on the discourse notion of topic. In this way we aim to throw light on the cognitive-textual nature of writing.*

**Keywords:** keystroke, pausing, productivity, fluency, topic, framing, discourse, word processing, L1, L2.

## 1 Introduction

Central to the description of online written language production, that is, the study of fluency, productivity and revision behaviour, is the notion of the pause. For the most part, following psycholinguistic tradition, studies have based their analyses of pausing on a definition of location using largely grammatical criteria. Such approaches have focused on pausing and associated planning, formulating and revision behaviour by considering units of language production defined in terms of word, clause and sentence spans. However, in this chapter I discuss an alternative scheme which complements the definition of units based on these

**Computer Key Stroke Logging and Writing: Methods and Applications**

**ISBN: 0-08-044934-4**

*Spelman Miller, K. (2006). Pausing, productivity and the processing of topic in on-line writing. In G. Rijlaarsdam (Series Ed.) and K. P. H. Sullivan, & E. Lindgren. (Vol. Eds.), Studies in Writing, Vol. 18, Computer Keystroke Logging: Methods and Applications (pp. 131–155). Oxford: Elsevier.*

grammatical concepts. The claim, made through reference to data collected in a keystroke study of a group of writers, is that that pauses may, in addition, be located at discoursally significant junctures, forming units of language which have a potential discourse role in introducing, maintaining and developing topic in the discourse produced. The notion of 'framing device' is proposed as a means of defining such units, and, when applied to the study of online formulation, allows the researcher insight into the association between text structure and the processes involved in handling topic.

In an attempt to evaluate the applicability of this proposed set of analytical categories, we present data from our study of 21 academic writers who have English as either their first (L1) or subsequently acquired (L2) language. Brief discussion is made of general features of subjects' pausing and formulating behaviour, before we turn to the findings concerning the framing device categories. Close analysis of individual writers' behaviours suggests interesting, but subtle differences in frequency and duration of pausing at key topic-related locations. The establishment and management of topic appears to be a critical concern for writers in their writing, and, we suggest, underpins characteristics of their pausing and formulating behaviour.

## 2 Analytical Developments in Keystroke Logging Research

### *2.1 Defining Pause Location: Grammatical Characterisation*

In the earlier discussion in Chapter 2 (Spelman Miller, this volume) of pausological studies of writing (e.g., Jansen, Van Waes, & Van den Bergh, 1996; Matsuhashi, 1981, 1982, 1987; Strömqvist, Ahlsén, & Wengelin, 1999; Warren, 1997) reference has been made to possible limitations in the locational categories used. In particular, is the problem of a lack of refinement in existing categorisations, especially in the definition of word-level locations, and the need to address more sensitively important distinctions, for example, between words of different classes (determiner, noun, disjunct, conjunction, and so on). The second area where attention is needed is in the representation of location in terms of potential as well as actual (produced) units of language. Given the online nature of the data being produced, it is necessary to account for the evolving, emergent status of the language. Text spans to be described are open to modification, as the writer adds, deletes and adjusts the message, and the descriptions and measurements of language produced need to account for this. Third, as has already been suggested, it is of potential interest to extend the notion of pause location to allow for the interpretation of the unit from the perspective of its function in establishing or introducing topic. To meet this aim, a discourse-oriented category, the framing device, is proposed.

The first steps in drawing up my framework involve the grammatical characterisation of language units. Identifying structural elements following Halliday's (1985, 1994) terminology, we classify stretches of text from morpheme to clause complex (or sentence), that is: character (morpheme), word, intermediate constituent (or phrase group), clause and sentence. The location of the pause is defined in terms of its position in the flow of the text in respect of the preceding structural element or elements produced. To accommodate the emergent nature of the data, location is referred to in terms of potential structural categories. For example, the location of the pause (indicated by the chevron bracket <>) in example 1

(1) student<>

may be described as following a noun phrase, or at a potential intermediate constituent boundary. However, this depiction may later be shown to be only temporarily true. If the writer makes modifications as s/he continues, for example, by adding s' to form student<>s', the location of the pause is now not phrase-final, but phrase-internal. How can we account, therefore, for the temporary status of language produced online? In response to this, we refer to the characterisation of units defined by pauses at a particular point in the construction of the text only. We refer to the units which may or may not survive in subsequent modifications to the text as potential completion points.

The levels we propose are as follows:

- character completion points (XCP) — after a morpheme or non-morpheme, but at a point which do not constitute a word in that context (i.e., word-internal);
- word completion points (WCP) — after a recognisable word, but at a point, which does not constitute a phrase (i.e., phrase-internal);
- intermediate constituent completion point (ICP) — after a nominal, verbal, adverbial or adjectival group, which is recognisable as a complete phrase (also after non-nuclear elements such as disjuncts and conjuncts), but at a point which does not constitute a clause (i.e., clause-internal);
- clause completion points (CCP) — after a clause unit, but which is not marked as a sentence;
- sentence completion point (SCP) — after a unit marked as a complete sentence.

Figure 1 provides a more detailed breakdown of these analytical levels using the following grammatical nomenclature: D = determiner; N = noun; Aux = auxiliary; MV = main verb; S = subject Prep = preposition; NP = noun phrase; Cl/Phr = clause/phrase; O/C = object/complement; rel pron = relative pronoun; Adj – adjective.

Further exemplification, discussion of background issues, and illustration of these categories applied to data are provided in Spelman Miller (2000a, 2002, pp. 123–128).

In summary, the grammatical categorisation we propose aims to provide a more delicate characterisation of pause location, which differentiates word class categories more appropriately. The next step in the design of our framework is to respond to the call for a discourse-oriented interpretation of units produced online through the concept of the framing device. This is the subject of the next section.

### *2.2 Framing Devices*

A central tenet of our approach is that a cognitive-textual analysis of writing should go beyond the traditional grammatical analysis of formulation. So far, pausological studies of writing have paid little attention to issues of text structure, concentrating on the description of pause occurrence in terms of surface or grammatical criteria. An exception to this is the work of Sanders, Janssen, Van der Pool, Schilperood, and Van Wijk (1996), mentioned

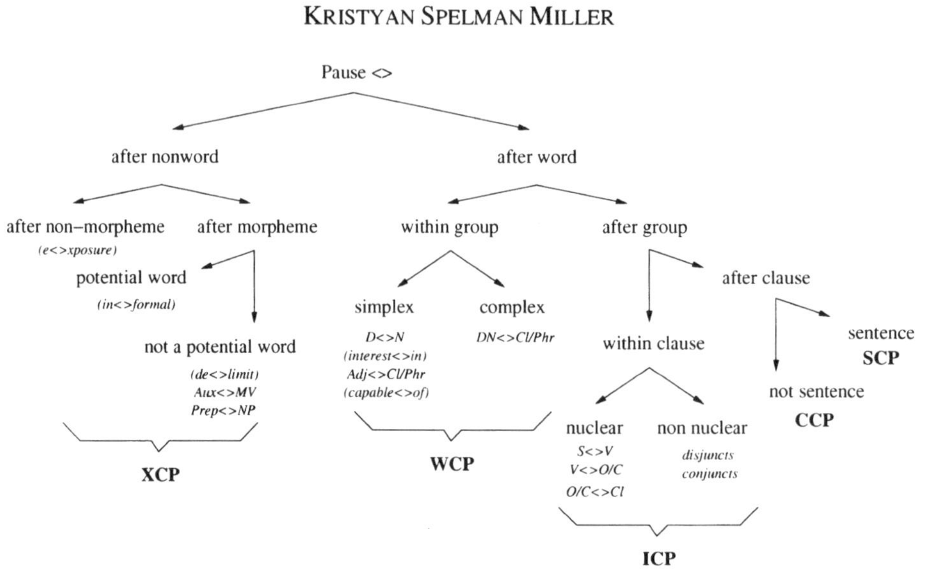


Figure 1: Identification of pause locations (main category contents: XCP = character completion point; WCP = word completion point; ICP = intermediate constituent completion point; CCP = clause completion point; SCP = sentence completion point happens at the critical juncture of planning and formulating (Witte & Cherry, 1986, p. 143).

earlier, which considers pause behaviour in relation to text structure from the perspective of hierarchical structure analysis (based on Mann and Thompson's [1988] Rhetorical Structure Theory).

While this offers a new direction for pausological research, as a proposition-based approach it makes limited use of linguistic markers explicitly produced in the text in order to identify text structure.[1] In seeking to make explicit connections between the substance of the writing output and the processes underlying text production, we therefore feel that there is scope for other. Drawing on Witte and Cherry's (1986) interest in relating text characteristics and writing processes involved in establishing topic, I set about exploring the types of strategies a writer may use in finding a focus for his/her message. This goal is inspired by Witte and Cherry's assumption that 'framing decisions, which must operate at the global level of whole discourse and at the local level of individual sentences or T-units, are reflected in writer's decisions about topicalization' (p. 141). This might allow us, in the context of on-line writing research, to investigate the association between the textual structure of output and the underlying processes of planning and formulating.

[1]The main linguistic markers used in Sanders et al.'s (1996) study to identify text structure components are temporal markers (then, the next day, later, and so on) and the semantic status of verbs ('stative' and 'event' verbs, p. 478).

I therefore propose a scheme to describe units of language produced from the perspective of certain discourse functions associated with the notion of topic, in particular in introducing and developing topic in the discourse. Starting with the grammatical characterisation of units described above, I introduce an additional category called the *framing device*, which allows us to consider the potential discourse function of certain units, principally from the categories of intermediate constituent category (nominal phrases in subject or adjunct position, and also conjuncts and disjuncts) and certain clause-level elements which may be seen as framing or setting up the rest of the message.

The concept of topic is defined in a variety of ways in the literature.[2] Most discussions focus on the notion of sentence rather than discourse topic, and employ a range of defining properties for its identification. Goutsos (1997, p. 5) summarises a number of different perspectives which may be taken in defining sentence topic: structural, presentational, logical, informational and pragmatic. The structural perspective specifies grammatical conditions for topic (in terms of it being a constituent dominated by S); the presentational approach considers topic in terms of the leftmost position in the clause or sentence, and its role as a point of departure for the message. The logical perspective (Reinhart, 1981) relates topic to the notion of what the sentence is about, and other approaches relate topic to information structure (i.e., the status of elements as given and new) or to pragmatic notions of prominence. From this wide range of perspectives offered in the literature, it is necessary to narrow down an approach for use in my framework.

It is sentence topic rather than discourse topic which I use in my own analysis, for the reason that much of the psycholinguistic work and pausological research in which our analysis is grounded focuses on sentence-level language production. Some writers (e.g., Lautamatti, 1987; Witte, 1983) have attempted to connect notions of sentence and discourse topic, assuming that analysis of the local sentence topic may lead to insights into the analysis of topic at a discourse level. Witte and Cherry (1986, p. 129), for example, include in their definition of sentence topic functions that of creating local coherence between individual sentences and guiding readers 'in constructing "gists" and identifying discourse topics for the texts they read' (p. 129). There may be some scope, therefore, for moving beyond the sentence to consider impact on the coherence of the discourse as a whole.

A more powerful argument is that because my analysis is concerned with units of text produced on-line, a local-level approach is the most appropriate perspective for the description of the data. As text is analysed at the point of production, we are not in a position to know the consequences in global, discourse terms of the selection of certain units in the text string. As has been discussed above, elements are likely to be modified or removed as the writer continues to compose, and the function of any item in the text string in contributing to the development of the discourse topic may be far from clear at the point of production. My perspective, therefore, as with the grammatical characterisation of the string, is to deal with topic from the level of sentence/clause.

As for the perspective taken in defining a topic-related unit, the framing device, this is strongly influenced by structural and presentational definitions of topic. In particular, I make use of the grammatical manifestation of topic within the clause or clause complex,

[2]For reviews, see, among others, de Beaugrande (1992), Keijsper (1985) and Reinhart (1981).

and issues of presentation (in terms of initial clause/sentence position) for the definition of framing device. Both of these perspectives are compatible with the Hallidayan view of *theme*, that is, of the first ideational element within the clause as the 'point of departure for the message' (Halliday, 1985, p. 38), although we have to ward against over-simplistic conflation of grammatical form (i.e., subjecthood) and sentence position in English.

I define a framing device quite simply as 'an element or structure (single word, phrase or clause) which serves to establish the starting point of the message at the clause/sentence level. This may be in one of a number of ways, either in constituting the topic itself, or in preparing the scene for the introduction of the topic' (Spelman Miller, 2000a, pp. 114–115). The proposed framework consists of five types of framing device which fulfil such functions:

- subject theme,
- adjunct theme/complement theme,
- non-experiential theme,
- empty theme (*it, what* and existential *there*), and
- thematised structure (e.g., finite/non-finite clauses).

In conception the framework bears some similarity to an approach to the modelling of topic in expository text (product) proposed by Goutsos (1997), published after our own framework was devised. Goutsos proposes a number of topic-related strategies visible in the text that he maintains are associated with topic framing, topic introduction, topic closure and topic continuation. In his model, topic framing devices include, for example, such signals as discourse markers similarly, moreover, metadiscourse items at this point, taking each in turn, sentence initial adjuncts, adverbials and clauses, encapsulating nominals this, this issue, and paragraph breaks, which fulfil a crucial role in preparing the ground for a shift of topic. Topic introduction may be marked by, among other things, specific sentence structure features such as the so-called light thematic structures, renominalisation through both full noun phrase and pronouns, and tense shift. Topic closure may be indicated by metadiscourse items, discourse markers, tense shift and encapsulation, and topic continuation by discourse markers, cohesive markers, use of parenthesis and tense continuity.

Goutsos's (1997) model goes beyond my purposes in relating the occurrence of these topic-related strategies to the development of the discourse topic. As has already been argued, such a goal is beyond the scope of this current analysis, which focuses on categorising the online data in terms of topic-related function. In other words, my focus is on describing text units at the point of production rather than in terms of the final product (as Goutsos does), although I acknowledge that this could be an interesting direction for future research.

In the discussion of framing devices that follows, I outline the main defining features of the five types before illustrating categories from data collected from the L1 and L2 writers in my study.

**2.2.1 Subject theme** The most frequently occurring category of framing device is the subject theme. This consists of elements which are both grammatical subject and initial sentence constituent. It contains both full nominal groups (including those which are postmodified) and proforms. In the illustrations below from our data the exponent is shown (underlined) in context (see also Spelman Miller, 2002, pp. 131–134).

(1) This hypothesis might be attributed to the claim of lateralisation [L2:A_E].
(2) This would be further discussed in terms of the claim of 'the Affective Filter Hypothesis' [L2:A_D].

In cases where the proform *it* occurs, preceding context is used to distinguish the case of subject theme from that of an empty theme construction as in *it is well-known that....* Where there is no obvious candidate for antecedent, the *it* may be viewed as part of such a construction (which is accounted for by the category of empty theme). Potential pronoun as opposed to determiner use of *this/these*, *that/those* is also decided from context. Whenever an item can stand as a proform, it is coded as such rather than as a determiner (whether or not the following text confirms this).

**2.2.2 Adjunct theme/complement theme** New topics are often introduced by sentence-initial adverbials, for example:

(1) Around puberty, human beings will face with lateralisation of the brain [L2:A_D].
(2) Among individual factors, those which are widely recognised by most scholars are: age, aptitude, attitude, motivation and personality [L2:K_D].
(3) With reference to Ellis (1994), he illustrates these differences with the aid of a framework [L2:C_D].

We include also the possibility of complement theme in this category, although this is not likely to be frequent in the data.

**2.2.3 Non-experiential theme** This category draws on the Hallidayan notion of the textual and interpersonal functions of theme, to describe those elements that appear in sentence initial position, but do not constitute part of the ideational content of the message. The category consists of those elements indicating textual structuring and interpersonal (evaluative) comment, which Goutsos notes are frequently used to signal topic shift, continuation or closure.

I include here disjuncts (sentence adverbials) and conjunctions, which in Hallidayan terms do not 'exhaust the thematic potential of the clause' (Halliday, 1994, p. 52, cited in Thompson, 1996, p. 134), but provide some kind of structuring or evaluative function on the content of the message. These items are often physically set apart from the rest of the clause or sentence by punctuation. Sentence adverbials consist of a wide range of structures, including adverbs, prepositional phrases, infinitive clauses, *-ing* and *-ed* participle clauses and finite verb clauses. Contextualised examples from our data are given below:

(1) To start with, in an attempt to present a theoretical view of motivation, Skehan put forward four hypotheses [L2:P_D].
(2) Moving on to some more general factors that influence the performance and the acquisition of the learners of a SL, we cannot avoid referring to motivation [L2:Ya_D].
(3) On the whole, research on SLA research has considerably contributed to our understanding of IDs of learners *but* there is still need for more valid and reliable data *before* we feel confident in labelling learners with various characteristics [L2:Ya_D].

**2.2.4 Empty theme (it, what and existential there structures)** This category includes in the notion of theme those elements such as existential *there*, pseudo-cleft structure or 'thematic equative', and the so-called 'empty' *it is X that* structure, which occur in subject position but do not in themselves fulfil the experiential function of theme. Examples of these in our data include:

(1) There are debates on the methodology of experiments carried out [L2:C_E].
(2) What is needed in this area of research is some longitudinal studies [L2:K_D].
(3) It is that young learners acquire a language more easily [L2:T_D].
(4) It is well known now that individuals acquire language in different ways [L2:R_D].
(5) It is beyond doubt that everyone apart from some exceptions can learn a language [L2:Yo_D].

**2.2.5 Thematised structure** This final category includes both clausal (finite and non-finite) and phrasal structures, which are fronted in the sentence. Unlike the non-experiential theme category that provides structuring or authorial comment outside the ideational content of the message, these structures are integral to the content of the text. Examples include:

(1) If the teacher knows that not all students have the same learning strategies, he/she will vary the material [L2:R_E].
(2) Since I was a child, his big dream was I to become an English teacher just like him [L2:T_D].

In summary, the framework proposed for the analysis of pause location is built on both grammatical and topic-related principles. My goal is to provide an extended and improved scheme for use in pausological research, and in particular for the definition of units of production, first, by offering a more elaborate scheme for the identification of elements, particularly at the word level; second, by introducing the notion of potential completion points to accommodate the emergent and often temporary status of text elements as they are produced online; and third, by introducing a discourse-sensitive category, the framing device, to interpret text units in terms of topic-related functions.

In the section that follows I present the context and summary findings of a study that has employed the framework outlined above. This allows us to explore the types of insights provided by my analysis in the context of the cognitive-textual study of writing processes.

## 3 A Keystroke Study of L1 and L2 Writers

### *3.1 Context: Subjects, Tasks and Research Design*

The key principles of a pausological approach to writing process research have already been established in previous chapters of this volume. The focus of my particular study is the planning and formulating processes of a group of writers who are working within an academic context. The participants differ in terms of language background: for half the writers English is their first language (L1), for the others it is a second or additional language (L2).

In very general terms I am interested in exploring the differences in the planning and formulating processes of these writers through a micro-analysis of data generated through keystroke recording.

The study is motivated by my own professional experience with students in a British university working towards award-bearing degrees in Linguistics. Typically students come from a variety of language backgrounds and during their university careers are required to produce a range of different tasks, including coursework essays, projects, dissertation and unseen written examination papers. The study as a whole is designed to address two research questions, one comparing performance on two contrasting task types, and the other concerned with L1 and L2 writing behaviour. It is the second of these dimensions which we will focus on in this paper.

The context of academic, particularly tertiary-level, writing is perhaps the most widely researched, especially from an educational perspective, and the range of research interests too broad to be reviewed here. We note in passing, for example, the work of O'Brien (1995), which inspires interest in the case of the undergraduate writer coming to terms with the demands of knowledge-transforming (Bereiter & Scardamalia, 1987) tasks in writing. O'Brien's comparison of coursework and examination performance analysed from a product (relational analysis) perspective highlights the problems of a writer (writing in his/her L1) unable to use source materials except in an 'uninterpreted, untransformed' manner (O'Brien, 1995, p. 471) and demonstrably weak at producing a coherent and accurate response to the essay prompt. Writers, even L1 writers, clearly have difficulties in meeting the demands of producing academic text. This domain appears to offer, therefore, scope for highly relevant and useful research on the features of individuals' writing behaviour.

As I have already suggested, the specific context established for my research concerns students from different language backgrounds (i.e., L1 and L2 writers of English) performing on a simulated authentic academic writing task, that of the timed, unseen examination essay. This is a familiar writing task format involving production of a structured written response (in continuous text) to a title prompt, produced within a fixed time-limit (typically 45 min). The manipulation of the task condition centres on the choice of mode, or method of addressing the subject matter, for the essay. In this study each student will be asked to produce two essays on the same topic, one defining/descriptive (presenting, classifying and defining ideas) and the other evaluative (presenting aspects of an argument, and deducing). In this $2 \times 2$ design, the language background of the writer constitutes the other independent research variable, and the focus (dependent) variable will be a number of pause-related phenomena, namely pause duration, pause frequency, pause rate, productivity (length of text span), and rate of production (within a text span). Crucial to this analysis is the definition of pause location, and to address this I have proposed the framework described above for the identification of pause location from both grammatical and topic-related perspectives.

The subjects involved in this study were all students in the Department of Linguistic Science, at the University of Reading, UK, at the time of the research. The data were elicited from 21 students, all of whom were following the same 20 h lecture course on Second Language Learning and Teaching. Participation in the data collection was voluntary. In an attempt to achieve face validity the experimental tasks were presented as an opportunity for students to prepare for their formal course assessment: informal feedback from the practice activity was offered concerning the subjects' understanding of the course content and their own essay writing practices. The experimental task conditions were designed to simulate those of the formal written examination both in format and procedure (i.e., in consisting of a previously unseen essay task to be completed within a fixed time frame). The medium of composition differed, however, from that of the typical examination since subjects would produce text on a word processor rather than with pen and paper. Motivation and commitment to participate in the experimental tasks were generally considered to be high because of the perceived importance of written assessment and the interest in receiving feedback prior to formal assessment, but students were aware that these tasks did not carry the weight of assessed assignments.

A number of constraints were placed on the sampling procedure. First, subjects were to be drawn from the same student group and were to be similar in age and exposure to the topic area. Second, they needed to be familiar with the computer keyboard and with the use of a word processor. Third, they had to be volunteers, since the data collection tasks were additional to the formal university assessment, and fourth, the subjects needed to be available for the two 1 h writing sessions conducted on separate occasions within the data collection period. These practical considerations limited the number of subjects available for inclusion in the study.

Of the 21 participants, 10 are L1 writers who share similar educational backgrounds. The remaining 11 subjects are referred to as the L2 group. This is a mixed group in terms of first language background. The largest subgroup consists of seven speakers of Greek as a first language; the other four comprise a Japanese, a German, a Russian and a Portuguese. All subjects in the study are approximately matched in terms of age (20–24 years). Nine of the participants are female.

The focus on subjects from both L1 and L2 writing backgrounds allows me to situate my work against the background of the extensive and expanding body of research. As Silva's (1993) synthesis of research suggests, several important trends emerge concerning differences between L1 and L2 writers in planning, formulating and revising. For example, planning appears to be more difficult for L2 writers, especially at the global level (Dennett, 1985; Jones & Tetroe, 1987; Moragne e Silva, 1989; Yau, 1989). Evidence points, too, to a slower rate of production and lower productivity for L2 writers, who pause more frequently and for longer (Hall, 1990; Hildenbrand, 1985). Revision also seems to occur more at the local level in L2 writing. Against this general background it is possible to anticipate differences in the observed writing processes of subjects in our study. In particular, we might expect, in the case of L2 writers, more pausing in general, more attention to lower order concerns and lower productivity or fluency.

Caution is also necessary, however, in forming these predictions. The L2 writers in this study are advanced users of English, and contrasts with L1 users, therefore, may not be so stark. Other individual factors, such as motivation, interest, fatigue, anxiety, for example, may also intervene. Some individuals may choose to economise rather than maximise their effort and reduce their engagement with the task, falling back on rehearsed responses and giving less attention to higher level concerns than might otherwise be expected. This is possible especially given the pressures of the timed writing condition (for discussion of a similar context, see O'Brien, 1995). In general, then, although some trends towards L1–L2 writing differences may guide the research question and hypotheses here, we might also anticipate a high degree of individual variation cutting across our L1 and L2 subject groups in response to the experimental tasks.

The keystroke logging tool used for the data collection is JEdit, devised at the IPLab, Royal Institute of Technology, Stockholm (see Severinson Eklundh & Kollberg, 1992, 1996b for details and Sullivan and Spelman Miller, this volume, for an overview) for use on the Macintosh computer. Underpinning the design of our study to compare the L1 and L2 writers are the following research question and hypotheses:

Do writers with different language backgrounds (namely L1 and advanced L2 writers of English) respond differently to writing tasks in terms of pause-related phenomena?

- Hypothesis 1 *(Pause duration)*. L2 writers of English will pause for longer than L1 writers at all locations, but especially at lower text unit levels.
- Hypothesis 2 *(Pause frequency)*. L2 writers of English will pause more frequently than L1 writers at all locations, but especially at lower level unit levels.
- Hypothesis 3 *(Fluency, Productivity, and rate of production)*. L2 writers of English will produce shorter text spans and their rate of production will be less than that of L1 writers.
- Hypothesis 4 *(Pausing at framing device locations)*. The frequency and distribution of pauses at framing device locations will differ across the two language groups, such that L2 writers of English will generate more simple subject theme pauses than L1 writers.

These hypotheses guide the presentation of general results summarised below in Section 4.2. For discussion of the hypotheses and findings relating to task type, see Spelman Miller (2000a).

### *3.2 General Findings Concerning Temporal Variables and L1/L2 Writers*

The issue of inter-subject differences in writing process research has frequently been addressed from the point of view of first/second language background. Debate centring on the potentially distinct nature of L2 writing processes has raged in the literature over the last two decades, with a number of contradictory positions emerging from the diverse body of research. With respect to pausological studies of writing, most research has focused on native speakers (Chanquoy, Foulin, & Fayol, 1996; Matsuhashi, 1981, 1987; Perrin, 1998; Sanders et al., 1996; Van der Pool, 1996, among others), although recently attention has begun to turn to the situation of the L2 writer. Phinney and Khouri's (1993) video-recorded observation of advanced L2 writers, for example, focuses on a number of aspects of the writing and revising activities (including pause time) of four individuals differing in proficiency level and degree of experience in using the word processor. Among findings exhibited by these four L2 subjects is evidence of 'a concern with form over substance' (p. 271), with the lower proficiency writers tending to pause more word-internally in order to focus on specific forms.

Warren's (1997) exploratory pausological study of L1 and L2 writers using keystroke logging reports a number of interesting findings, including the observation that learners (L2 writers) spend a greater percentage of time pausing than L1 writers and tend to produce longer pauses. In terms of pause distribution, Warren suggests that differences in the lexical, structural and organisational locations of pauses reflect learners' 'more conscious decisions and revisions compared to the relative ease of native speakers' (p. 166).

Similar keystroke studies of L2 writers by Pålson (1998), Sullivan and Lindgren (2002) and Sullivan, Kollberg, and Pålson (1998) have focussed on the writing patterns and revision activities of Swedish learners of English at a number of age levels. Again, attention to local issues such as spelling and grammatical problems is most frequently associated with the L2 writers. Broekkamp and Van den Bergh (1996), in their study of L2 revision strategies, interpret differences between L2 and L1 writers in terms of 'trade-off effects of lower-level processes and higher-level processes' (p. 170). The authors claim that 'Attention conflicts between lower and higher text levels are expected to be especially apparent in L2 writing. [...] [E]xtensive attention required by linguistic demands seems to reduce the attention of the L2 writer to higher-level text demands' (p. 171). Finally, in a comparison of German L2 and English L1 revision behaviour in North America using the JEdit logging software, Thorson (2000) reports that, when writing in the L2, writers produce less text and in general revise more.

Against this background of interest in L1 and L2 writing processes explored through pausological analysis, I present a summary of the key findings. The first two hypotheses are concerned with pause duration and frequency, and draw on the grammatical characterisation of pause location in terms of the five linguistic levels (from character to sentence). With respect to pause duration [Hypothesis 1], the prediction that pause length would be greater in the case of the L2 writers is borne out by the data. Statistical analysis confirms a significant overall difference between language groups in terms of pause duration ($p = 0.002$), and this difference is apparent at all text unit levels except the clause (CCP) level. Where we would expect to find greatest difference, at the lower text unit levels, results are not clear cut, however. At the lowest (word-internal, or XCP) text unit level pauses do appear to be significantly longer in the case of the L2 writers, a finding which fits well with the explanation that L2 writers may pay more attention to lower level (often spelling and morphological) concerns. Striking differences between the groups are also attested at the intermediate constituent (ICP) level, although not to the same degree at the lower, word (WCP) level. We need to consider why the two groups should display such clear differences in pause length at the ICP level but not at the lower, word level. Insight into this issue is provided later in the discussion of pausing at framing device locations.

Hypothesis 2, that L2 writers pause more frequently than L1 writers, is supported in general terms by my results, although, contrary to expectations, differences between groups fail to reach levels of statistical significance with respect to the lowest text unit level (XCP). Pause frequency counts at this location display an extremely high degree of individual variation within the L2 group, suggesting a lack of consistency in pausing behaviour at this level. Fine-grained analysis of specific performances (as we provide in our case-study analyses) will help to shed more light on such behaviour. Note that the information generated from the calculation of pause frequency alone becomes more meaningful when considered in terms of proportion of opportunity for pausing, or, as in the case study analyses, when viewed in conjunction with information concerning pause duration and production.

With respect to fluency measures (Hypothesis 3), the expectation that productivity and rate of production would be lower in the case of the L2 writers is clearly supported by the findings. Both Silva (1993) and Thorson (2000) report similar findings with respect to L2 productivity. The task of producing text appears to be slower and more effortful, in line with findings of Hildenbrand (1985), Moragne e Silva (1989) and others, although we are reminded that higher productivity is not necessarily equated with better writing (Reppen, 1995).

The fourth hypothesis concerns pausing behaviour at the specific location defined as framing devices. Since this is one of the main features of the framework presented in this paper, the findings from this hypothesis are discussed in more detail below.

### *3.3 General Findings Concerning Framing Device*

The final hypothesis to be addressed concerns the interpretation of certain units in my categorisation from the point of view of topic-related function, referred to here as topic framing. The following devices, which coincide with either ICP or CCP level units, are identified in the data:

(1) subject theme (e.g., This hypothesis <>);
(2) adjunct/complement theme (e.g., Around puberty <>);
(3) non-experiential theme (e.g., Historically, <>);
(4) empty theme (e.g., It is stated that <>); and
(5) thematised structure (e.g., Since I was a child, <>).

Based on the assumption that production of these devices may be important in determining the discourse structure of the message, I seek visible evidence in the temporal behaviour of our writers that pauses at certain locations coincide with the production of such devices.

As Table 1 indicates, the most frequent framing device location at which pausing occurs is the subject theme category. Some of the other categories (notably adjunct/complement themes and empty themes occur infrequently (4.3% and 7.1% of the total, respectively).

Table 2 allows us to consider the effect of language group on pausing at all framing device locations. Calculation of an ANOVA reveals no evidence of statistically significant difference in mean frequencies according to language group. The p values for the five framing device categories respectively are: 0.39, 0.14, 0.42, 0.39 and 0.34 (1 df).

Table 1: Summary of pausing at framing device categories.

| | **Subject theme** | **Adjunct/ complement theme** | **Non-experiential theme** | **Empty theme** | **Thematised structure** | **Total** |
|---|---|---|---|---|---|---|
| *n* | 528 | 37 | 154 | 61 | 80 | 860 |
| Mean | 12.57 | 0.88 | 3.67 | 1.45 | 1.90 | 20.47 |
| SD | 5.07 | 1.35 | 2.35 | 1.78 | 2.26 | 7.82 |
| % | 61.4 | 4.3 | 17.9 | 7.1 | 9.3 | 100 |

Table 2: Mean frequencies of pausing at framing device by language group.

| Lang group | Subject theme | Adjunct/ complement theme | Non-experiential theme | Empty theme | Thematised structure |
|---|---|---|---|---|---|
| L2 mean | 13.23 | 1.18 | 3.95 | 1.68 | 2.23 |
| SD | 5.64 | 1.37 | 2.82 | 1.96 | 2.33 |
| L1 mean | 11.85 | 0.55 | 3.35 | 1.2 | 1.55 |
| SD | 4.38 | 0.28 | 1.73 | 1.58 | 2.19 |

Since raw frequencies are small, no firm claims may be made concerning the pattern of framing device pause occurrence in these data. However, it is possible to note that in all categories the L1 group appears to produce fewer pauses at framing device boundaries than the L2 subjects. This is in line with the L1 group's comparatively lower mean pause frequency in general, and in particular with respect to ICP locations. The possibility remains that differences in framing device pausing between subject groups may obtain, but have not been revealed in this general frequency count. Further investigation focusing on the case of the most frequent category, subject theme, will seek to explore more closely the issue of the association between pausing and framing device location.

It has already been noted that the most frequently occurring category of framing device in the data is that of the subject theme: 61.4% of all recorded instances of pausing at framing devices are categorised as subject themes. Of the 528 instances of subject theme pausing, the vast majority (458, or 86.7%) consists of full noun phrases rather than pronoun subjects. It is clear from this that there is a tendency for pauses to coincide with subject themes when they are full noun phrases.

A second issue is the susceptibility of subject themes to pause occurrence. Since the raw frequency data alone provide limited information, we need to consider actual pause occurrence as a proportion of potential occurrence at available subject theme locations. Calculation of such a proportion reveals a considerable range across individuals: from 7% in the case of the fluent writer, L1:S, who pauses at only 8 of the 110 potential subject theme locations, to 88% in the case of L2:Yc, for whom 23 of the potential 26 subject themes coincide with production of a marked pause. The mean proportion for subjects overall is 33%. In other words, in general one third of the available subject theme locations coincides with the location of a pause. This rate of uptake is generally constant across tasks.

This finding lends support to the establishment of a discourse-oriented category for the analysis of pause location. As an alternative means of interpreting pause occurrence to the grammatical categories traditionally used in pausological studies of both speech and writing, the notion of framing device (and subject theme, in particular) appears to be useful in accounting for pause location from a topic-framing perspective. Although patterns of pausing at such locations vary according to individuals, the general impression is that the (full noun phrase) subject theme is a likely location for pausing. Individual differences in the uptake of this position for pausing will be considered in more detail below according to subject group.

The third issue in the analysis of the subject theme framing device concerns the duration of pauses occurring at this location. Will pauses at this location be longer than other equivalent pauses? Since all subject themes by definition fall within the ICP text unit, the mean pause length of ICP pauses coinciding with subject themes is compared with those which do not coincide with production of this framing device. Table 3 summarises the results of an ANOVA conducted in order to investigate the interaction effect of task, language group and task/language on pause duration at subject theme and non-subject theme ICP locations. Results suggest evidence of a significant effect of language group on pause duration at subject theme locations, but not with respect to non-subject theme locations. No significant differences with respect to task and task/language on pause durations at these locations were revealed. The nature of the inter-group differences with respect to pause duration at subject and non-subject theme locations may be clarified by considering the mean values by language group (see Table 4).

This information reveals that in the case of the L1 writers, means for subject theme and non-subject theme pauses are very similar (5.13 and 5.24 s, respectively), but for the L2 writers, pauses are markedly longer at subject theme locations than at the non-subject theme ICP locations (7.26 and 6.16 s, respectively). This points once again to inter-group differences with respect to pause behaviour. A possible interpretation of these findings is that the L2 writers appear to make use of the subject theme-framing device location to produce longer pauses,

Table 3: ANOVA mean pause durations at subject theme and non-subject themes.

| Location | Source[a] | *F* | *P* |
|---|---|---|---|
| Subject theme | Task | 0.20 | 0.654 |
| | Language | 12.22 | 0.001* |
| | Task/language | 2.17 | 0.149 |
| Non-subject theme ICP | Task | 1.75 | 0.194 |
| | Language | 3.72 | 0.061 |
| | Task/language | 0.82 | 0.372 |

[a]For both task and language there is 1df.
*Denotes significance at $p < 0.001$.

Table 4: Mean pause durations at subject theme and non-subject theme ICP locations by language group.

| | Subject theme | Non-subject theme |
|---|---|---|
| L1 mean | 5.13 | 5.24 |
| SD | 0.44 | 0.34 |
| L2 mean | 7.26 | 6.16 |
| SD | 0.42 | 0.33 |

whereas in the case of the L1 writers, in general, the subject theme location does not attract substantial pausing. Indeed, in the case of the L1 subjects mean durations of subject theme pauses are slightly lower than those of other (non-subject theme) ICP pauses.

Such findings ought to be carefully handled, however, given the degree of individual variation which we have noted in the data. A more tentative observation might be appropriate, that for certain individuals within the L2 group the framing device slot appears to coincide with marked pausing. A finer grained exploration of individual writing episodes, as we propose in the following Section 3.4.

In summary, the conclusions we can arrive at from the analysis of framing device analysis are as follows:

- Hypothesis 4, that there will be language group differences in use of framing devices, is supported by the results. In particular in the case of the subject theme category, where numbers are most substantial, the L1 writers produce fewer pauses at framing device locations, although this difference does not reach a level of statistical significance. When mean duration of pauses at these locations is considered, a further distinction between the groups becomes apparent, with the L2 writers pausing for considerably longer at these locations ($p = 0.001$). This suggests that, in contrast to the L1 writers, the L2 subjects use the framing device location as an important pausing point in the production of the message.
- On average, one third of all potential subject theme framing devices in the text coincides with a pause location. This reinforces my claim that this may be an important unit in the construction of the message for certain subjects.
- There is a strong tendency for subject theme framing devices to consist of full noun phrases rather than pronouns.

Such potentially interesting findings are, as I have stressed above, tempered by the problems of small sample size. Although the differences which emerge with respect to the L1 and L2 writers across all measures appear to complement well existing research findings on L2 writing processes, I acknowledge the need for caution in interpreting small scale comparative studies, particularly given that writing behaviours tend to show considerable individual variation.

With this concern in mind, we proceed to studying in detail the performances of a small number of subjects through case study analysis, and these are discussed in the following section. Through such a qualitative approach the aim is to complement the findings generated from the quantitative data analysis, and to address the interest in identifying patterns of pausing and productivity within the context of the specific writing episode.

### *3.4 Case Study Findings*

In an attempt to provide a more detailed micro-analysis of the data within the context of the writing episode as a whole, the quantitative group-level analysis is complemented by the close description of the pausing and production data of a small subset of subjects. The type of detailed analysis of pausing and production activity over the history of the writing

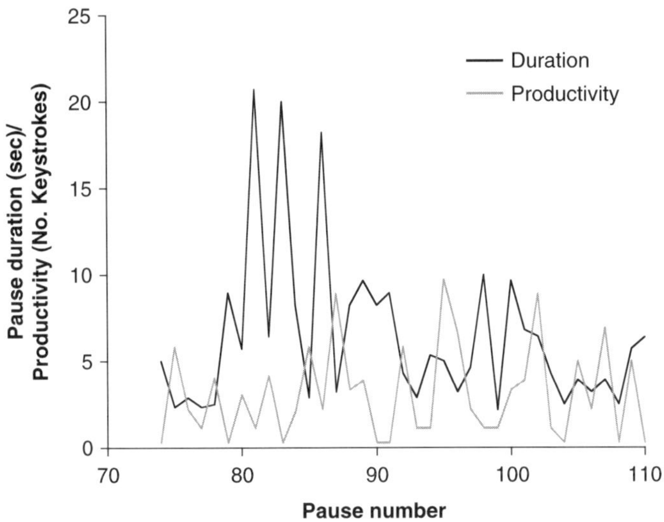


Figure 2: Pause duration and productivity over a stretch of writing for one L2 writer.

episode, as illustrated in the graph of one case study writer, L2: Ya (Figure 2), allows us to consider the following questions:

- Do periods of high pause frequency coincide with high pause duration to suggest disfluent or problematic phases of the writing? Are these associated with periods of low text productivity?
- Do phases of low pause frequency co-occur with low duration pausing to suggest fluent stretches of the writing episode? Are these associated with high text productivity?
- Do increases in productivity follow periods of significant pausing?

Such considerations take us back, of course, to the discussion of early research on planning in spoken language production (Beattie, 1983; Butterworth, 1980; Goldman-Eisler, 1968, 1972; Henderson, Goldman-Eisler, & Skarbek, 1966, and so on), which highlights the presence of alternating phases of hesitant and fluent phases of speech. When frequencies of non-fluencies in spoken data are represented graphically (e.g., as a cumulative plot over some linear measure such as time or number of syllables produced, as in Garman, 1990, p. 125), clusters of non-fluencies are seen to occur at certain points, interspersed with phases of fluent production. These alternating phases of fluent and non-fluent production have been described as representing the speaker's 'encoding cycles'.

The interpretation of the planning activity occurring during these phases is not straightforward, however. As has been discussed earlier, pauses during hesitant phases may generally be associated with forward planning for content, but this is not the complete picture. The more complex reality is that major constituent boundaries act as loci not only for major conceptual macroplanning, but also for local, microplanning activity. During more fluent phases, pauses are likely to reflect local level syntactic planning and lexical selection, with pauses tending to group at clause and constituent boundaries. In brief, then, the different determinants of pausing, as Garrett (1982) outlines (summarised by Garman [1990]), relate to:

(1) *Overload*: distal pauses linked to the encoding cycle, arise from the demands of conceptual planning which momentarily overload the system [...].
(2) *Establishing frames*:[3] [...] Establishing a frame yields pauses that [...] tend to gather at major constituent boundaries (frame-joints), particularly those that are clause-initial.
(3) *Filling the frames*: Filling a frame, word by word, yields pauses that tend to gather at prelexical points (p. 376).

Analysis of the data reveals support for the notion of cycles of pausing and producing during writing. In a way reflective of the cumulative plots of spoken language production, pause duration and frequency data show alternating peaks and dips over the history of the writing episode. Disfluent phases, that is, where pauses are both relatively long and frequent and productivity decreases, occur at paragraph transitions in all the observed episodes, and also in some cases at the end of the writing event when individuals may be rereading and editing. While the pattern of disfluency at paragraph transitions is common to all subjects, there is variation between individuals in the acuity of these contours.

At points other than paragraph transitions, individuals also display noteworthy features of disfluency. The specific interpretation of disfluent stretches may be made through the examination of the text produced and revision operations made on the text. Through detailed paragraph-level analysis of the pausing data, it is possible to arrive at likely explanations for disfluency within paragraph stretches. For example, pausing in Example 2 before and after the 'that' reflect the writer's hesitation concerning the continuation of the sentence (with a relative clause) or its termination:

(2) learners of a second language <>are characterised by various <>IDs <6.8> [that] <2.1>.<14.6> <11.1> These Ids ... (L2:Ya_D: 5–8).

Decision-making concerning the formulation of the text string in the following Example 3 centres on the selection of the starting point for the sentence. The deletion of 'there must be' after the pause of 2.6 s adjusts the thematic and syntactic status of 'different environments and situations', which now becomes the subject (and theme) of the sentence:

(3) [there <>must be] different environments and situations in which <3.4> learners are involved with <2.6> <3.8> might also be varied. (L2:A_D: 25–28)

In Example 4, attention to spelling appears to explain the substantial word internal pausing (15.7 and 2 s):

(4) Langua<>ge<2.8> A<15.7>c<2.0>quisition is affected... (L2:An_E:6-8)

In Examples 5 and 6 we associate the pre-lexical pausing with the selection of specific lexical items, the terms 'variables' and 'Critical Period Hypothesis':

[3]Garrett's use of the term frame is clearly distinct from our notion of framing device. In Garrett's sense, a sequence of frames makes up a plan. Frames generally correspond to clauses and are specified locally in terms of their syntactic properties. 'A frame is a sequence of elements of which some, particularly the major lexical items, are also specified locally' (Garman, 1990, p. 376).

(5) a very wide <>range of <24.6> variables (L2:Ya_D:3-4)

(6) This claim is <> thought to be based on <>, what is called <2.0> "<3.0>the Critical Period Hypothesis <>" (L2: A_D: 60-64).

The intention behind the detailed paragraph level descriptions, as these illustrations show, is to consider the occurrence of pauses within their specific linguistic/discoursal context, and thus to forge a clear link between processes of production and textual output. The paragraph-level analyses are organised around the discussion of pause occurrence and productivity with respect to a number of specific locational categories: paragraph transitions, clause and sentence boundaries, framing device locations, and locations prior to immediate revisions of the text.

The motivation for the selection of these locations is that they all are potentially important in accounting for the development of the unfolding discourse. The goal of this part of the analysis is to consider to what extent the temporal features of production (pausing and productivity) may be interpretable in terms of catagories associated with the development of the discourse. By way of illustration of the type of paragraph-level representation we work with, Figure 3 shows the duration of pauses coinciding with framing devices for one paragraph (L2: Ya).

Of these categories, the importance has already been noted of paragraph and clause/sentence boundary locations, which attract significant pausing, as transition points within the discourse. Where my study departs from other studies of pausing in writing, however, is in considering these locations (and others, namely the framing device and pre-revision locations) from the perspective of their potential contribution to the development of the discourse. In other words, the notion of pause location is extended beyond the solely grammatical characterisation on which pausological work has traditionally been based to

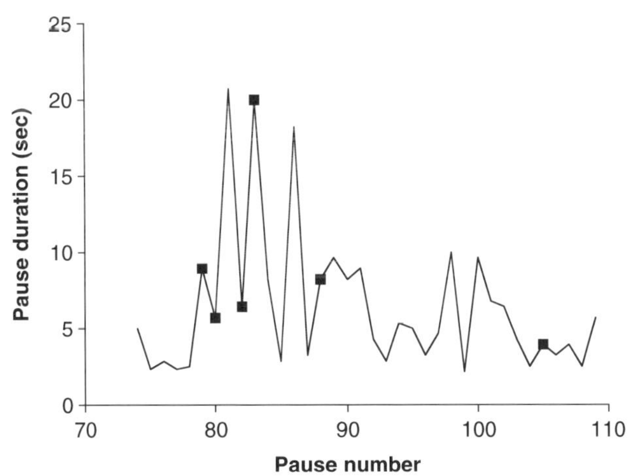


Figure 3: Pause duration (in seconds) with framing device locations marked by black squares. The stretch of writing is one paragraph written by an L2 writer.

incorporate a consideration of the discourse function of such units. This is an innovative and therefore exploratory move in the analysis of pause location in writing, although others (Sanders et al., 1996; Schilperoord & Sanders, 1999) have approached the correspondence between pausing and discourse topic from a different perspective.[4]

The approach to topic taken in our study has more in common with Goutsos's (1997) notion of topic signals in his modelling of sequential topic structure in English expository texts. Although Goutsos is concerned with the final product of writing rather than the data of on-line production, his notion of topic signals (i.e., metadiscourse items, discourse markers, certain types of nominals, empty theme structures, and so on) suggests an important connection between the occurrence of items in the text string and the writer's techniques for presenting and managing topic within the discourse. This provides a backdrop to the notion of framing device, which has been proposed above, as a unit which may serve to frame or establish topic within the discourse.

Finally, included in our paragraph-level analysis is the identification of pauses immediately preceding revision operations. Since revisions may have an impact on the development of the discourse, I am interested in exploring pausing and productivity associated with such operations. The consideration of revision here is restricted to the identification of activity immediately adjacent to pausing.

As has already been suggested, the data point to consistent patterns of increased pausing and decreased productivity associated with paragraph transitions. In addition, there is a general tendency for dips in productivity to occur at or close to sentence boundaries. Observations concerning the association between pause duration and clause/sentence and framing device locations suggest an intriguing and complex picture. The detailed analysis of the three individuals (two L2 writers and one L1) reveals different tendencies across the subjects. For both L2 writers, but not for the L1 writer, the framing device location appears to be a natural location for pausing, although the nature of the pause behaviour differs. In the case of one L2 writer, subject themes are particularly susceptible to pausing although pauses at these locations tend not to be lengthy. For the other L2 writer, pausing is less frequent at these framing device locations but when it does occur, especially at subject theme locations, pauses tend to be very long. For this writer, particularly lengthy pausing occurs at sentence boundaries, where rereading and planning activity appear to coincide. Finally, in the case of the L1 writer, extensive pausing occurs almost exclusively at these clause and sentence locations and not at framing device locations.

How might we interpret such observations? One possible explanation draws on the notion of differential attention to higher and lower level planning concerns. In other words, the occurrence of marked pausing activity at framing device locations in the case of the L2 writers may reflect a greater concern with micro-level planning to do with the selection and formulation of elements of the text string. The evidence of pausing at framing device locations suggests that, at least for some writers, there is a tendency for more local level decision-making once the starting point for the text string has been established. Such an interpretation is necessarily tentative, however, given the selective data on which it is

[4]Their approach focuses on continuity and discontinuity of discourse topic considered in terms of hierarchically arranged relations within the discourse.

based, but it would fit well with other observations concerning differences between L1 and L2 writers with respect to attention to lower level concerns (see Broekkamp & Van den Bergh, 1996, Pålson, 1998, Phinney & Khouri, 1993; Warren, 1997, for example), with findings from the quantitative part of my current study and with broader perspectives on the distinct nature of L2 and L1 writing (see Silva, 1993).

On the basis of these observations, then, the notion of framing device appears to offer a window on strategy differences between writers which is worthy of further investigation. While satisfying the aim set for this study to develop a framework incorporating a discourse-oriented categorisation of pause location, it is clear that more definitive claims about the significance of the framing device unit depend on further exploration through larger scale study of their distribution in pausological data. For example, as has already been suggested, different patterns of pause duration and frequency may be associated with the different types of framing device, but more data are necessary before any clear picture emerges. One issue for consideration, for example, may be the degree to which the framing device is integral to the structure of the clause. Is it that pauses are longer at the site of an empty theme (*it is...that*) structure than at a subject theme, for example? Or might there be differences in pause duration and frequency depending on the function of the framing device, for example in signalling authorial stance, or not?

Other observations from the paragraph-level analyses offer tentative support for the prediction that revision behaviour will be anticipated by lengthy pausing. Again, however, such a claim is tempered by the acknowledgement that only immediate revisions are represented here. It is clear that revisions may be planned at places other than at the immediately preceding pause, and that a more complete analysis would have to incorporate the notion of distance between pausing and revising. Although in the current analysis I have only been able to work with a partial picture of revision behaviour, the promise of more sophisticated keystroke logging and revision analysis tools, however, brings with it the opportunity for more detailed analysis through the integration of pausological and revision data.

Productivity, that is, the number of words produced between pauses, has been discussed with respect to pauses at both pre-revision and framing device locations [2d]. I have noted some evidence of increased productivity following framing device pauses, offering support for the notion of the framing device as a springboard for the production of the text string. Such is not the case, however, in the case of stretches of text following pausing for revision. The more detailed analysis of revision, in particular, involving the identification of levels or units of revision, would be a further step towards clarifying the relationship between planning and producing.

The case study analyses have attempted to demonstrate the application of certain locational categories to data as a means of exploring and explaining text production processes. The locations used in our analysis are selective, derived from considerations of writer strategy in presenting and managing topic. Although these selected categories appear to capture a large proportion of significant pauses in our data, it may be argued that alternative approaches to the data could have been taken. One such possibility might be to give more prominence to the role of lexis in accounting for pausing. Indeed, such a perspective might offer the future analyst alternative angles on the interpretation of the data. Within the bounds of the perspective chosen for this current research, however, I have investigated general patterns of pausing and production across writing episodes and, through the detailed analysis of sections of the writing, demonstrated how planning interacts with other component processes of writing, namely text generation and interpretation (or revision). In this way this research contributes to our understanding of the link between textual output and planning activity.

## 4 Discussion and Conclusions

In this final section I reflect briefly on the goals of this research and consider future directions for research in this vein. I have argued that in focusing on the temporal features of text production, my work fits within the well-established cognitive psychological research paradigm. In general terms, I approach 'writing from a psycholinguistic viewpoint as language behaviour unfolding in time' (Kowal & O'Connell, 1987, p. 110), exploring the component processes of text production, and planning in particular, through the investigation of the 'overt, measurable indications of processing activity' (Chafe, 1980, p. 170). In doing so, I am both following and extending the traditional psycholinguistic interest in idea generation and responding to specific calls for research with respect to writing itself. This presents an opportunity to relate concerns addressed in cognitive process writing research to the broader psycholinguistic domain, which for many years has been seen to focus more on spoken than on written language production.

While I acknowledge, with Candlin and Hyland (1999) and others, the need for an integrated approach to writing research, since

> Writing as text is thus not usefully separated from writing as process and interpretation, and neither can easily be divorced from the specific local circumstances in which writing takes place nor from the broader institutional and socio-historical contexts which inform those particular occasions of writing (p. 2).

I define the scope of this study as principally concerned with the interaction between cognitive and textual dimensions. Hayes (1996) lends support to such a position by arguing that cognitive analyses continue to have an important place in writing research: 'Our research problems are difficult. We need all available tools, both social and cognitive' (p. 13). Furthermore, it is of course possible to propose ways in which this research may lead on to and connect with interests from a more socio-contextual research perspective.

In the tradition of psycholinguistic research into (spoken) text production, temporal features are viewed as 'naturally displayed sources of evidence' of language processing (Garrett, 1982, p. 23), although the nature of this evidence is clearly indirect. In the case of writing, this point needs to be underlined for two important reasons. First, pausing is an indirect indication of planning in the sense that when a writer is pausing s/he may not be planning at all, but rereading, or thinking off-task. In other words, planning activity needs to be inferred from pausological data and cannot be simply equated with occurrences of off-time writing. Second, even when planning is associated with pausing, the nature of the planning activity is not directly visible from the data themselves.

The first issue, that is, which cognitive process underlies the overt behaviour, opens up the question of how to define the construct of planning. For example, how distinct is planning from the other major components, text generating and reviewing, proposed in models of cognitive writing processes? Where are the boundaries between rereading and idea generation? From existing discussions in the literature, the specifications of the processes of writing, and in particular those 'critical juncture[s]' (Witte & Cherry, 1986, p. 127) between planning, text generating and revising are far from fully elaborated. As Caccamise (1987) summarises,

> Perhaps, then, the most interesting and important phase identified by Flower and Hayes, but the least understood psychologically, is the planning process [...] (p. 225)

Hayes and Nash (1996) and Hayes (1996), however, offer useful recent contributions to the definition of planning. First, Hayes and Nash extend the notion of planning beyond abstract, conceptual (preverbal) concerns to include decision-making concerning the specific language to appear in the text itself. Such planning, in earlier models, would have been part of the formulating or text generation component. Second, in Hayes (1996) the concept of planning itself is revised in such a way that it becomes subsumed in a more general component of reflective processes, which includes problem solving, decision making and inferencing. This moves us towards a more integrated representation of the components of text production than that of Flower and Hayes (1980), among others, and forms the basis for the investigation of the pausological data elicited in our study.

The second issue concerning the indirect nature of pausological data as evidence of planning has been summed up by Hayes and Nash (1996, p. 46) in the following terms: 'even when pauses do correspond to planning, the pause provides few clues about what is being planned and what kind of planning is involved'. Interpretation of the planning pause can of course be made on the basis of the text generation and revision activities surrounding the pause, that is, with reference to 'proximate overt behavior' (Kowal & O'Connell, 1987, p. 113). Such an approach demands the close consideration of the interrelations between planning and production processes and places an emphasis on an aspect which is typically underspecified in existing models of writing: the nature of the textual output of the writing process. The selection of a methodology, which elicits pausing, formulating and revising data in real-time, and the design of both general quantitative and case study analyses, allows us to address this concern directly in this research.

The issue of interpreting pauses as indirect evidence of planning is raised by Warren (1997), who in presenting her keystroke pause study, characterises the process as 'informed speculation [...] from the context that the pause arose in' (p. 160). Some categorisation of pause type appears relatively uncontroversial (e.g., associated with production or correction of idiosyncratic spelling or typographical error, or pauses for lexical selection), although this remains an inferential process of analysis. In some cases what appears to be a pause at a T-unit boundary for organisational planning may in fact be associated with a number of complex decisions concerning, simultaneously, multiple levels of the message. This perennial issue, which was described earlier with reference to spoken language production, remains one of the characteristics of pause analysis. Such a potential limitation may be seen as being offset, however, by a number of advantages offered by this approach, and it is to these that we now turn.

The choice of methodology through which to explore planning in writing is the subject more generally of this collection of papers. As I have argued here, pause analysis using observation-generated data offers an alternative approach to the popular think-aloud tool for exploring the writing process, and the options presented through computer-based observation in particular keystroke logging, allow the elicitation of a vast quantity of data automatically, and therefore discreetly, without interfering with the activity of the writer. The keystroke logging tool, JEdit, selected for this study is robust and easy to use. What is more, the electronically stored data generated may be used for further analysis to extend the focus of investigation.

In sum, as a data elicitation tool, keystroke logging offers a powerful means of capturing the dynamics of text production in a way unavailable to studies of speech production. The analyst is provided with a detailed pretranscriptional record of the production process in real-time, which allows us to further our understanding of the integrated nature of the processes of formulation, planning and revising. Textual output, displayed in relation to the cognitive processes from which it is generated, is readily available for close analytical scrutiny.

Pause analysis requires a framework for the description of pause occurrence. In two important ways the current study departs from approaches used in other pausological studies of writing. First, I propose an analytical approach which is specially devised to account for dynamic, online data rather than static, fixed textual product. The notion of potential completion points allows us to account for location at the point of inscription, regardless of subsequent changes made to the grammatical characterisation of the location as a consequence of subsequent working on the text (e.g., through revision operations).

Second, a framework is created which includes not only units defined by traditional grammatical characterisations (character, word, intermediate constituent, clause and sentence), but also by functions related to the development of the discourse. Whereas location in the text string has been most commonly discussed with respect to major (T-unit) junctures or in terms of sentence, clause or word level units, we introduce an additional, alternative means of interpreting location in a more discourse-sensitive way. The exploratory unit, the framing device, is proposed as a way of accounting for some of the means by which topic is established and maintained within the discourse.

Several types of framing device offer themselves for inclusion in my analysis: subject theme, adjunct theme, non-experiential theme including disjuncts and conjunctions, empty theme (e.g., '*it is ... that*), and thematised structures (fronted clausal and phrasal structures). As an exploratory approach to the data analysis, this is clearly not a definitive framework. The selected list of devices was arrived at on the basis of consideration of the type of structures associated with the establishment, maintenance and development of topic, and may be seen to correspond to the type of topic signals discussed in Goutsos (1997). Once applied to the data in my study, however, it is clear that not all types of framing device occur frequently; indeed, quantitative analyses were only possible in the case of the subject theme category.

I maintain that the notion of the framing device offers a novel and potentially important means of interpreting the pausological data beyond solely grammatical characterisation. Indeed, investigation of the susceptibility of such framing device locations to pausing suggests that in general approximately one third of all such slots attract pausing in our data. There is a clear tendency for such pauses to coincide with full noun phrase (rather than pronoun) subject themes. What is more, the analysis of framing device pauses appears to offer insights into individual differences in planning behaviour during writing: there was evidence that, for some writers, the subject theme location coincided with noticeably longer pauses than at equivalent non-framing device locations. This may point to different strategies, particularly across L1 and L2 writers, with respect to the distribution of pauses at these locations.

As a concept, the framing device, as presented here, may benefit from refinement and development. One such direction for development might be to consider the occurrence of framing devices from a socio-contextual rather than linguistic point of view, that is, reflecting choices concerning authorial stance and the interaction between writer and reader. Hyland (1999), for example, presents a scheme for analysing features of academic text in terms of the projection of the writer's involvement, credibility, and position *vis-à-vis* the subject matter. Some of his selected features, such as hedges (*it may be that*), emphatics (*it is obvious, definitely, of course*), relational markers (*it is seen that)*, and person markers (*we report*), for example, appear to overlap with and crosscut the types of framing devices we have used in our analysis. Although this would take the data analysis in a very different direction from the present analysis, there appears to be ample scope for extending the interpretation of certain text units arrived at through pause analysis to the discussion of the data as reflecting 'constraints on a writer's representation of self and others' (Hyland, 1999, p. 121), in other words, broadening the discussion to 'the different social practices of disciplinary communities in constructing knowledge' (p. 121). Although beyond the scope of this present study, it would seem interesting to relate aspects of text construction to such socio-contextual concerns, as discussed in the work of Hyland (1999), Myers (1989), Thompson (1996), Thompson and Thetela (1995), and others.

In drawing this chapter to a close, I point to a number of ways in which this study could be extended or modified. In order to improve the design of the research, for example, the selection of subjects might be refined. The heterogeneity of the L2 group in the study may be seen as a potential weakness. More controlled subject selection, and possibly the use of larger cohorts of participants would clearly strengthen the claims I can only tentatively make here about group differences in writing behaviour. Furthermore, the focus of the study on pausological features has necessarily limited attention to only a number of local-level features of writing. Further study could focus more directly on revision behaviour and the role of revisions in shaping the final written product. Keystroke recording clearly offers much scope for the analysis of the association between characteristics of the dynamic process of construction and features of the final text product. Through this exploratory investigation of topic through the notion of framing devices, I have only just opened the debate on the ways in which planning can affect text structure.

Beyond such research potential, the value which keystroke recording appears to have for writing pedagogy should be recognised. Although there is little discussion as yet of applications of keystroke logging to teaching contexts (except perhaps Sullivan et al., 1998; Sullivan & Lindgren, 2002 and in this volume), the versatility of keystroke logging offers much potential as a classroom tool. In a number of ways the use of the interactive replay facility to focus on the planning and revising activity of individual writers offers potential value in diagnosis and consciousness-raising. For example, developing with the writer the notion of the (conceptual) paragraph and of the progression of the whole text beyond the individual sentence and paragraph may help to relieve sentence-level planning pressures, and may help to increase fluency and productivity. Furthermore, considering the role of certain devices, which here we have referred to as framing devices, in establishing and maintaining topic development may be useful for some writers in understanding topic progression throughout the paragraph and text. Awareness of the occurrence in their writing of subject themes, conjuncts, and framing constructions such as *it has been stated that*, for example, may be a useful step in developing awareness of the impact of certain devices on the progression of the whole text. Finally, close consideration of individuals' writing performances may reveal points of difficulty or uncertainty in the formulation of the message, which may then be the focus of specific pedagogic attention. Problematic grammatical and lexical items, such as the selection of reporting verbs or differences between semantically close terms, for example, may be highlighted through such work.

Chapter 9

# Analysing Online Revision

Eva Lindgren and Kirk P. H. Sullivan
*Umeå University, Umeå, Sweden*

*This chapter presents, discusses and illustrates a method for the analysis of revision of form and concepts in online writing. Keystroke logging was coupled with stimulated recall to assist the development of the LS-taxonomy for online writing revision. Revisions are fundamentally divided according to their position in the text and according to their effect on the developing text. Revision occurs either within the previously written text or at the point of inscription. Revisions at the point of inscription are characterised by being only preceded by written text; the revisions occur in the course of transcription. During the writing process, revisions interact actively with pauses and other revisions. The complex nature of discourse in development, the issues of multiple categorisation of revision and the linking of revisions and pauses together as revision episodes, and how these impact upon the use of the LS-taxonomy is overviewed. All LS-taxonomy categories are thoroughly exemplified by examples from a corpus of keystroke-logged data of first language Swedish and English as a foreign language (EFL) compositions.*

**Keywords:** online revision, pre-contextual revision, contextual revision, revision units, revision episodes, revision taxonomy.

## 1 Introduction

In order to enhance the understanding of how a text develops, the writing process can be studied in real time as it unfolds. Keystroke logging affords the collection and analysis of online writing (Leijten & Van Waes, this volume; Severinson Eklundh & Kollberg, 1996b; Strömqvist & Malmsten, 1998). The replaying of keystroke-logged writing sessions makes possible the online analysis of pauses and revisions. Such an analysis enables detailed examination of the routes writers take through the developing discourse in order to create the

**Computer Key Stroke Logging and Writing: Methods and Applications**

**ISBN: 0-08-044934-4**

*Lindgren, E., & Sullivan, K. P. H. (2006). Analysing on-line revision.*
*In G. Rijlaarsdam (Series Ed.) and K. P. H. Sullivan, & E. Lindgren. (Vol. Eds.), Studies in Writing, Vol. 18, Computer Keystroke Logging: Methods and Applications (pp. 157–188). Oxford: Elsevier.*

final text. In this chapter we propose a scheme for revision analysis, the LS-taxonomy, which categorises revisions according to their content and position in the on-going text production. Traditional revision taxonomies analyse revisions in the context of the final text. Using keystroke logging allows revisions undertaken during a writing session to be viewed in the context of their occurrence, and analysed according to their content and position in the developing text. The position in the developing text can be both within previously written text and at the end of the current text. Moreover, both of these revision types can occur in text, which is ultimately deleted and forms no part of the final text. These deleted revisions are, however, an integral part of a text's discoursal development; keystroke logging affords the possibility to analyse the deleted revisions in the context of the text in which they are undertaken.

Some keystroke-logging software packages include revision-analysis tools. The discourse and/or syntactic level of the revisions are analysed automatically by the program; these can be combined with information about the time of occurrence and the location of the revision within the text (Kollberg & Severinson Eklundh, 2001; Strömqvist & Ahlsén, 1999). As outlined by Spelman Miller and Sullivan (this volume), the keystroke-logging program JEdit (Cederlund & Severinson Eklundh, nd.; Severinson Eklundh & Kollberg, 1996a) and its associate analysis program Trace-it (Kollberg, 1998; Severinson Eklundh & Kollberg, 1996b) analyse revisions in terms of insertions and deletions. A substitution of one word for another is, thus, defined by Trace-it as a deletion of one word and an insertion of another word, and counted as two revisions. However, a manual analyst using, for example, Faigley and Witte's taxonomy (1981), would regard this sequence of deletion and insertion as single revision operation, the substitution of one word for another. Kollberg (1998) distinguished between revision defined automatically only in terms of deletion and insertion actions and revisions defined after a researcher has categorised them in terms of insertion, deletion and sequences of deletion and insertion. She called automatically defined revisions as 'elementary' revisions and those defined by the researcher as 'interpreted' revisions.

Automatic revision analysis has been used in the study on L1 and L2 revisions (e.g. Thorson, 2000). However, it is important to bear in mind when interpreting automatically generated revision-analysis data that not only are revisions defined in terms of elementary revisions but also that syntactic categories are difficult to define computationally in developing text. Moreover, and of central importance when developing a revision taxonomy that supports categorisation of revisions based on their content and effect on the developing text, automatic analysis provides no information about the effect a revision has on the developing text. Manual analysis is necessary to define the content of revisions.

In some cases it is impossible to define the content of a revision without complementary data collection. Stevenson, Schoonen, and de Glopper (submitted) used think-aloud protocols to collect complementary data to assist in the categorisation of unclear external revisions in their keystroke-logged data and to gain an insight into internal revisions that do not leave explicit traces in the log data. Stevenson et al. demonstrated that keystroke logging is a powerful tool for the analysis of revision and that complementary data are necessary to categorise unclear revisions.

The importance the LS-taxonomy places on pausal information is greater than that of the taxonomy developed and used by Stevenson et al. Pause information is affected by thinking aloud, for example when writers stop writing to talk (Jansen, Van Waes, & Van den Bergh, 1996). Think-aloud protocols are, thus, an inappropriate complementary data collection method for use with the LS-taxonomy.

A complementary data collection method that leaves the writer undisturbed during writing is stimulated recall (Gass & Mackey, 2002). After a keystroke-logged writing session, the keystroke log is replayed and the writer comments on the events that occurred during writing. The events include pauses and revisions. The method has been used in the interpretation of keystroke-logged revision data in several studies (Lindgren & Sullivan, 2002, 2003; Perrin, 2003; Sleurs, Jacobs, & Van Waes, 2003). As the use of retrospective accounts of events has been criticised and their reliability questioned, they need to be carried out carefully (Levy, Marek, & Lea, 1996). Stimulated recall prompted by keystroke logs fulfils three important criteria that support accurate retrospective recall. First, it follows directly upon the writing session (Greene & Higgins, 1994). Second, it re-creates the original writing session by replaying the text (Levy et al., 1996). Third, it includes carefully chosen prompts (Gass & Mackey, 2002; Greene & Higgins, 1994).

As stimulated recall does not impact upon the temporal aspects of writing and as the criteria for reliable stimulated recall could be met, stimulated recall was used as the complementary data source to be used alongside keystroke logging for the development and testing of a taxonomy for the analysis of online revision.

## 2 The LS-Taxonomy: An OnLine Revision Taxonomy

The online revision taxonomy we present here, the LS-taxonomy, is product- and process-oriented and focuses on both the location of the revisions and their effect on the online text. An earlier version of this taxonomy (see Lindgren, 2004, 2005; Lindgren & Sullivan, 2002, 2003; Sullivan & Lindgren, 2002) was primarily product-oriented and defined revisions according to their effect on the text. In the earlier version of the taxonomy, revisions at the point of inscription were recognised as items that shape, that is balance the text, and were included as a sub-category of 'balance revision'.

In many respects the LS-taxonomy is similar to those of Allal (2000); Chanquoy (2001) and Stevenson et al. (submitted), but the LS-taxonomy takes a different starting point. Revisions are first defined as to their location and then according to their effect on the text. The LS-taxonomy covers externalised revisions (see Figure 1, Lindgren & Sullivan, this volume, Chapter 3) and defines revisions as 'pre-contextual', that is those revisions made before an externalised context is completed or 'contextual', that is those revisions made within a completed externalised context. The distinguishing features of pre-contextual revision are (1) that at the time a pre-contextual revision occurs the only externalised text is before the place of revision, (2) that at the time of the revision there is no externalised text following the place of revision and (3) that at the time of the revision, the revised text represents the writer's last externalised text item. Features (1) and (2) are identical, but for clarity both perceptions are presented. Both pre-contextual and contextual revisions can further be divided into form or conceptual revisions, depending on their effect on the text written thus far and/or the writers' own explanations.

As revisions in online writing are actions that shape an on-going text product and that at any point in the writing process before the completion of final version, neither the writer nor the researcher analysing the keystroke data knows the final outcome of a revision, the LS-taxonomy defines revisions according to the text written thus far. Further, in order not to impose subjective interpretations of the function of revision, the LS-taxonomy defines revisions only according to the effect the revisions have on the written text. Without additional information from the writer, the researcher can only speculate at the intended function of a revision. In the examples we present to illustrate LS-taxonomy categories, writers' reasons for a revision will only be posited when additional information to that in the keystroke data can support the claims. Two independent coders analysed ten randomly selected first and foreign language texts; the inter-coder reliability was 79%.

In the following sections we describe, exemplify and discuss the pre-contextual and contextual revision categories and their sub-categories in detail. All the examples we present come from a corpus of logfile data. The corpus consists of 237 texts written in L1 Swedish and EFL by 27 Swedish writers between 13 and 15 years of age. The corpus consists of 16,026 elementary revisions.

We begin by placing pre-contextual revision in a theoretical framework and, in particular, within the model of writing proposed by Van Gelderen and Oostdam (2004) before proceeding to present and discuss six examples of pre-contextual revision. After the presentation of these examples, how pre-contextual revisions function in the shaping of discourse structure and can form an integral part of revision units is discussed. Then, before exemplifying conceptual revision in detail, an empirical study that investigates the validity of pre-conceptual revisions is presented. Finally, the possibility of multiple categorisation of online revision and the notion of revision episodes are considered.

All the examples in this chapter are present in a simplified notational system for the representation of revision. The examples include the text before the revision and the text after the revision divided by an arrow (→). Pauses are indicated within brackets < >. For example, <4.5> indicates that a pause of 4.5 s occurred at that position in the writing. Pauses are defined as a period of 2 s or more, when the writer is not pressing a key on the keyboard or using the mouse. The same definition has been used in several keystroke-logging-based studies (Hadenius, 1992; Spelman Miller, 2002; Sullivan & Lindgren, 2002; Warren, 1997; Wengelin, 2002). For a critical discussion of pause-time definition, see Wengelin (this volume). Deletions are indicated by '⌫', and preceded by the number of deleted characters. Thus, '6⌫' indicates that the previous six characters were deleted.

## 3 Pre-Contextual Revisions

Online revisions can occur at the end of the current text, that is, at the end of the text produced thus far. In the literature these revisions have been called revisions 'at the point of inscription' (Matsuhashi, 1987). These revisions occur as a result of an on-going text production process that is constantly in a state of development. The writer moves between conceptual and sequential (form) plans, and revisions made at the point of inscription would hint at the writer's focus at a particular point in the writing process:

> ...the writer moves from thought to language in a highly flexible manner defined by the current goals for the text. Yet, when a writer interrupts a

> relatively fluent production process to evaluate the plan for the text, he or she has an option to revise. The content of that revision suggests whether the writer's focus is primarily on the conceptual or sequential nature of the plan. (p. 206)

Before presenting examples of pre-contextual revision, this category is placed in a theoretical framework and, in particular, within the model of writing proposed by Van Gelderen and Oostdam (2004).

At the end of the current text, the writer has several options for how to proceed with the text. The writer could choose to leave the text-generating process for a while to engage in re-reading and revision of already written text. In the logfile this process would be represented as a pause followed by contextual revision. If the writer chooses to continue to produce new text, several challenges occur at the point of inscription. First, the content of the text under construction has to be fit into the overall plan for the text. This process entails retrieval of linguistic and extra-linguistic information from long-term memory. Second, the writer has to find an appropriate way to transport the meaning into a form that can be externalised (Chenoweth & Hayes, 2001; Van Gelderen & Oostdam, 2004). During writing, features such as orthography and syntax have to be manipulated in relation to the concepts to be presented and the chosen style. Third, the proposed text has to be evaluated according to global representations of both the text and the task. At any point during the writing process the global task representation as well as its external representation can be evaluated and, if need be, changed (see Flower & Hayes, 1981).

Revision at the point of inscription, pre-contextual revision, occurs when the writer notices and decides that something that has just been or is in the process of being transcribed needs to be adjusted. Assuming that the functions of pre-contextual revision are the same as for revision in general, pre-contextual revisions can serve as modifiers of concept or form. Conceptual revision of, for example, plans and ideas is cognitively more demanding than revision of form. Re-reading of previously written text often precedes these revisions (see Hayes, 1996; Kellogg, 1996). Revisions of form, such as spelling or grammar, can be undertaken automatically, provided that the writer is fluent in the writing language. When the writer is not fluent in the writing language, these revisions are not automatic and demand working memory capacity. When pre-contextual revisions occur within transcription, they are directly affected by writers' working memory capacity.

Van Gelderen and Oostdam's (2004) posited a model of writing revision that accounts for working memory capacity, revision location (i.e. internal, external, contextual and pre-contextual) and revision content (i.e. form and meaning). The model distinguishes between revision of form and revision of meaning. In the model these are processed differently. Van Gerlderen and Oostdam proposed that the writing process consists of three components processed in working memory: the *planner*, the *translator* and the *reviewer*. The planner has the overall responsibility for conceptual plans and ideas, and handles conceptual revisions of, for example, coherence or extra-linguistic features. The translator is responsible for the linguistic forms designated to the message presented by the planner and carries out revision of form. The reviewer acts as a gatekeeper and checks the relation between meaning and form in text passages that have been proposed by the translator.

In Van Gelderen and Oostdam's (2004) model, the revision process on a local level starts when the reviewer detects a discrepancy in the proposed text. This text can be either internal or external. Depending upon the type of discrepancy, the reviewer assigns the responsibility of diagnosing it either to the planner or to the translator. This component then decides whether to make a new proposal or not. If the discrepancy found is between the intended meaning and the proposed form, the passage is sent back to the translator for diagnosis. If the discrepancy found lies in the meaning represented in the externalised text, the passage is sent back to the planner for diagnosis.

As Van Gerderen and Oostdam's reviewer is able to check both internal and externalised text, it is able to diagnose text that is in development. The reviewer can thus check a sentence or word that is half-written — half internal and half external. If the reviewer diagnoses the passage not suitable, the transcription process can be interrupted for revision. This entails parallel processing of transcription and reviewing. Parallel processing demands capacity from working memory and there is always a risk of cognitive overload if several processes occur simultaneously. In order for parallel processing to occur one of the processes has to be automatised (Olive & Kellogg, 2002). In computer-based online writing, revision can continue during transcription when the writer is familiar with the computer software, the keyboard and the writing language.

According to Van Gelderen and Oostdam's model (2004), conceptual revisions are more complex in terms of cognitive constraints than formal revisions. Conceptual revision entails both the planner and the translator, while the translator alone undertakes revision of form. The division of pre-conceptual revision into conceptual and form revisions can, thus, be justified within the framework of Van Gelderen and Oostdam's (2004) model of revision as revisions that differ in cognitive operation. Moreover, it can be hypothesised that pre-contextual revisions carried out by the translator alone during transcription (form revisions) are likely to be carried out without considerable pausing, and that pre-contextual revisions carried out by the planner that alters the global text representation and entails linguistic control from the translator (conceptual revisions) are likely be preceded and/or followed by pauses.

### *3.1 Examples of Pre-Contextual Revisions*

It is not always an easy task to classify the content of a revision made at the point of inscription, that is a pre-contextual revision. In this section, the complexity of categorising pre-conceptual revision will be exemplified with six examples of pre-contextual revision taken from our young writers' corpus. The examples will be discussed, when appropriate, both in the light of the comments made by the writers during post-writing stimulated recall sessions (Lindgren, 2004; Lindgren & Sullivan, 2003) and in relation to the Van Gelderen and Oostdam's model of revision.

#### 3.1.1 Example 1

(1') I want you to come to sweden therefor Sweden <4.8> 6⌫ → the summer holidays in Sweden <3.0> are really great.

Example (1) illustrates that it is not always an easy task to classify the content of a revision made at the point of inscription. In the example the writer was trying to persuade a pen-friend to visit Sweden and started by writing 'I want you to come to sweden therefor sweden', here the writer stopped and deleted 'Sweden' before continuing and completing the sentence. At the point this revision occurred, that is, when the writer stops after writing the word 'sweden', it is, for the researcher, unclear what the initial intentions of the writer were.

When considering this pre-contextual revision, it is important to know that incorrect use of 'therefore' is a frequent EFL error made by Swedish speakers. The Swedish word 'därför' is incorrectly translated to 'therefore' rather than 'because'. The writer's initial intention may have been to write something similar to the revised version: 'I want you to come to sweden therefor sweden is so nice in the summer holidays'. However, it is equally possible that the writer had a completely different initial intention: 'I want you to come to sweden therefor sweden is such a nice country'. If the first hypothesised version were true, the revision would alter the formulation of the sentence and the revision would be categorised as a form revision. The writer knew what to write, but was not sure about the best form to use to express the intended meaning. In the second hypothesised version, the revision changes the conceptual meaning of the intended message. In this case the writer revised to adjust the content of the text, perhaps in accordance with the overall plan or the intended reader, and the revision would be categorised as a conceptual revision. The categorisation of this pre-contextual revision is thus unclear without complementary data.

### 3.1.2 Example 2

(2) In <2.6> 2⌫ → We are doing alot of fun things around Christmus.

Another example of a pre-contextual revision that is difficult to interpret is illustrated in Example (2). The writer starts a new sentence by writing 'In'. The writer deletes 'In' and finishes the sentence. This example illustrates the difficulty of defining the effect that some revisions have on the text. Again the categorisation of this pre-contextual revision is thus unclear without complementary data as it is impossible to categorise the revision from the context preceding the revision. Without complementary data this revision can only tell us that for some reason something had to be changed in the course of production. The writer was shaping the text in order to meet one or more of the many goals involved in writing.

### 3.1.3 Example 3

(3) That should make almost everyone happy, at least make people <2.5> feel more at h 4⌫ → comfortable in the classrooms... ¶ I think it's something to invest in.

In Example (3) the writer is writing a letter to the municipality in order to convince them to give more money to the school. She starts writing 'at least make people', pauses for 2.5 s, writes 'feel more at h', deletes 'at h' without pausing and finishes the sentence. In the stimulated recall session the writer explained the pre-contextual revision of 'at h' to 'comfortable' as a re-formulation. At first she intended to write 'at home', but decided to use the synonym 'comfortable' instead because she felt it more suitable in the context. The unfamiliar audience and the character of the task implied a more formal writing style than that she had first suggested. The revision was undertaken without pausing, which indicates that she was re-formulating the sentence at the same time as she was typing.

This pre-contextual revision could be explained as a revision of an extra-linguistic character that adjusts the text on a stylistic level towards the intended reader; the revision adjusts the proposed text towards the global text representation. In order to accomplish the revision, the Van Gelderen and Oostdam (2004) *reviewer* detects the discrepancy and assigns the tasks of diagnosis to the Van Gelderen and Oostdam *planner*. The *planner* checks the intended message with the extra-linguistic knowledge and the global task representation stored in long-term memory after which an alternative solution is proposed.

The revision is carried out without any observable pausing, which means that the revision would have to be processed at the same time as the text was being transcribed, or in the short intervals of less than 2 s between keystrokes. This writer's teacher reported this writer to be proficient in writing, typing and English. It is likely, therefore, that she has the well-developed automatic linguistic and typing skills necessary for parallel processing of transcription and revision.

### 3.1.4 Example 4

(4) I have a room by my self and next to my room my brother has his room. ¶ I have <5.4> 6⌫ <2.7> → The co 6⌫ <2.0> → Almost everything in my room is white and orange.

Example (4) illustrates a revision sequence of two revisions. The writer is describing her house and her room. She starts the second sentence in the example with 'I have', pauses for 5.4 s before the phrase is deleted. After the deletion she pauses for 2.7 s before she writes 'The co', which is immediately deleted and followed by another 2-s pause after which the sentence is completed without any pause. The writer explained these revisions in a post-writing stimulated recall session as 'I was going to start with something else'.

The pauses before and after the deletion indicate how the processing of the revision was carried out. After writing 'I have' the writer paused for 5.4 s, during which it is possible that the *reviewer* detected a discrepancy and signalled to the *planner* to propose a new idea. During and/or after this processing, the writer executed the deletion. After this deletion, a pause of 2.7 s occurred. This pause could indicate that the *translator* was considering how to present the new idea in externalised text. This appears in text as 'The co' and is immediately deleted. The speed of deletion reflects a process that is less demanding than the one involved in the previous revision. Assuming that the writer intended to write 'The colour', the revision could not have been due to a conceptual change, but rather reflect the writer's re-formulation of the idea. As such, the *reviewer* could have put the *translator* in charge of the revision, a process that could be rapidly undertaken in parallel with transcription. This would mean that as the writer typed 'The co', she made the decision to delete the phrase and that graphomotoric activity and formulation occurred simultaneously.

### 3.1.5 Example 5

(5) I hope we can do something about the toilets. They really are disgusting..., at least some of them. <7.0> B 1⌫ → And in th<2.9>e up 13⌫ → ¶ We also have this room where students can hang when they don't have class.

Example (5) is another instance where it can be argued that parallel processing is occurring. The female writer is composing a letter to the municipality in order to convince them to give more money to the school. After the first sentence in the example, she paused for 7 s before she wrote and immediately deleted 'B'. Without pausing she continued by writing 'And in the up', which is then deleted without a pause. She continued by inserting a new line and describing a room in the school where students can spend time during breaks. In the stimulated recall session, she explained that the reason for these revisions was that the first attempts 'were not good ideas'. The function of these rapid pre-contextual revisions was, according to the writer, to present new ideas, that is, to create new content. In order to do this, it was necessary for the original plans, or parts of them, to be revised.

The writer had, thus, discovered a problem on a conceptual level in her text. She was not content with the text she had started to transcribe; she felt the ideas were 'not good'. In order to deal with this problem, she had to revise; an operation that entails several processes. First, she had to engage the *reviewer* in order to detect the problem in the text, in this case the ideas that were 'not good'. Second, the *planner* was called upon to revise the plan and propose new content that was more in line with the global task representation. Third, the new content had to be transformed by the *translator* into linguistic form before new text could be proposed and externalised. In this example, the first pause indicates the position at which the writer detected the problem with the ideas, the *planner* started revising the plan and internally proposing new text. The lack of pauses involved in the deletion of 'B' and the phrase 'And in the up' hint at a process, in which the *reviewer* is checking the proposed text, which has been only partly externalised, in accordance with the text written thus far. A discrepancy was found either in terms of linguistic form or in terms of intended meaning and a second revision is executed.

The second revision in the example can be explained in two ways. The partly written word 'up' is likely to be the first two letters of the word 'uppehållsrum', which is the type of room the writer describes in the sentence following the revision. The phrase 'And in the up' implies that the intended reader is familiar with the concept of 'uppehållsrum', while the revised version does not. Instead, it explains the concept to the reader. This revision could be interpreted as demonstrating awareness of audience and style as well as the knowledge of how to adapt these accordingly to the text written thus far. In order to process the revision the writer has to draw on extra linguistic as well as linguistic knowledge. The other explanation would be that the writer realises that she does not know the English for 'uppehållsrum' and therefore describes the room to overcome her EFL lexical retrieval difficulty.

The externalised revisions in this example represent revision carried out by the *reviewer*, with the function of adjusting the plans to the text written thus far, while the revision of the ideas not judged to be good ones was carried out internally by the *planner*, represented as pausing in the writing process. Further the rapid execution of the revisions undertaken in this example shows how revision can be performed during transcription and thus be closely related to both planning and formulation processes (Van Gelderen & Oostdam, 2004).

### 3.1.6 Example 6

(6) So please give us some money for a <18.6> 1⌫ <2.3> → two <8.9> 3⌫ <13.0> → a football for <6.6> every <2.0>c<2.0>lass.

An example of a pre-contextual revision that reflects difficulties in generating content in combination with EFL lexical retrieval difficulties is shown in Example (6). The male writer is composing an argumentative text. The instructions were to persuade the municipality to give more money to the school for break activities. In the stimulated recall session he said that he wanted to write what they needed the money for, but that he found this difficult to define. He started a sentence, paused for more than 18 s, then wrote the indefinite article 'a', deleted the indefinite article and paused again before writing 'two'. This typing was followed by another pause before 'two' was deleted. The writer paused again before he proceeded with the sentence. He explained that at first he intended to write 'a skate-board ramp', but changed his mind because he wanted the school to have something else. He then decided to write 'two football fields', but reported that he could not recall the word 'field' in English. This was why he finally decided to suggest a football for every class.

This example illustrates how EFL content in some cases has to be adapted to the writer's present EFL linguistic ability. It was not until he was about to formulate and transcribe the content that this writer realised that he could not express his ideas in English. In order to solve the problem he decided to revise the content.

This revision sequence presented in Example (6) illustrates the importance of complementary information to that presented in the keystroke log in order to ascertain the function of pre-contextual revisions. Without the stimulated recall data, the revision from 'a' to 'two' to 'a football for every class' could not have been appropriately categorised. However, even without the complementary information from the stimulated recall session, this sequence of pauses and revisions indicates to the researcher that this was a position in the text where the writer was struggling to find a suitable way to proceed with the composition.

Taken together Examples (1–6) demonstrate that from a keystroke log alone it is not possible to know the exact reason(s) behind a pre-contextual revision. However, that writers choose to revise at the point of inscription indicates that, at that point in the writing session, some form of decision process is occurring that relates to how the composition is to proceed.

### *3.2 Shaping the Discourse Structure*

The locations within the writing process where pre-contextual revision occurs can be referred to as junctures (Givón, 1983). Revision at such a juncture can either shape the linguistic conception of the text written, or partly written, thus far or it can shape the discourse in terms of topic.

A pre-contextual revision that serves to maintain, or develop, the topic shares several characteristics with those of 'framing devices' (Spelman Miller, 2002). Framing devices build on notions of topic and discourse-related units of production and are used as tools to categorise the location of pauses in online writing. Spelman Miller defined a framing device as

> an element or structure (single word, phrase or clause) which serves to establish the starting point of the message at the clause/sentence level. This may be in one of a number of ways, either in constituting the topic itself, or in preparing the scene for the introduction of the topic. (pp. 114–115)

During composition, a writer has to handle several writing specific issues simultaneously, one of them is topic. At certain points in the production process the writer stops, pauses, revises or conducts a combination of all these actions, in order to introduce, maintain or develop the topic. In order to ascertain the type of location within the discourse, Spelman Miller has defined five types of framing devices: subject theme, adjunct theme/complement theme, non-experiential theme, empty theme (*it, what* and existential *there*) and thematised structure (e.g. finite/non-finite clauses).

In Example (1), the writer stopped after the subject in the sub-clause 'Sweden', and revised it into 'the summer holidays'. The writer used revision at this point in the writing session as a framing device to assist in the development of the topic. The deletion of 'Sweden' was preceded by a pause, and according to Spelman Miller's taxonomy, this pre-contextual revision occurred at the 'subject theme' location. The occurrence of a pause and a revision at the same location indicates that they have been used together as a revision unit to frame the topic and develop the discourse (Spelman Miller, Lindgren, & Sullivan, 2004).

### *3.3 Revision Units*

Writing and revision analysis schemes generally consider pauses and revisions as single distinct entities and, as such, they are analysed separately (e.g. Spelman Miller, 2002a, 2002b; Thorson, 2000). However, as revision is not only represented in the externalised text a pause that precedes a revision can be a part of that revision. During the pause, the writer can have revised internally before the revision becomes externalised.

While writing, writers revise internally, in the externalised written text or by combination of internal and external revision. Revision of externalised text is represented in the logfile as a deletion or an insertion of text or as a sequence of deletions and insertions. Internal revision, on the contrary, is not clearly visualised in a logfile, but is in many cases represented as a pause. In Example (6) above, the revision sequence can be analysed as either one unit consisting of three pauses and two revisions 'a <18.6> 1⌫ <2.3> → two <8.9> 3⌫' or two units: 'a <18.6> 1⌫' and '<2.3> → two <8.9> 3⌫'.

Example (6) illustrates that revision can be represented in the logfile as sequences of pauses, and deletions or insertions; externalised revision can be preceded and followed by internal revision. In online writing, it is, therefore, useful to view external revisions and their surrounding pauses as single revision units rather than as distinct entities to be analysed separately. Precisely which sequences of pauses and revisions can form revision units and which cannot is a topic that demands further research.

### *3.4 Testing Pre-Contextual Revision Empirically*

As the concept of pre-contextual revision is new, it is important to validate this revision category empirically. We decided to validate the function of pre-contextual revision as adjusting form and concepts, and to investigate whether pre-contextual revision is affected by writing language and text type. To do this we used keystroke logged data along with post-writing tape-recorded stimulated recall session transcripts from a project investigating 13-year-old writers' descriptive and argumentative writing (Lindgren, 2004; Lindgren & Sullivan, 2003). Thirty-six of the texts from this corpus were analysed using the LS-taxonomy.

The selected texts were written by nine 13-year-old writers using the keystroke logging software JEdit (Cederlund & Severinson Eklundh, nd.). They wrote four texts each: one L1 (Swedish) descriptive, one EFL descriptive, one L1 argumentative and one EFL argumentative. Descriptive topics were addressed to a familiar audience, a pen-friend of their own age, and the task was to write a letter and describe something familiar, that is their room, their school or their family. Argumentative topics were addressed to an unfamiliar audience, that is a TV company or the municipality and the task was to write a letter and persuade the reader to publish an article or to give the school more money. The design was balanced for text type and writing language (in this chapter writing language refers to whether the writer is working in their first of other language). The writers were instructed to write around half an A4 page of text and write for about half an hour.

All writing sessions were directly followed by a tape-recorded stimulated recall session. The writers used JEdit to replay their text and were instructed to talk as much as possible about what was happening on the screen. A researcher/teacher (the first author) and a peer were present. The peer was instructed to ask questions if anything appeared unclear and the role of the teacher was to prompt talk when necessary and to confirm, for example, a revision if the students were uncertain about its outcome. Only open prompts, such as 'What are you doing now?' and 'Can you talk about that revision?' were used. If the writers could not recall the item at once, no further questions were asked. In order for recalled items to be considered accurate in the present study, the writer must have recalled them spontaneously or after the researcher/teacher's prompts.

All 2769 elementary revisions, as defined in Trace-it, were analysed manually according to the taxonomy presented in this chapter and the tape recordings were analysed in order to ascertain which revisions were discussed and what explanations the writers gave for their pre-contextual revisions. The manual analysis defined some deletion–insertion, that is two elementary revisions, sequences as one substitution and after the manual analysis 2418 interpreted revisions remained. Typographical revisions and revisions that were a result of the writers playing around with the computer were not included in the analysis. The remaining 811 interpreted revisions were divided according to whether they were discussed in the post-writing sessions or not.

**3.4.1 General analysis and results** Table 1 shows the overall results of the general analysis. The table includes the total number of revisions in each revision category together with the number and percentages of revisions that were discussed and/or explained by the writers. The percentage of discussed revisions is similar for pre-contextual and contextual revisions 41% versus 44%. The writers apparently found it equally easy (or difficult) to recall both revision types.

From this general analysis of the logfiles and stimulated recall data we can conclude that pre-contextual and contextual revisions are similar in terms of writers' ability to recall them in a post-writing stimulate recall session. Hence, it is as valid to use stimulated recall data to analyse pre-contextual revision, as it is to use this data to analyse contextual revision.

Table 1: Total number of revisions and number of revisions discussed.

| Revision type | Number of revisions | Number of discussed revisions | Percent of discussed revisions |
|---|---|---|---|
| All revisions | 811 | 348 | 43 |
| Pre-contextual | 292 | 120 | 41 |
| Contextual | 519 | 228 | 44 |

**3.4.2 Pre-contextual revision of form and concepts** The transcripts of the tape recordings from the stimulated recall sessions were used in order to understand the function of the pre-contextual revisions recorded in the 36 logfiles. Table 2 presents a summary of the writers' explanations for their pre-contextual revisions and is divided into three main categories depending on the functions of the revisions. A total of 120 pre-contextual revisions were discussed and analysed. The function 'form' refers to revisions that the writers explained as a result of formulation when writers chose a correct way to externalise the content. Comments the writers made for this function included: 'It didn't sound right' and 'I didn't know how to write that'. The function 'concept' refers to revisions that were undertaken because writers adjusted the content and revision that were undertaken because writers generated new content that they decided had to precede what had just been written. Common comments that the writers made for these revisions were 'I didn't know what to write, so I tried different things', 'I didn't want to write that there' and 'I came up with the idea of writing something else first'. Some revisions have been labelled 'unclear' as the writers could not explain their function.

The descriptive statistics in Table 2 show that the writers made more conceptual revisions than form revisions at the point of inscription. Forty percent of the revisions were due to formal issues and 48.3% to conceptual issues. Thus, pre-contextual revision seems to represent a position in the composition process, in which content is frequently being either generated or elaborated on in order to suit, for example, the audience or the task. The writers were unable to explain 11.7% of the revisions and were assigned to the category unclear.

The data were further analysed in three separate repeated measures ANOVAs: form revision, conceptual revision and unclear revision. Apart from the different dependent variables, the designs were identical: the within subject variables were text type, with two levels (descriptive and argumentative) and language, with two levels (L1 and EFL). In order to account for text length the number of pre-contextual revisions in each text was divided by the total number of typed characters in the text.

Table 3 presents the average number of pre-contextual revisions and the standard deviation for the four conditions. The results show that pre-contextual revisions were sensitive to language. During writing, form and concepts were revised significantly more in EFL than in L1 (($F_{form}$ (9.18); $p < 0.05$; $\eta_p^2 = 0.53$) and ($F_{concepts}$ (5.56); $p < 0.05$; $\eta_p^2 = 0.40$)). The differences within the category unclear were not significant. There was no significant effect of text type on any dependent variable.

Thus, the results indicate that the foreign language induced writers to revise more at the point of inscription. During transcription, writers adjusted forms as well as concepts more

Table 2: Number and percentages of form, conceptual and unclear pre-contextual revisions in L1 and EFL descriptive and argumentative texts according to writers' explanations.

| | Form | | Conceptual | | Unclear | | All revisions | |
|---|---|---|---|---|---|---|---|---|
| **Text type** | **No.** | **%** | **No.** | **%** | **No.** | **%** | **No.** | **%** |
| Descriptive L1 | 9 | 7.5 | 18 | 15.0 | 4 | 3.3 | 31 | 26 |
| Descriptive EFL | 22 | 18.3 | 17 | 14.2 | 4 | 3.3 | 43 | 36 |
| Argumentative L1 | 6 | 5.0 | 4 | 3.3 | 2 | 1.7 | 12 | 10 |
| Argumentative EFL | 11 | 9.2 | 19 | 15.8 | 4 | 3.3 | 34 | 28 |
| All texts | 48 | 40.0 | 58 | 48.3 | 14 | 11.7 | 120 | 100 |

Table 3: Frequency of pre-contextual revisions per 100 typed characters according to writing language and text type. Mean and standard deviation (in brackets).

| | Form | | Concept | | Unclear | |
|---|---|---|---|---|---|---|
| **Text type** | **Mean** | **SD** | **Mean** | **SD** | **Mean** | **SD** |
| Descriptive L1 ($N=9$) | 0.10 | (0.13) | 0.16 | (0.12) | 0.05 | (0.07) |
| Descriptive EFL ($N=9$) | 0.21 | (0.17) | 0.18 | (0.19) | 0.04 | (0.06) |
| Argumentative L1 ($N=9$) | 0.05 | (0.08) | 0.05 | (0.06) | 0.02 | (0.03) |
| Argumentative EFL ($N=9$) | 0.13 | (0.12) | 0.22 | (0.22) | 0.03 | (0.05) |

in EFL than in L1. These results concur with those of other revision researches that has shown revision in general to be more frequent in foreign language writing as compared with first language writing (Silva, 1993; Thorson, 2000).

This result can be interpreted from a number of perspectives: a language acquisition perspective (e.g. Pienemann, 1998), a fluency perspective (e.g. Chenoweth & Hayes, 2001) and a working memory capacity perspective (e.g. McCutchen, 1996, 2000). However, it is clear that pre-contextual revisions are language dependent and that they function as a means to adjust the form of the written message as well as a means to adjust the message itself.

### *3.5 Concluding Remarks on Pre-Contextual Revision*

Pre-contextual revisions represent revision of form and revision of concepts. They point at important discoursal locations in the writing process where internal text is being externalised, and they are sensitive to writing language and text type.

It is possible that pre-contextual revisions could also be sensitive to writer type. According to Galbraith (1999), the process of generating content is twofold. Either it can "be retrieved from episodic memory or it can be synthesised in the course of translation" (p. 146). The latter form has further been described as a knowledge-constituting process, in which "... ideas are seen as being constructed in the course of text production rather than existing prior to it" (Galbraith & Torrance, 2004, p. 70).

Depending on the type of writer, the revision process can be more or less interactive. Some writers, defined by Galbraith (1999) as high self-monitors, tend to prefer to plan before writing, while others, low self-monitors, prefer to work more interactively with the text and generate content as they write. In terms of online revision, the interactive writers would probably revise extensively pre-contextually, as this is the location in writing at which content and ideas are most easily elaborated upon.

Hayes (2004) suggested that revision could be stimulated by writers' discoveries of new connections or new arguments in their texts. He suggested that revisions triggered by discovery could "mark those occasions when the writer learns something through the act of writing" (p. 20). Pre-contextual revision could thus assist the writer in targeting locations of possible discovery and hence facilitate the analysis of discourse development for the researcher.

## 4 Contextual Revisions

Contextual revisions are defined as revisions undertaken when writers move away from the point of inscription to insert new text or to delete, substitute or rearrange already written text. When a contextual revision is undertaken, writers are operating within an externalised context; a contextual revision is conducted within a previously written and completed sentence. Hence, a contextual revision is both preceded and followed by text. The effect of a contextual revision on the text can be on a form or on a conceptual level depending on the type of the contextual revision.

As a starting point for our categorisation of contextual revisions we used Faigley and Witte's (1981) taxonomy. In order to apply this taxonomy to 'online' revision categorisation we both extended and re-labelled some of Faigley and Witte's categories. The distinction 'surface' versus 'text-base changes' was retained, yet re-labelled as 'form revision' and 'conceptual revision'. This change results in terminological consistency for pre-contextual and contextual contexts, and between our LS-taxonomy and Lindgren and Sullivan's (this volume, Chapter 3) Figure 1 that was developed in conjunction with Stevenson (Stevenson et al., submitted).

The category 'form revision' is more detailed than Faigley and Witte's 'surface changes'; our extension to this category accounts for form revisions when writers are writing in languages other than their first language. The phrase 'different languages' is used in this chapter to refer to difference and similarities between writing and revision in first and second languages, and is not used to suggest that there is a difference in writing and revision between first language writers of different languages due to the language.

A new category — 'balance changes' — has been added to the conceptual revision category in order to give a more detailed account of revisions undertaken that affect the text on a stylistic rather than a formal or text-based level. The detailed structure of the taxonomy we are proposing (see Table 4) facilitates re-structuring of categories into the revision taxonomies developed by Allal (2000), Chanquoy (2001) and Stevenson et al. (submitted).

Table 4: LS-taxonomy of contextual revision.

| **Form revision**<br>***Conventional/optional***<br>***Correct/erroneous/neutral*** | | **Conceptual revision** | |
|---|---|---|---|
| Typography | Punctuation and format | Text-based | Balance |
| Spelling | *Punctuation marks* | Micro-structure | Topic |
| *Revision* | *Capitalisation* | *Addition* | Audience |
| *Substitution* | *Paragraph* | *Deletion* | *Register* |
| *Deletion* | *Other format* | *Substitution* | *Other* |
| *Homophone* | Meaning-preserving | *Permutation* | |
| Grammar | *Addition* | *Distribution* | |
| *Verb* | *Deletion* | *Consolidation* | |
| *Agreement* | *Substitution* | Macro-structure | |
| *Preposition* | *Permutation* | *Addition* | |
| *Conjunction* | *Distribution* | *Deletion* | |
| *Article* | *Consolidation* | *Substitution* | |
| *Pronoun* | *L2 to L1* | *Permutation* | |
| *Genitive* | *L1 to L2* | *Distribution* | |
| *Adjective* | | *Consolidation* | |
| *Adverb* | | | |
| *Other* | | | |

The taxonomy for the contextual online revision that we are proposing (the LS-taxonomy) and that is presented in Table 4 will be exemplified in detail in the remainder of this section. This detailed presentation will assist the research to both apply the taxonomy and re-categorise revisions labelled according to the LS-taxonomy into other taxonomies.

### *4.1 Form Revision*

The category 'form revision' is divided into five categories: typography, spelling, grammar, punctuation and format, and meaning-preserving. The categories spelling, grammar, punctuation and format are further categorised as 'conventional' or 'optional' following Allal's (2004). All conventional revisions are coded for correctness, that is, whether the result of the revision is a correct or an incorrect text item (Allal, 2000). Optional formal revisions have an effect on the text that is different to conventional formal revisions. Conventional formal revisions adjust the text towards language-specific conventions whereas optional revisions are of a stylistic or an argumentative character.

**4.1.1 Typography** Typography includes revisions undertaken as a result of a typing error. The definition of a typing error used here is the same as in Kollberg (1998):

> A typing error occurs when the writer presses the wrong key, even though she knows what she *should* write. (p. 68)

Categorisation of a typing error can be problematic. For example, if a writer types a character and then immediately replaces it with another character, which is a neighbouring key on the keyboard, it is often possible to assume that it was a typing error. However, if there is a spelling, grammatical or lexical aspect attached to the exchanged characters, the categorisation of the revision is more complex. An example is the replacement of an 'i' for its neighbouring key 'o' in an English text changing 'in' to 'on'. This revision can be the result of a slip, that is a typing error, but it can also be the result of the revision of a grammatical character, that is changing prepositions. As most typographical revisions are undertaken immediately and at the point of inscription, if the writer types a letter, pauses and replaces it by a letter on a non-neighbouring key, the revision is most likely to be something other than a typographical error. It could be, for example, a spelling or grammar correction.

Stevenson et al. (submitted) have developed a checklist for ambiguous typographical categorisation. In order to classify a revision as a typing mistake one or more of the following should apply: (a) the pre-revision form does not conform to the orthographic rules of the language, (b) the pre-revision form involves a letter string which does not conform to a likely pronunciation of the word, (c) the semantic context indicates that the pre-revision form could not have been intended, (d) the same word has been written correctly at an earlier point in the text, and (e) a letter is replaced by an adjacent letter on the keyboard. If there is still uncertainty about how to classify the revision Stevenson et al. suggest that if a pause of less than 1 s lies between the preceding keystroke and the revision, it should be classified as a typing revision. Thus, in the example of 'in' and 'on' above, the pause information together with the semantic context of the revision would be necessary for appropriate categorisation.

Stevenson et al.'s (submitted) checklist has limitations. For example, that a word has been written correctly at an earlier point in the text does not necessarily mean that the writer knows the spelling of that word. The writer could have guessed and when the word occurs again the writer experiences the same difficulty, but chooses an incorrect spelling. This scenario undermines Stevenson et al.'s checklist point 'd'. Hence, even when using a checklist, one cannot mechanically apply it.

Similar awareness is demanded when using automatic typing revision filters such as the one developed by Kim (1996) and implemented in the revision-analysis software Trace-it (Kollberg, 1998). Kim's automatic typing revision filter is based on eight rules for typing error detection. In an evaluation undertaken by Kim, the filter detected 88% of the typing revisions, of which a human interpreter judged 96% as typing revisions. It is thus clear that the typographic error problem can be reduced automatically.

**4.1.2 Spelling** Spelling revisions are revisions that affect the orthography of a word in such a way that it cannot be categorised as a typing revision. There are several ways in which spelling revisions impact upon a text. The LS-taxonomy defines four types of spelling revision: revision, substitution, deletion and homophone.

***Revision*** The original word that includes the spelling mistake, is kept but revised, as shown in Example (7). The writer writes 'brash', but revises into the correct orthographic representation 'brush'.

(7) brash → brush

***Substitution*** The original word is substituted with a semantically similar word or phrase after several attempts to correct the spelling of the word. Examples (8, 9) show a spelling revision sequence that ends with the substitution of the original word. In Example (8) the writer intends to write the word 'both', but cannot find the correct spelling. After three attempts the original word is deleted and the entire passage is rephrased (9).

(8) Do you live whit your mother or father or do you live whit bouht → buth → buoth → bouth.
(9) Do you live whit your mother or father or maby your parents is togather.

***Deletion*** The word is deleted after several attempts to correct the spelling of the word. In Examples (10, 11) the writer is discussing the different options for language studies in the Swedish compulsory school system. After two attempts at getting the word 'French' spelt correctly (10) the writer deletes the word (11).

(10) When you start school you can chose a language to. ex. Germany, English, Fransh. → Franch. → Fransh.
(11) When you start school you can chose a language to. ex. Germany, English. Homophone

***Homophone*** Spelling revisions involve homophones as exemplified in Example (12). A female writer tries to persuade a pen-friend to come and visit her during the summer holidays but experiences difficulties in distinguishing between the homophones 'there' and 'their'.

(12) The best thing with summer in Sweden is that you get to see all good looking boys, in just there underwear. →... their underwear.

**4.1.3 Grammar** A grammatical revision is defined as a revision that involves a grammatical item that is defined by conventional language rules for the written variety of the writing language. Grammar revisions are divided into ten sub-categories according to the grammatical aspect under revision: verb, agreement, preposition, conjunction, article, pronoun, genitive, adjective, adverb and other.

***Verb*** Verb revisions include revisions of tense, verb form and auxiliaries. Example (13) shows a revision sequence, in which the writer produced two consecutive conventional tense revisions in order to correct the grammar of the sentence. She first revised 'don't' into 'diden't' and second revised 'cared' into 'care'. Both revisions are categorised as grammar/verb/conventional/correct. Although the spelling of 'didn't' was incorrect in the first revision, the revision is regarded correct as the focus of the revision, and hence its categorisation was grammatical and not spelling.

Example (14) illustrates an optional verb revision. The writer revised from the present tense into the present progressive, which from a grammatical point of view was not necessary. The task was to write a letter to the municipality to convince them to give more money to the school in order to improve break-time activities. The use of the present progressive instead of the present tense gives the letter a more direct tone and helps convey the urgent need for break activities. This example illustrates how a grammar revision can be used as a discourse device to create a certain atmosphere in the text and strengthen the argumentation. The revision is classified as grammar/verb/tense/optional.

(13) On the weekend I was a little sick but I don't cared. → ... diden't cared. → ... diden't care.
(14) Now we only stand in a corner → Now we are only standing in a corner.
Agreement

***Agreement*** Agreement revision includes both subject/verb agreement and agreement between the determiner, the adjective and the noun within the noun phrase. Both types are included in the analysis in order to account for agreement in both English and Swedish, as well as other languages with similar agreement systems. The two types of agreement are different in structure; the subject/verb agreement involves both the noun phrase and the verb phrase as in English, and the determiner/adjective/noun agreement involves agreement within the noun phrase as in Swedish.

Example (15) illustrates a subject/verb agreement revision. The writer revises the verb 'be' at the end of the sentence into the correct past tense form. This revision is categorised as grammar/agreement/conventional/correct.

(15) I've talked to two of them yesterday, their names was Anna and Marlene. → I've talked to two of them yesterday, their names were Anna and Marlene.

***Preposition*** Preposition revisions can be both conventional and optional. A conventional preposition revision is shown in Example (16); the writer has used the direct Swedish translation, a strategy that resulted in an incorrect preposition. This was noticed by the writer who revised the preposition into the correct English version. The revision is categorised as grammar/preposition/conventional/correct. In Example (17) the writer chose to change the correct preposition 'i' into another equally correct preposition 'på'. The result is a correct sentence with a slight shift in meaning. The categorisation is grammar/preposition/optional.

(16) On the winter → In the winter
(17) Det biblioteket finns här i skolan → Det biblioteket finns här på skolan [That library is here in the school → That library is here on the school].

***Conjunction*** The conjunction revision sub-category contains both conventional and optional revisions. This category includes both revision within a sentence, revision of a comma into a conjunction and revision of a conjunction into a comma. A revision of a full stop into a conjunction, and vice versa, involves two sentences and is not categorised by the LS-taxonomy as a conjunction revision, but as a meaning-preserving revision.

In Example (18) the writer ends the first sentence with three dots, followed by a sentence starting with a conjunction. This type of writing gives an impression of spoken language. In Swedish it is not considered appropriate to start a written sentence with a conjunction. This writer is aware of this and deletes the conjunction 'And' that at the start of the sentence and thus adjusts the text towards the written standard. Example (18) is categorised as grammar/conjunction/conventional/correct. Example (19) shows a revision of an optional character. The writer finishes the sentence, moves and replaces the conjunction 'and' with 'or'. This example is categorised as grammar/conjunction/optional.

(18) ... make people feel more comfortable in the classrooms ... And I think it's something to invest in. →... make people feel more comfortable in the classrooms ... I think it's something to invest in.
(19) In the night we may play some games with the neighbours and go swimming in the lake. → In the night we may play some games with the neighbours or go swimming in the lake.

***Article*** Article revision can take the form of conventional revision of the indefinite article or optional revision of the definite and the indefinite articles. Example (20) illustrates a conventional revision of the indefinite article in English. In the description of a future occupation, the EFL writer does not include the obligatory indefinite article in the first version of the sentence. In Swedish, words describing occupations do not need to be preceded by the indefinite article. The writer revises by inserting the correct article. The revision is categorised as grammar/article/conventional/correct. In Example (21) the writer describes her spare-time riding activities by referring to the dressage group in the definite form. The revision into the indefinite article adds a more general character to the statement. The revision is categorised as grammar/article/optional.

(20) I'd like to be designer → I'd like to be a designer
(21) på stor häst i dressyrgrupen → på stor häst i en dressyrgrup [on a horse in the dressage group → on a horse in a dressage group].

***Pronoun*** Pronoun revisions include both conventional and optional revision of the pronoun. In Example (22) an incorrect form of the pronoun is revised into the correct form, which is categorised as a grammar/pronoun/conventional/correct revision. Example (23), on the other hand, illustrates the writer's apparent conscious choice to replace a noun phrase with its corresponding pronoun and thus is categorised as a grammar/pronoun/optional revision.

(22) she's → her
(23) the school → it

***Genitive*** Revision of the genitive is exemplified in Example (24). The EFL writer is describing an event at the local school of music where the public is invited to participate and listen to concerts. In the first version of the sentence the genitive construction is written without the apostrophe following the Swedish writing rules. When revising, the writer adds an apostrophe, however in the wrong place. The revision is categorised as grammar/genitive/conventional/incorrect.

(24) During the music schools day last year → During the music schools' day last year.

***Adjective*** Adjective revision includes revision of comparison. In Example (25) the writer revises the comparative form of 'expensive'. The result is double comparative marking, a feature that is not allowed in English. The revision is, thus, categorised as grammar/adjective/conventional/incorrect.

(25) Vila is a very small city that have some shops but not any big shops so it can get pretty more expensive than →... pretty more expensiver than.

***Adverb*** Adverbial revision includes revision of an adjective into an adverb or vice versa. An example of a revision of an adjective into an adverb is shown in Example (26). This revision is classified as grammar/adverb/conventional/correct. Another type of revision included in the grammar sub-category adverb are word order revisions resulting from adverbial usage. In Example (27), the word order is altered when the adverb 'really' changes position. The revision is considered 'optional' as both versions are correct. The categorisation is grammar/adverbial/optional. This revision sequence also includes a spelling revision: 'relly' is revised into 'really'.

(26) The teachers was very good. High qualified → The teachers was very good. Highly qualified.
(27) so it relly is full house → so it is really full house.

***Other*** The grammar revision sub-category 'other' includes revision of contracted forms, abbreviations, compounds and number. The revision in Example (28) has a stylistic effect when the writer chooses to use the contracted form. It is thus categorised as a grammar/other/optional revision. In Example (29) the revision is, on the other hand, categorised as conventional; the writer adds a space between the words 'each' and 'other', resulting in a grammar/other/conventional/correct revision. In Example (30) the noun 'group' is revised into the plural form. This revision was immediately followed by the addition of three more examples of techno groups. As such, the revision could be defined as a revision of number (singular to plural). The categorisation of this number revision is, thus, grammar/other/optional.

(28) They almost play the same songs, so it is no use to buy all their cd's →... so it's no use to buy all their cd's.
(29) And they all hate eachother → And they all hate each other.
(30) I would be very happy if you could write about my favourite techno group, ATB! →... my favourite techno groups, ATB, Mushroom, Braindead or mistake!

**4.1.4 Punctuation and Format** The revision category punctuation and format includes four sub-categories: punctuation marks, capitalisation, paragraph and other format.

***Punctuation*** The sub-category punctuation includes revisions that involve adjustment towards the conventional language rules for the usage of punctuation marks and the use of capitalisation to indicate the start of a sentence. Note, however, that if a conjunction is involved in the revision LS-taxonomy categorises this revision as a conjunction revision.

***Capitalisation*** The sub-category capitalisation covers capitalisation in non-sentence initial position. A difference between Swedish and English is the capitalisation of nationality words, school subjects, days and months; these are capitalised in English, but not in Swedish. As shown in Example (31) this can be a cause of a revision. The male Swedish writer is composing the final sentence in his text describing a typical school day. Earlier in his text he has written school subjects correctly with capital letters. However, in his final sentence that is shown in Example (31), the capital is incorrectly revised to the lower-case letter. This could indicate difficulty in keeping language-specific rules apart. The revision is coded as punctuation and format/capitalisation.

(31) But it is dark sides to, you gonna have Math. → ... gonna have math.

***Paragraph*** Revision of paragraph entails dividing or merging paragraphs. The paragraph is an important entity in written discourse, which divides text according to argumentative or content-based subsets. A paragraph revision changes the structure of the text and can affect both content and argumentation.

***Other format*** Revision of other format includes revisions that affect the text on an aesthetic level, such as tabbing, font, margins and text justification.

**4.1.5 Meaning-preserving** For the LS-taxonomy we have adopted Faigley and Witte's (1981) definition of meaning-preserving: Faigley and Witte defined meaning-preserving changes as ". . . changes that 'paraphrase' the concepts in the text but do not alter them" (p. 403). These changes can include one or more words, and are divided into six Faigley and Witte's sub-categories: addition, deletion, substitution, permutation, distribution and consolidation, and two sub-categories that account for revisions particular to second and foreign language writing: 'translation L2 to L1' and 'translation L1 to L2'.

***Addition*** An addition meaning-preserving revision is exemplified in Example (32). In the first version of the sentence the writer only included her first name 'Anna'. The reader is likely to know that Anna has a surname and that that it is not necessary to state that fact explicitly. Anna then adds her surname. The addition of her surname does not alter the meaning of the sentence; 'Anna' and 'Anna Svensson' refer to the same person.

(32) My name is Anna and I'm thirteen. → My name is Anna Svensson and I'm thirteen.

***Deletion*** A meaning-preserving deletion is illustrated in Example (33). The deletion of 'the last time' does not affect the content; it removes repetition, both on a word and a content level. The word 'time' was used at an earlier position in the sentence and by removing it, repetition is avoided. Further, the statement 'since you were here' carries the meaning of 'the last time' and by deleting the noun phrase, 'the last time', unnecessary repetition of content is avoided.

(33) It has been such a long time since you were here the last time. → It has been such a long time since you were here.

***Substitution*** Example (34) illustrates a meaning-preserving substitution. The writer replaces the word 'gifts' with 'presents'. This is a revision that does not alter the meaning of the text as the words represent similar concepts.

(34) After we have given eachother gifts → After we have given eachother presents.

***Permutation*** A meaning-preserving permutation is shown in Example (35). Two text segments 'fick jag' (got I) and 'förra året' (last year) are rearranged within the sentence. Both versions carry the same meaning and are correct according to Swedish word order rules. The second version is, however, the most commonly used formulation.

(35) I födelsedagsprest av mamma och pappa *fick jag förra året* ... [As birthday present from mum and dad *got I last year* ...]. → I födelsedagsprest *förra året fick jag* av mamma och pappa ... [As birthday present *last year I got* from mum and dad ...].

***Distribution*** In Example (36) a meaning-preserving distribution is illustrated. The revision distributes one sentence of three clauses into two sentences. By deleting the conjunction 'but' the passage is divided into two sentences; the first with two clauses and the second with one clause. This revision facilitates ease of reading by reducing the number of clauses involved in each sentence.

(36) So much different that you can't even imagine but if you travelled there I know for sure that you would love it! → So much different that you can't even imagine. If you travelled there we know for sure that you would love it!

***Consolidation*** Example (37) illustrates a meaning-preserving consolidation revision in which two sentences are combined into one. Although the revision does not affect the meaning of the text, it affects the reading of the passage by reducing the unnecessary repetition of 'north'.

(37) Hey my name is Anders and am 13 years old and I live in the north of Sweden. I live in north part of Sweden in a town called Vila. → Hey my name is Anders and am 13 years old and I live in the north of Sweden in a town called Vila.

***Translation L1 to L2*** Examples (38, 39) illustrate revision of Translation L2 to L1. The revision sequence is undertaken over a period of two writing occasions. During the first writing session, the writer correctly wrote the word 'cellar', but revised it by Translation L2 to L1 (38). A post-writing discussion revealed that the writer was not sure about the word and as he knew that he was going to work again with the text the following day, he decided to write the Swedish word and look up the English translation at home. The word 'våning' (floor) was written in Swedish for the same reason. During the second writing occasion, he translated both words into English (39).

(38) The biggest building is the building with all the classrooms it have a second våning and a cellar. → ... it have a second våning and a källare.
(39) The biggest building is the building with all the classrooms, it have a first floor and a basement.

***Translation L2 to L1*** Revision of Translation L2 to L1 operates in the opposite direction to revision of Translation L1 to L2. This revision type did not occur in our corpus, however, it would be a revision in which the writer translates an L1 aspect into an L2 without resulting in a change of meaning.

### *4.2 Conceptual Revisions*

The LS-taxonomy contextual revision category conceptual revision is divided into text-based and balance revisions. Faigley and Witte (1981) defined 'text-base changes' as changes that affect the content of the text. This is the definition applied here. The text-based revision corresponds to similar revision types in other taxonomies, such as 'semantic revision' (Allal, 2000; Chanquoy, 1997) and 'content revisions' (Stevenson et al., submitted). Balance revisions are those revision that adjust the topic or the text in order to make it more (or less) appropriate for the intended reader.

**4.2.1 Text-based revisions** A change of meaning that is implemented into the text by a text-based revision can affect the text on different levels. The revision can impact upon the text on a local or on a global level. Even when a revision is of minor overall importance for the understanding of the text, it can still impact on the content locally. Faigley and Witte (1981) defined two text-based revision types 'micro-structure' and 'macro-structure'. Micro-structure revisions affect the text locally and macro-structure revisions affect the global summary of the text. This distinction needs refining for online revision analysis. Faigley and Witte analysed pen-and-paper-written drafts, in which the revisions were analysed in the context of the draft versions. When analysing online writing, revisions are analysed in the context of the text written thus far; a revision made to the half-written text could be analysed differently if it were to be analysed in the context of the finished text. However, at the point of the revision, it is impossible to infer the writer's global intentions for the entire text. Therefore, we have used the following definitions for the two levels of text-based revision in the LS-taxonomy for online writing revision: Micro-structure revisions locally affect the text written thus far, and macro-structure revisions affect the global summary of the text written thus far.

Similar to the division of meaning-preserving revisions, text-based micro- and macro-structure revisions are further divided into addition, deletion, substitution, permutation, distribution and consolidation depending on the type of operation involved. In other revision taxonomies, these revisions have been grouped together — permutation revisions into a single category 'rearrangements' (Allal, 2000) or combination (Stevenson et al., submitted).

In our corpus of compositions by young writers, that we are using to exemplify the revision categories, no examples of distribution or consolidation revisions on a text-based level were found. This is not unexpected; Faigley and Witte (1981) found distribution and consolidation revisions to be more frequent in experienced writers' compositions. An example of a distribution revision is the distribution of the material in one paragraph into two paragraphs that places the moved information into focus. The effect of the revision on the content in the text produced so far can be local or global.

The other text-based revisions categories are exemplified in our corpus. Micro-structure addition, macro-structure deletion, macro-structure substitution and micro-structure permutation will now be illustrated. In the Examples (40–43) the revisions are italicised for clarity.

***Micro-structure addition*** Example (40) illustrates a micro-structure addition. In the first version the writer lists activities they engage in while at their friend's house. In the revised version another activity, eating, is added to the list. The revision does not affect the summary of the text, as the information given in the first version of the sentence is sufficient to include in a summary of the text written thus far. However, at the local level the reader is informed in greater detail about the activities.

(40) And after that we use to go home to someone, to talk, tell jokes, and we always stay up very late. → And after that we use to go home to someone, to talk, tell jokes *and eat*, and we always stay up very late.

***Macro-structure deletion*** A macro-structure deletion revision is illustrated in Example (41). The writer deletes two sentences at the end of the first version of her letter. The deletion includes information about what she would like to become. This information is not included elsewhere in the text. Paragraph symbols (¶) have been inserted to indicate the paragraph structure in the original text layout.

(41) Have you been to sweden sometime? I guess not, but maybe you have been to Europe. Last year I was on New Zealand, near Australia. It is a beautiful country! I guess Australia is least as beautiful as New Zealand. ¶ *What do you want to work with when you grown up? I'd like to be a designer I think.* ¶ Bye, Bye C Ya!! →

Have you been to sweden sometime? I guess not, but maybe you have been to Europe. Last year I was on New Zealand, near Australia. It is a beautiful country! I guess Australia is least as beautiful as New Zealand. ¶ Bye, Bye C Ya!!

***Macro-structure substitution*** A substitution that affects the macro-structure of the text is exemplified in Example (42). A female writer has written a letter about herself to a penfriend. The example is taken from the end of her letter. Two sentences that contain information about her interests are substituted by one sentence with another content. If a summary were to be made of the text prior to the revision, the deleted information would have been included.

(42) ... And my class is so wonderful. Everyone is so nice. ¶ *I write sometimes, I can write a story on the computer or a song. It's fun.* ¶ Cya./ Linda → ... And my class is so wonderful. Everyone is so nice. ¶ *Hope you know what you want about me.* ¶ Cya./ Linda.

***Micro-structure permutation*** A micro-structure permutation is shown in Example (43). The revision entails both re-structuring and substitution of information. The 'too' at the end of the sentence is replaced by 'even' and moved to a position between the verb and the object. These two words have similar, but slightly different meanings; 'even' has an evaluative meaning, while 'too' does not. The revision thus affects the content of the text on a local level.

(43) I think the teachers would like it too. → I think *even* the teachers would like it.

**4.2.2 Balance revisions** During writing, writers have to consider their writing from several perspectives. The text has to be as linguistically correct as possible, the content has to be coherent and the text has to be adequately presented according to the intended reader. In order to handle such a complex task, writers use both their linguistic and their extra-linguistic knowledge (Van Gelderen & Oostdam, 2004).

In our LS-taxonomy for revision, we have designated revisions of extra-linguistic discourse features to the category 'balance revisions'. As described by Nystrand (1986) throughout writing, the writer has to balance the text both towards the topic itself and towards the intended audience:

> The shape and direction of discourse are configured by the communicative need of writers to balance their own purposes and intentions with the expectations and needs of readers. (p. 36)

Revision of balance features such as style, audience, politeness and genre does not necessarily affect the form or the content of the text, but rather shapes the character of the text on a discourse level. The balance revision category is divided up into Topic and Audience.

***Topic*** Topic revisions are those that modify the view of the topic presented in the text. Example (44) shows a revision that modifies the writer's view of school. The first sentence gives the reader the impression that the writer is positive towards school, but by removing the exclamation marks and adding three dots together with 'oh no!', the initial positive view is reversed. The revised passage presents a negative attitude towards school. Another example of a topic orientation revision is found in Example (45). The positive attitude towards the topic, the class, is strengthened by the addition of the adverb 'so'. A third example of this category is the removal of capitals for emphasis in Example (46).

(44) ... then I remember: SCHOOL!!! → ... then I remember SCHOOL ... oh no!
(45) And my class is wonderful → And my class is so wonderful.
(46) I Sverige har det varit ISKALLT hela vintern. → I Sverige har det varit iskallt hela vintern. [In Sweden it has been ICE COLD all winter. → In Sweden it has been ice cold all winter.]

***Audience*** The category audience orientation consists of revisions that balance the text towards the reader by giving the text a more or a less formal character. An example of this is given in Example (47). The opening phrase 'Hi' in a letter to a fictive person is revised into 'Dear'. This revision was undertaken at a late point in the writing process when most of the letter had been written. The style had changed during writing and the revision adjusted the style of the opening phrase to the context and style of the entire letter.

(47) Hi Marie → Dear Marie

Example (48) illustrates a revision sequence that involves audience orientation. The first version of the passage has the character of an informal chat or email, with exclamations and smilies. In the revised version, these are removed together with the word 'well' at the beginning of the second sentence. The revisions adjust the text towards a more formal writing style. According to the post-writing discussions with the writer, this passage was revised because she thought the formal style would be more suitable for the task.

(48) Do you have a big or a small house?! HaHa ... Maybe a stupid question ...)) ¶ Well we have a quite big house. → How do you live?? ¶ We have a quite big house.

**4.2.3 Concluding Remarks on Contextual Revisions** Contextual revision includes revision of both form and concepts that occur within a previously written context. Writers move around in their texts as they delete old or insert new text. This revision type is often preceded by a pause, which can reflect re-reading processes. Re-reading of text does not necessarily result in revisions, but when it does, the revision can both correct and create mistakes.

Revisions of form include revisions that do not affect the meaning of the text. Conceptual revision develops the content of the text in various ways by revision of, for example, content or style. Since these revisions occur within a context, they are easier to analyse than pre-contextual revision of concepts. Both preceding and following text can be used in the interpretation of contextual revision.

Conceptual revision occurs throughout writing. The recursive character of the writing process makes writers stop every now and then to evaluate what has been written thus far and make necessary adjustments (Chenoweth & Hayes, 2001; Flower & Hayes, 1981; Van Gelderen & Oostdam, 2004). As with pre-contextual revision, contextual revision varies both between and within writers for the reasons discussed in Lindgren and Sullivan (this volume, Chapter 3).

## 5 Other Aspects of Online Revision Analysis

Some of the complexities of online revision analysis and the categorisation of revision according to the LS-taxonomy have been illustrated in our presentation of pre-contextual and contextual revision categories. However, there are two other aspects of online revision analysis that warrant specific discussion owing to influence on the application of the LS-taxonomy. These aspects are the possibility of multiple categorisation of revision, that is one revision can be categorised as to belonging to two, or more, LS-taxonomy categories, and that revisions can occur in episodes.

### 5.1 Multiple Categorisation of Revision

Some revisions are ambiguous and can belong to more than one revision category. This aspect of revision categorisation reflects the complex nature of writing revision and that one revision can be undertaken to resolve more than one form or conceptual issue. Examples (14) and (49) illustrate this.

The revision in Example (49) occurred within the writers' last produced sentence. The male writer is composing in his L1, Swedish, and the task was to go back 200 years in time to convince someone to travel 200 years into the future with him in a time machine.

(49) Jag ska förklara hur en TV → Jag ska förklara vad en TV är senare [I will explain how a TV → I will explain what a TV is later.]

The initial version gives the writer a range of options for continuing the sentence, for example he could explain how a TV works or what a TV looks like. After a short pause, the writer choose none of these, but decided to explain what a TV is. This revision could be interpreted as (1) a macro-level change affecting the content, (2) an audience-orientation revision as the writer realised that it was not appropriate to describe how a TV works or what it looks like if the reader does not know what a TV is and (3) a topic orientation revision. The writer could have realised at the point of this revision that there were no TVs 200 years ago and revised to adjustment the content towards the topic. All three possibilities, however, are sub-categories of 'conceptual revision'.

Form revisions that are categorised as optional, that is, not necessary in order to create a linguistically correct text, often have to be assigned multiple categories. In Example (14) the writer revised the present tense '...we only stand...' into the present progressive '...we are only standing...'. This grammatical verb revision was not necessary in order to correct the grammar of the sentence, but it created a different atmosphere in the text. Thus, form revision can be used as a means to balance the text towards the topic. In this case the revision is categorised as both a balance and a verb revision. Multiple categorisation provides detailed information about the tools writers use to create discourse that is consistent with their view of the topic, the genre and the intended audience.

### 5.2. Revision Episodes

During the creation of a text, its form, content and discourse structure have to represent the intentions of the writer and be presented according to task requirements. Revisions are undertaken throughout a text's evolution as the writer struggles to meet with these goals. Some revisions are single additions or deletions, with no relation to other revisions in the text. Other revisions, however, form units or groups of revisions in which the revisions are related to each other. These groups are called 'revision episodes'. One revision can trigger another, which in turn can trigger a third revision. A text-based revision of a sentence can include several surface level revisions of spelling and typography. A revision of form can, for example, trigger a change of plan and result in a text-based revision, and a revision of style can, for example, trigger a chain of revisions that tighten the text's discoursal consistency.

Severinson Eklundh and Kollberg (2003) used revision episode analysis to study task-specific discourse development in university writing. Twenty university students wrote four texts of different task type and were keystroke logged. The general revision patterns, revision episodes and the specific content of the episodes were analysed for all the texts. The students writing strategies were affected by the task characteristics, which were reflected in their writing as, by among other things, revision episodes. Severinson Eklundh and Kollberg argued that

> The analysis of revision episodes reveals the successive considerations that writers face while trying to find a structure for their texts. In particular, it shows how a certain change often triggers new revisions to fulfil general and task specific text norms. (p. 888)

Severinson Eklundh and Kollberg's work was assisted by the automatic analysis of the three revision episode categories that Kollberg (1998) had implemented in Trace-it. The definitions of the revision episode categories drew on the work of Monahan (1982) and Williamson and Pence (1989). The three categories that can be automatically analysed in Trace-it are (1) episode with repetitive revision at one cursor location, (2) episode with embedded revision and (3) episode with a sequence of revisions in previously written text.

**5.2.1 Episode with repetitive revision at one cursor location** In order for revisions to be defined as a revision episode with repetitive revision at one cursor movement, the revisions "should be performed in a temporal sequence and bring the cursor to the same location between the revisions, or to a location to the left of an earlier revision in the episode" (Kollberg, 1998, p. 89). According to Kollberg, these revisions often occur when writers are trying out a spelling or a formulation of a word or when writers are "thinking with their fingers" (p. 91). It has been posited that the computer facilitates experimentation of formulations, allowing for writers to try out and look at the written passage before deciding whether to include it in the text or not (Severinson Eklundh, 1994). If the repetitive revisions occur at the end of the on-going text, they correspond with pre-contextual revision. An example of such a revision sequence consisting of two consecutive revisions is shown in Example (50).

(50) The da → We alway <7.2> → Everything we do on Christmas goes after the same old tradition.

The writer started writing a sentence, deleted it and started again. After a 7.2-s pause the writer continued and completed the sentence. One interpretation of the revision episode is that the writer intended to present the content of the completed sentence at the start of the revision episode. It is, however, equally possible that the writer started the episode with an intention that changed during the course of the revision episode. Although it is not possible to draw any conclusions about the writer's intention on the basis of a keystroke logfile without complementary data, the location of repetitive revision can provide the research with an insight into the development of discourse during writing.

**5.2.2 Episode with embedded revision** An embedded revision is a revision that is undertaken within an insertion. The writer inserts a text item into previously written text, and in the course of this insertion revisions are undertaken. Thus, several levels of embedding can occur. The insertion is superordinate to one or more levels of embedded revisions. Example (51) illustrates a revision episode in which a meaning-preserving distribution revision is embedded in a micro-level addition (insertion). The writer adds one text unit to the previously written text, the information that the dog Ella is 4 years old. If this unit had been added to the original sentence, it would have resulted in a sentence including four units that are joined together with a conjunction 'and'. The writer chose to divide the units into two sentences, which makes the description less repetitive. Hence, the embedded revision is an effect of the addition; in order to incorporate the new information unit into the previously written text, the structure of the passage has to be revised.

(51) Ella is a pretty dog and she loves to ran and she is black. → Ella is a pretty dog and she loves to ran. She is blackand she is 4yers old.

Embedded revisions often entail surface revisions undertaken in previously written text or surface revisions undertaken within a text-based addition. In order to revise, the writer must have located the inadequacies in the text either by re-reading the previously written text or by remembering, for example, the spelling of previously written words or the structure of passages. By locating revision episodes in previously written text the degree of recursiveness of the writing session can be reflected (Kollberg, 1998).

**5.2.3 Episode with a sequence of revisions in previously written text** Another type of revision episode is characterised by a sequence of revisions after which the writer resumes writing at the point of interruption. A final round of revision at the end of a writing session would fall into this category, as well as the re-reading and revision of paragraphs and sentences during writing. Severinson Eklundh and Kollberg (2003) studied this revision type in university students' writing. They found that global revision sequences that affected the text beyond the current sentence often involved discoursal revisions of, among other things, consistency, coherence, emphasis, clarity and structure.

Other revisions in this category appear to be triggered by something the writer just wrote. In Examples (52–54) the writer performs a revision sequence based on the word 'music', starting at the point of inscription.

(52) it's a pleas we can go to and lisen to music and bay candy [...160 words] and on swedhich you can chemistri, paint,so and mucic.
(53) mucic <4.8> → mucik <7.9>.
(54) <2.0> music → mucic → mucik.

The word 'music' was correctly spelt at the beginning of the text. However, 160 words later the word was written again, but this time with the spelling 'mucic' (Example 52). After a 4.8-s pause the writer revised this into 'mucik' (Example 53). The writer paused again, this time for nearly 8 s, before the cursor was moved back 160 words in the text to the first occurrence of the word 'music' (Example 54). The writer paused again, and revised the 's' into a 'c' and the 'c' at the end of the word into 'k'. The revisions adjusted the spelling to concur with second occurrence of the word. Although the revision is on a surface level and creates a spelling error in the text, it reflects the writer's global perspective of the text. The first revision made the writer recall the previously written, but differently spelt word, move, revise for consistency and resume the writing at the point of inscription.

## 6 Discussion

Revision of internal and externalised text occurs throughout writing and it is "[i]n the act of writing people regenerate or recreate their own goals in the light of what they learn" (Flower & Hayes, 1980, p. 381). Revision can occur at any time during writing and accounts for writers' need to develop their ideas or the form in which the ideas are presented.

In this chapter, the LS-taxonomy for online revision analysis has been presented and illustrated. The taxonomy defines revisions according to their position relative to the point of inscription and whether the revisions affect the text on a form or a conceptual level. In the taxonomy, revisions are divided into two major categories, pre-contextual revisions and contextual revisions; pre-contextual revisions occur at the point of inscription before a full context has been externalised as text and contextual revisions occur within previously written text. Both revision types can be undertaken to adjust form and conceptual issues in the developing text.

This approach to revision analysis provides insight into how revision at different locations is undertaken, and when during the writing process writers focus on forms and concepts. Revision not only shapes the forms and concepts of previously written text through contextual revisions, but also shapes the forms and concepts of text that is in the process of being formulated and transcribed through pre-contextual revision.

The formulation process has been described as a point in the writing process that is particularly sensitive to writing language (L1 or L2) (Roca de Larios, Murphy, & Marin, 2002). Writers who use a foreign language interrupt their writing to pause or revise more often than when they use their L1 (Chenoweth & Hayes, 2001). These interruptions can be a result of writers trying to find a linguistically suitable way of expressing their ideas in the foreign language or of the writers having to change their ideas when they lack the sufficient foreign language knowledge to express their original plan. The writers need more time to express ideas effectively in a foreign language owing to the increase in cognitive effort that not writing in a first language brings (see Piolat, Roussey, Olive, & Amada, 2004 for a discussion of processing time and cognitive effort in revision). The results of the empirical study testing the validity of pre-conceptual revision category presented in this chapter also found that pre-contextual revision of both form and concepts were affected by writing language and that at the point of inscription writers revised form and concepts more in the EFL texts than in the L1. These results indicate that the writers processed form and concepts more during transcription when writing in a foreign language than when writing in their L1.

As illustrated in Examples (4–6), pre-contextual revisions of partly written words are often preceded by pauses. During such pauses, writers can formulate or revise the intended text internally before it is transcribed. When the transcription starts, the writer changes his or her mind about the text and revises before the word had been completed. Such a revision sequence can be represented in a logfile as a pause followed by a pre-contextual revision and can be analysed as a revision unit. The relationship between pauses and revision needs to be further investigated in order to better understand the cognitive processing that they can represent. In most keystroke logging programs pre-contextual revisions are detectable. In the logfiles that are generated from JEdit, the occurrence of a pre-contextual revision is indicated by a deletion at the point of inscription without cursor movement. This deletion is frequently followed by new text production at the point of inscription. Similar representations can be found in other keystroke logging software, such as ScriptLog (Strömqvist & Malmsten, 1998).

In this chapter, stimulated recall was coupled with keystroke logging in order to assist in the development of the LS-taxonomy and in the interpretation of revisions. The importance of using complementary data collection when analysing online revision was confirmed. Even though think-aloud protocols impact upon the temporal aspects of writing and revision, future studies could triangulate keystroke logging, think-aloud protocols and stimulated recall data to provide another perspective on revision, its causes and its effects on the developing textual discourse. These data could be analysed for new relationships through, for example, visualisation and data mining, perhaps using Geographic Information Systems as suggested by Lindgren, Sullivan, Lindgren, and Spelman Miller (in press). Such a broad approach to online revision analysis would be able to support the interpretation of the complex revision patterns consisting of deletions, insertions, movements and pauses in the keystroke logfiles. It would further permit stringent testing of the LS-taxonomy, lead to improvements in the taxonomy for analysing online revision and validate studies based on the LS-taxonomy as they feed into writing theory.

## Acknowledgements

The authors thank Anders Steinvall, Marie Stevenson, Ingela Valfridsson and two anonymous reviewers for their useful comments on an earlier draft of this paper.

Chapter 10

# Segmentation of the Writing Process in Translation: Experts Versus Novices

Birgitta Englund Dimitrova
*Stockholm University, Stockholm, Sweden*

*This study analyses differences between professional translators and students in how they segment the writing process. Four professional translators and four students participated, translating a text from Russian into Swedish. The professionals were found to divide their writing process into fewer and larger segments than the students. Professionals with very long translation experience differed markedly in these respects from all other subjects. Values for pause length did not correlate with translation experience. Facilitation effects were found during the task for all subjects, leading to fewer and larger segments towards the end of the task.*

**Keywords:** translation process, expert-novice, segmentation, facilitation effect, Russian-Swedish translation.

## 1 Introduction

Translating means producing a text, the target text (TT), which is modelled upon another text, the source text (ST) written in the source language (SL), and which aims at reproducing pertinent features of the ST in the target language (TL). Which features will be reproduced depends upon the purpose (or *Skopos*, see Reiss & Vermeer, 1984) of the particular TT. The exact manner in which they will be reproduced depends upon many factors, including norms for translations in the given society (Chesterman, 1997; Toury, 1995).

Various aspects of the translation process have been studied, for instance with concurrent verbalisations (think-aloud-protocols, TAPs), since the 1980s; for overviews, see Bernadini (2001), Jääskeläinen (1999) and Tirkkonen-Condit (2002). From the 1990s (but see the early study by Tommola [1986]), keystroke logging of the writing process has also been used in studies on the translation process (see the articles in Hansen, 1999, 2002).

**Computer Key Stroke Logging and Writing: Methods and Applications**

**ISBN: 0-08-044934-4**

*Englund Dimitrova, B. (2006) Segmentation of the writing process in translation: experts vs. novices. In G. Rijlaarsdam (Series Ed.) and K. P. H. Sullivan, & E. Lindgren. (Vol. Eds.), Studies in Writing, Vol. 18, Computer Keystroke Logging: Methods and Applications (pp. 189–201). Oxford: Elsevier.*

The present paper will present and discuss data on how subjects with different amount of experience in translation, from professional translators to language students at university level, segment their writing process in translation. The research reported in this chapter is part of a larger study (Englund Dimitrova, 2005).

## 2 Pauses and Segmentation of the Writing Process

### *2.1 Monolingual Writing*

In online studies of monolingual writing, for example by computer logging of the writing process (e.g., Sanders, Janssen, Van der Pool, Schilperoord, & van Wijk, 1996; Strömqvist, 1996; Van Waes, 1991), by video recordings (Chanquoy, Foulin, & Fayol, 1996; Matsuhashi, 1982) or by studies of dictation (Schilperoord, 1996), one prominent feature that has been analysed is pauses, that is moments of inactivity in the process of writing down or dictating. Their convenience lies in being both observable in the process and measurable. Pauses are interpreted as evidence for, or traces of, underlying processes, such as planning, retrieval, problem-solving and decision-making. Several studies have shown that pause length can be seen as an indicator of the cognitive complexity of various aspects of the task. Thus, it has been shown that the length of pauses correlates with their location in the textual structure. Longer pauses tend to occur immediately before more extensive syntactic constituents (Chanquoy et al., 1996) and before hierarchically higher units in the discourse (Matsuhashi, 1982; Sanders et al., 1996; Schilperoord, 1996). Such locations in the text presumably require a larger amount of planning, which explains the longer pause length.

Breaks and pauses during the writing process take up a considerable share of the whole writing process, more than half of the time spent on the task (Baurmann, 1989). These moments of keyboard or pen inactivity divide the actual writing process into segments, which are often quite small. The subjects in the study by Kaufer, Hayes, and Flower (1986) produced segments, delimited by pauses, varying in size from 4.5 words to 16.8 words. Expert writers produced larger segments than did novices. Good and weak writers differ in the number of pauses, but not in pause length (Baurmann, 1989, p. 271).

### *2.2 Translation*

In writing down a translated text, there are important differences in comparison with writing one's own text, and it can be assumed that this influences the pause pattern as well. Whereas in monolingual writing, an important part is the planning of content, that is finding and further developing the ideas that will be expressed in the text, in translation this planning of content is done beforehand, by another writer, the writer/author of the ST. Other aspects instead have to be planned in translation, such as for instance the pragmatic and stylistic adjustment of the TT (Englund Dimitrova, 2005). There is also the need for reading the ST and the segments that are to be translated, to understand them (perhaps with the help of dictionaries and other aids, an important part of the translation process of experts as well, see Künzli, 2001) and to retrieve and perhaps evaluate TL linguistic material, before writing it down. Once these TL words, phrases, clauses and expressions have been mentally formulated, there can be assumed to be important similarities between monolingual writing and the writing down of translated text. Thus, Matsuhashi (1982) concluded that planning in monolingual writing, as evidenced by pause patterns, does not correspond to grammatical units, but rather to psychological processing units which are based upon underlying conceptual content. Therefore, surface structure constituents are seldom produced as a unit (Matsuhashi, 1982, p. 286; *cf.* Gerloff, 1987, p. 147f. for a similar observation of units in TAPs in translating).

In contrast to monolingual writing, the length of pauses in translation can be assumed not necessarily to correlate with boundaries between hierarchical units on different levels in the text. This is because translation is usually considered a text which is supposed to follow the overall formal patterns of the ST rather closely. (There are of course exceptions to this, and how translations are viewed and evaluated depends also on the text type involved.) This being the case, the amount of planning required before starting a new paragraph, for instance, is not necessarily greater than that required before starting to write a sentence or a clause.

The issue of pauses and segmentation can be connected with a claim frequently made in studies on translation, *viz.* that experienced professional translators tend to work at the sentence or at the text level, whereas students tend to work at the word level. These claims are to a large extent intuitively based, being deduced either from the practical experience of translation teachers and scholars, or from observations of certain features in translated texts, for example lack of idiomaticity in the TL or downright ungrammatical constructions, even when the translation is done into the translator's/student's L1 (Krings, 1986; Lörscher, 1991; Toury, 1986), and which are attributed to interference from the ST and the SL.

A segment of the TT which a subject writes down without a pause, in one go, can be assumed to have been planned cognitively as a whole. Therefore, an analysis of the pause patterns of different subjects can give indications both of general cognitive patterns typical of translating, and of individual variations. Since the cognitive effort can be assumed to be larger for novices than for experts, the writing process of novices can be assumed to have more pauses and longer pauses for writing their translated text. The first assumption, that professional translators segment their writing process in translation into fewer segments, was confirmed in Jakobsen (2003), where the differences in this respect between professionals and semi-professionals (advanced translation students) were found to be statistically significant. This chapter investigates segmentation in the writing process in translation of subjects with a larger variation in translation experience, translating between another language combination.

## *2.3 Aspects Studied*

The number of pauses, as well as their total length, will thus be assumed to be a measure of the amount of cognitive effort involved in translating. Obviously, pauses are not equally indicative of such effort. Shorter pauses, 1–2 s, seem to be due to monitoring, detecting and correction of typing errors, etc. To be able to compare segmentation of the writing process in translation in different individuals, a pause length value must be chosen as the basis for the segmentation. A length should be chosen which excludes, for example pauses owing to individual differences in skill and speed in typing, and it should capture relevant aspects of processing. There is at present not sufficient research on writing in translation to provide indisputable evidence what this pause length value should be. Jensen (2000) suggested ≥4 s, Jakobsen (2003) ≥5 s. All suggested values are to some extent arbitrary. For this study, I have chosen the length ≥5 s, to allow some comparisons with Jakobsen's results.

One *segment* in the log is here defined as "a pause of ≥5 s + all keystrokes and mouse movements until the next pause of ≥5 s". This is an operational definition, which should not be taken to imply that the segment initial pause would always be due to planning what will be written after the pause. It can also be due to monitoring and evaluating what has been written before the pause.

One aspect which will be studied is the number of segments in the logs, given both for the writing phase (starting when the subject starts to write down the first integral version of the TT and finishing when the last sentence of the first version of the TT has been written down) and for the task as a whole (thus including any revisions made after the writing phase). This can also be illustrated by another measure, the number of segments required to complete the task in relation to the number of characters in the ST. This is of course not of interest as long as the same ST is translated into the same TL by all participants, since the values will say nothing more than is already said by the values for the number of segments. However, for comparisons across languages as well as across different texts, a measure independent of the involved languages must be used. For this, the notion of *ST unit*, introduced by Jakobsen (2003), will be used. It is defined as "100 characters in the source text, including blanks". The ST used here contains in all 3330 characters including blanks, making the number of ST units according to this measure 33.3.

There will also be a quantitative analysis of the average size of segments during the writing phase. Although the participants translate the same ST, it cannot be assumed that they will write the same total number of characters when translating it, for several reasons. Different translations, within the same language pair, differ in relative length, and it is possible to discern patterns in this respect related to individual translators (Englund Dimitrova, 1994). This is to say that if *one* ST is translated by several translators into one and the same TL, their TT's will differ in length.[1] Furthermore, all participants do some amount of concurrent revision during the writing phase, but the precise amount is subject to individual variations (see further Englund Dimitrova, 2005). Also, different individuals make differing numbers of typing errors, and correct them not to the same extent. Individuals might also skip translating parts of the ST without intending to do so.

For this analysis, the number of characters written within each segment will be the measure. Using *word* as the unit of measurement turned out to be impossible, since the loggings abound with examples of words written only partly, before being revised. The *character* was therefore considered a more appropriate unit of measure, having the additional advantage of facilitating comparisons with data and results from other language combinations. It is expected that on the average, the more experienced participants will write a larger number of characters within each segment.

[1]This is also shown by the length of the TT's of the subjects in this project, which varies between 473 and 565 words, counted in characters (including blanks) they vary between 3180 and 3745.

The values for length of the segment initial pauses, that is the mean length of all pauses ≥5 s, will also be given. It is expected that the pauses of professional translators will be shorter, since their process can be assumed to be characterised by a higher degree of automaticity.

Furthermore, it will be studied whether there is any facilitation effect during the writing phase of the translation task, resulting in differences in segmentation and/or number of characters per segment between the beginning and the end of the task. Facilitation effects have been found in monolingual writing (Strömqvist, 1996) and can be expected in translation as well, for at least the following reasons:

- Certain global decisions regarding the TT and the task are taken at the beginning of the task, and can be expected to facilitate processing towards the end, thereby speeding up processing.
- Certain words or phrases might occur several times in the source text, which will potentially facilitate retrieval of translation equivalents.
- The growing text representation (mental and in the form of a TL version) will facilitate certain aspects of both ST comprehension and TT production.

### *2.4 Hypotheses*

The following hypotheses will be tested:

- The log files of the professional translators will contain fewer segments, as defined above, both during the writing phase and for the completion of the whole task, than those of the students.
- The log files from the writing phase of the professional translators will contain more characters per segment (as defined above) than those of the students.
- The average length of the pauses ≥5 s during the writing phase will be shorter in the log files of the professional translators than in those of the students.
- A facilitation effect will appear during the writing phase leading to:
  - a decrease in the number of segments per ST unit in the log files of all groups of participants for the last 50% of the ST units compared to the first 50% of the ST units;
  - an increase in the number of characters written per segment in the log files of all groups of participants in the last 50% of the segments compared to the first 50% of the segments;
  - a decrease in the mean length of the segment initial pause in the log files of all groups of participants in the second 50% of the segments compared to the first 50% of the segments.

## 3 Data and Method

### *3.1 Data*

The study had eight participants: four professional translators and four students, all with Swedish as their L1. They translated into Swedish a Russian text of 438 words, describing the life of a 19th century Ukrainian artist and poet. The stated purpose of the translation was that the text would be used by a Stockholm art museum, which was planning an exhibition of 19th century art from Central and Eastern Europe. The subjects had as their disposal a wide array of dictionaries and other aids. There was no time limit for completing the task. The data was collected within a larger project (for a fuller description, see Englund Dimitrova, 2005), with the aim to study various aspects of the translation process. For this reason, a combination of data was used (triangulation of data). The subjects thus performed the task with concurrent verbalisations (TAPs) and wrote their target text on a Macintosh computer with the logging software ScriptLog, version 2.1, 1993 (see Strömqvist, 1996; Wengelin, 2002).

The subjects can be divided into two groups: professionals and students, as reflected in the hypotheses. However, the individual values obtained (see Section 4) showed considerable variation within the group of professionals, which can potentially be related to amount of professional experience in translation. Two subgroups can be distinguished, *senior professionals* and *junior professionals*. The senior professionals have well over 10 years of experience working more or less full time as translators, whereas the junior professionals have somewhat shorter experience. Within the student group, two subgroups were also distinguished, *translation students* and *language students*. The translation students were attending a three-semester translator training programme, with the entrance requirement of 2 years of previous university level study of Russian. The language students were in their second and third semester, respectively, of Russian at university level.

Thus, the results will be presented on three levels: individual, group and subgroup levels. Due to the small size of the data, no test for statistical significance has been made. The study has an exploratory character, and is to be regarded as a pilot study. It should be remembered that the segmentation data are taken from performing a task under concurrent verbalisation. This condition increases the number of segments (Jakobsen, 2003), but since this effect can be assumed for all groups, the values can still be used for between-group comparison.

### *3.2 Method*

The method consisted in generating from the log file of each participant a text file with the software, showing all pauses equal to or longer than 5 s in the writing process. The characters written within each segment (as defined in Section 2.3) were counted with the word count function of the software Word; the figures include blanks between words.

## 4 Results

Tables 1–3 give the values for number of segments for the writing phase and for completing the whole task. On this measure, there is considerable individual variation (*cf.* Table 1). Tables 2 and 3 show that the first hypothesis is verified on the group level, where there are substantial differences between the two groups. On the subgroup level, however, only the values of the senior professionals stand out, whereas those of the junior professionals, the translator students and the language students show only small differences.

Table 1: Number of segments, writing phase and whole task, individual data.

| | Number of segments | | | |
|---|---|---|---|---|
| | Writing phase | Per ST unit, writing phase | Whole task | Per ST unit, whole task |
| Senior professional | 115 | 3.45 | 122 | 3.66 |
| Senior professional | 88 | 2.64 | 115 | 3.45 |
| Junior professional | 123 | 3.69 | 271 | 8.14 |
| Junior professional | 217 | 6.52 | 294 | 8.83 |
| Translation student | 218 | 6.55 | 286 | 8.59 |
| Translation student | 150 | 4.50 | 290 | 8.71 |
| Language student | 195 | 5.86 | 313 | 9.40 |
| Language student | 216 | 6.49 | 318 | 9.55 |

Table 2: Number of segments, writing phase and whole task, group level.

| | Number of segments | | | |
|---|---|---|---|---|
| | Writing phase | Per ST unit, writing phase | Whole task | Per ST unit, whole task |
| Professionals | 135.75 | 4.08 | 200.50 | 6.02 |
| Students | 194.75 | 5.84 | 301.75 | 9.06 |

Table 3: Number of segments, writing phase and whole task, subgroup level.

| | Number of segments | | | |
|---|---|---|---|---|
| | Writing phase | Per ST unit, writing phase | Whole task | Per ST unit, whole task |
| Senior professionals | 101.50 | 3.05 | 118.50 | 3.56 |
| Junior professionals | 170 | 5.10 | 282.50 | 8.48 |
| Translation students | 184 | 5.53 | 288 | 8.65 |
| Language students | 205 | 6.16 | 315.50 | 9.47 |

It is interesting to compare the value for segments per ST unit with the values from Jakobsen (2003), whose subjects translated from English into Danish.[2] His professional subjects had between 3.68 and 7.24 segments per ST unit for the whole task, thus a range quite similar to that found in the professionals here (*cf.* Table 1 above). His group of semi-

[2]Only those of Jakobsen's results are taken into account, which were obtained under the same experimental conditions as those in the present study, that is where the subjects translated from L2 into their L1, and under concurrent verbalisation.

professionals can be compared to the translation students here. Their values in his study ranged from 3.80 to 7.49, thus lower than the values of the two translation students in this study (see Table 1). The differences in results for the translation students can perhaps be attributed to the different language combinations and to the fact that the languages in the present study, Russian and Swedish, are typologically more distant than Danish and English, which can be assumed to cause less experienced subjects, such as translation students, more problems.

The rest of the results presented are based only upon the logs from the writing phase. Tables A.1–A.3 (see Appendix A) show the number of characters written per segment during the writing phase. On this measure as well, there is a clear difference on group level between professionals and students. Hypothesis 2 is thus verified on group level. The value of the subgroup of senior professionals stands out, whereas those of the junior professionals and the translation students are very close to each other, the language students showing the lowest value. The values for mean length of segment initial pauses during the writing phase are given in Tables B.1–B.3 (see Appendix B). On this measure, the individual variation, as shown by Table B.1, is quite small, with the exception of one language student. At group level, the length of the segment initial pauses is shorter in the professionals' logs, as hypothesised, but at subgroup level, the difference between both senior and junior professionals and the translation students is small. The language students have on average the longest pauses. On this measure, there is virtually no difference between the two subgroups of professionals.

Values concerning the possible facilitation effects during the writing phase will next be presented and discussed. The first measure is the number of segments required for writing down the TT of the first 50% and the second 50% of the ST units, respectively. If there is a facilitation effect, we expect that fewer segments will be required per ST unit towards the end of the writing phase, here defined as the second 50% of the ST units. Tables C.1–C.3 (see Appendix C) give the pertinent values.

As expected, the number of segments required to write the translation of the second half of the ST decreases in comparison to the number of segments required to write the translation of the first half of the ST. A decrease is found in the data of all participants, with the exception of one language student, and as a consequence also in the group and subgroup values. The decrease is especially conspicuous in the group of translation students.

The possible facilitation effect is also studied through another measure, *viz*. the number of characters written per segment, during the first 50% and the second 50% of the segments of the writing phase. On this measure, facilitation would result in an increase from the first to the second 50% of the segments. The values are shown in Tables A.1–A.3. In all groups and subgroups, there is in fact an increase in the average number of characters written during the second half of the segments in the writing phase. On the individual level, however, this increase is very slight in some cases.

Finally, it was also hypothesised that facilitation would lead to shorter segment initial pauses towards the end of the writing phase. Tables B.1–B.3 show the mean length of segment initial pauses for the first 50% of the segments and the second 50% of the segments. Here, the results are contrary to what was hypothesised. The average pause length does decrease, but not in all subgroups: this happens only in the subgroups of junior professionals and translation students. In the other subgroups, there is a slight increase, contrary to what was predicted. On group level, no effect was found.

## 5 Discussion

In most aspects studied here, the hypotheses are borne out by the data. Thus, the more experienced participants divide their writing process when translating into fewer segments (as defined here) than the less experienced participants. This goes both for the whole task, and for the writing phase. Also, during the writing phase, the more experienced participants wrote more characters within each segment. The values of the subgroup of senior professionals were in these respects particularly outstanding.

The results also point to facilitation effects during the writing phase of a translation task, and these were found in *all* groups and subgroups of subjects. Thus, all groups and subgroups use fewer segments to write the translation of the second half of the ST than they do to write the translation of the first half of the ST. On another measure, the number of characters per segment, this facilitation effect shows in an increase in the average number of characters written per segment in the second half of the writing phase as compared to the first half of the writing phase.

The analysis of the length of the segment initial pauses did not give the expected results. The mean pause length in the language students' log files was the longest. However, the differences between the other subgroups were small, and, more importantly, did not mirror the results from the other analyses, that is the subgroup of senior professionals did not here differ markedly from the other groups. Neither could any facilitation effect on pause length during the writing phase be found, that is there was no clear tendency for it to decrease. Perhaps the increase that was found in mean pause length in the logs of several of the participants, reflects the fact that they also show an increase in the number of characters written in each segment. When more linguistic material is included in each segment, more time for processing is required.

The three subjects with the highest number of segments for the writing phase (one junior professional, one translation student and one language student) are not homogenous in translation experience. They do, however, work in a very similar way when translating. An important reason for their relatively fragmented writing phase and process seems to be that they tend to do dictionary searches mainly as they "happen upon" the need for it, often in the middle of sentences. On the other hand, the case of the language student with the lower amount of segments is particularly illuminating. The reason for her segmentation is, paradoxically, her rather low competence in the SL Russian. Due to this, she often does not understand enough even to make a very literal translation when first reading a sentence. Instead, she has to read the sentence through thoroughly, looking up words in the dictionary, and by the time she has done all this, she is often able to write down relatively large segments. As a consequence of this, her pauses during the writing phase are on the average very long. Thus, segmentation pattern is influenced also by other factors than professional experience. The number of segments during the writing phase can also be assumed to depend upon how the ST has been read and approached. In fact, the junior professional and the translation student who have a relatively low number of segments in the writing phase, both start their task performance by reading the source text quite thoroughly, combining this reading with a partial, oral translation into Swedish.

Conspicuous and to some extent unexpected were the very large differences found in many respects between the subgroup of senior professionals, who can be considered experts in terms of their experience (well over 10 years of experience in the profession), and the other subgroups. It was also unexpected to find relatively small differences between the two groups of junior professionals and of translation students on many of the measures. Whereas it might be tempting to see these results solely as due to the senior professionals' degree of expertise, there can be some other reasons as well. It is possible that the translation task, more specifically the text type and some of its stylistic features, were more of a routine task for the senior professionals than for the junior ones. Furthermore, the TA condition may have influenced the results. Jakobsen (2003) shows that in that condition, the number of segments (defined in the same way as in this study) increases significantly; in his group of expert translators, the average increase of segments was 21.7%. To be sure, in the present study, *all* subjects did their translation with concurrent verbalisations, so that should potentially not have any bearing on the results. However, it is clear from the data that the two senior professionals verbalise less than all other subjects. This is in protocol studies usually taken to indicate that the processes in such subjects are to a large extent automated, and therefore not available for introspection (Ericsson & Simon, 1984/1993), an explanation which is quite compatible with the degree of experience in the senior professionals. However, most researchers using introspection have certainly encountered subjects who seem to have more difficulties to verbalise than others. If the smaller amount of verbalisations in the two senior professionals' protocols in this study is in fact due to automated processes, their results and figures are comparable to those of the other subgroups, but if they are due to a difficulty to verbalise, matters stand differently.

Finally, there is an alternative tentative explanation for those measures which are here attributed to a facilitation effect, namely that the second part of the ST might perhaps be easier linguistically to translate. Since no exact measures for text difficulty have been applied here, such an explanation cannot be completely excluded, although the character of the text (syntactically, lexically, etc.) seems quite homogenous. Obviously, further research testing facilitation effect in translation is needed, as well as on other aspects studied here.

## 6 Acknowledgements

This study has been financed by grants from the Swedish Research Council for the Humanities and Social Sciences and the Bank of Sweden Tercentenary foundation. Parts of this study have been published in Englund Dimitrova (2005). Published here with kind permission by John Benjamins Publishing Company, Amsterdam/Philadelphia.

## Appendix A: Tables A.1–A.3

Table A.1: Number of characters written per segment, for the whole writing phase, and for first half and second half of ST, individual level.

| | Mean number of characters | | |
|---|---|---|---|
| | **Per segment, whole writing phase** | **Per segment, first 50% of segments in writing phase** | **Per segment, second 50% of segments in writing phase** |
| Senior professional | 29.39 | 27.77 | 30.98 |
| Senior professional | 46.05 | 38.18 | 53.91 |
| Junior professional | 29.28 | 26.90 | 31.69 |
| Junior professional | 19.52 | 19.16 | 19.87 |
| Translation student | 18.00 | 15.57 | 20.43 |
| Translation student | 29.63 | 29.60 | 29.67 |
| Language student | 21.81 | 19.44 | 24.19 |
| Language student | 18.42 | 17.90 | 18.94 |

Table A.2: Number of characters written per segment, for the whole writing phase, and for first half and second half of ST, group level.

| | Mean number of characters | | |
|---|---|---|---|
| | **Per segment, whole writing phase** | **Per segment, first 50% of segments in writing phase** | **Per segment, second 50% of segments in writing phase** |
| Professionals | 31.06 | 28.00 | 34.11 |
| Students | 21.96 | 20.63 | 23.31 |

Table A.3: Number of characters written per segment, for the whole writing phase, and for first half and second half of ST, subgroup level.

| | Mean number of characters | | |
|---|---|---|---|
| | **Per segment, whole writing phase** | **Per segment, first 50% of segments in writing phase** | **Per segment, second 50% of segments in writing phase** |
| Senior professionals | 37.72 | 33.00 | 42.44 |
| Junior professionals | 24.00 | 23.03 | 25.78 |
| Translation students | 23.82 | 22.59 | 25.05 |
| Language students | 20.12 | 18.67 | 21.56 |

## Appendix B: Tables B.1–B.3

Table B.1: Length of segment initial pause, whole writing phase, first and second 50% of segments, individual level.

| | Mean length of segment initial pauses (sec) | | |
|---|---|---|---|
| | Writing phase | First 50% of segments, writing phase | Second 50% of segments, writing phase |
| Senior professional | 26.95 | 28.58 | 25.34 |
| Senior professional | 23.96 | 19.76 | 28.15 |
| Junior professional | 25.74 | 30.49 | 20.92 |
| Junior professional | 24.31 | 24.71 | 23.91 |
| Translation student | 30.09 | 29.12 | 31.05 |
| Translation student | 24.33 | 27.51 | 21.15 |
| Language student | 42.90 | 40.86 | 44.95 |
| Language student | 25.48 | 25.63 | 25.33 |

Table B.2: Length of segment initial pauses, whole writing phase, first and second 50% of segments, group level.

| | Mean length of segment initial pauses (sec) | | |
|---|---|---|---|
| | Writing phase | First 50% of segments, writing phase | Second 50% of segments, writing phase |
| Professionals | 25.24 | 25.89 | 24.58 |
| Students | 30.70 | 30.78 | 30.62 |

Table B.3: Length of segment initial pauses, whole writing phase, first and second 50% of segments, subgroup level.

| | Mean length of segment initial pauses (sec) | | |
|---|---|---|---|
| | Writing phase | First 50% of segments, writing phase | Second 50% of segments, writing phase |
| Senior professionals | 25.45 | 24.17 | 26.75 |
| Junior professionals | 25.02 | 27.60 | 22.42 |
| Translation students | 27.21 | 34.19 | 26.10 |
| Language students | 34.19 | 33.25 | 35.14 |

## Appendix C: Tables C.1–C.3

Table C.1: Number of segments for writing first and second part of the ST, writing phase, individual level.

| | Segments per ST unit | |
|---|---|---|
| | **First 50% of ST units** | **Second 50% of ST units** |
| Senior professional | 3.60 | 3.30 |
| Senior professional | 2.88 | 2.40 |
| Junior professional | 3.78 | 3.60 |
| Junior professional | 6.67 | 6.37 |
| Translation student | 7.87 | 5.23 |
| Translation student | 4.56 | 4.44 |
| Language student | 6.49 | 5.17 |
| Language student | 6.37 | 6.61 |

Table C.2: Number of segments for writing first and second part of the ST, writing phase, group level.

| | Segments per ST unit | |
|---|---|---|
| | **Segments for first 50% of ST units** | **Segments for second 50% of ST units** |
| Professionals | 4.23 | 3.92 |
| Students | 6.32 | 5.36 |

Table C.3: Number of segments for writing first and second part of the ST, writing phase, subgroup level.

| | Segments per ST unit | |
|---|---|---|
| | **Segments for first 50% of ST units** | **Segments for second 50% of ST units** |
| Senior professionals | 3.24 | 2.85 |
| Junior professionals | 5.22 | 4.99 |
| Translation students | 6.21 | 4.84 |
| Language students | 6.43 | 5.89 |

Chapter 11

# Supporting Learning, Exploring Theory and Looking Forward With Keystroke Logging

Kirk P. H. Sullivan and Eva Lindgren
*Umeå University, Umeå, Sweden*

*Keystroke logging is an approach to writing research that can also be used in teaching and exploring existing theories. This chapter overviews how keystroke logging can be used, and has been used, in the writing, language and translation classroom, illustrates how keystroke logging can provide new insights that can be used to interrogate theory and considers how keystroke logging's capabilities can be extended to provide a bright future for this technology.*

**Keywords:** Learning, writing, translation, theory, keystroke logging, processability theory, corpus, ERP.

## 1 Introduction

As we have seen throughout this book when an individual is writing a text, a large number of cognitive processes interact leaving traces in the keystroke log. The processes creating these traces may relate to the solving of the writing task, per se, or to combinations of solving the writing task, the learning of more appropriate writing-task solution techniques, and the noticing of linguistic problems that need to be addressed and resolved. We have further seen in this book that computer keystroke logging can be used to study a multitude of aspects of the processes of writing and translation. In this chapter we explore two domains and look forward to the future. The domains we examine are: (1) how computer keystroke logging can be used in the teaching of writing and translation and (2) how keystroke logging can be used to test, explore, extend and strengthen theory.

**Computer Key Stroke Logging and Writing: Methods and Applications**

**ISBN: 0-08-044934-4**

*Sullivan, K. P. H. & Lindgren E. (2006). Supporting learning, exploring theory and looking forward with keystroke logging. In G. Rijlaarsdam (Series Ed.) and K. P. H. Sullivan, & E. Lindgren. (Vol. Eds.), Studies in Writing, Vol. 18, Computer Keystroke Logging: Methods and Applications (pp. 203–211). Oxford: Elsevier.*

## 2 Supporting Learning Using Keystroke Logging

Computer keystroke logging can be used in teaching both writing and translation. In Sullivan, Kollberg, and Pålson (1998), we first presented our pedagogical work using keystroke logging. This work focused on how keystroke logging could help the modern language teacher "gain extra insights into the student's unique situation with regard to second language acquisition" (p. 22). More recently our focus has shifted to investigating how keystroke logging can be used to increase noticing and language awareness for the individual language learner (e.g. Lindgren & Sullivan, 2003). Spelman Miller (this volume, Chapter 8) motivated the use of keystroke logging in the writing classroom in the following way:

> In a number of ways the use of the interactive replay facility to focus on the planning and revising activity of individual writers offers potential value in diagnosis and consciousness-raising. For example, developing with the writer the notion of the (conceptual) paragraph and of the progression of the whole text beyond the individual sentence and paragraph may help to relieve sentence-level planning pressures, and may help to increase fluency and productivity. Furthermore, considering the role of certain devices, which here we have referred to as framing devices, in establishing and maintaining topic development may be useful for some writers in understanding topic progression throughout the paragraph and text. (p. 168)

In 2000, Rijlaarsdam and Couzijn pointed out that "if students are not even aware of their writing strategies and their results, they can hardly be expected to evaluate them — and thus deliberately change, maintain or abandon — them" (p. 176) and in this section we present ways in which keystroke logging can be and has been (e.g. Deutschmann, Lindgren, Steinvall, & Sullivan, 2005; Lindgren, 2004, 2005; Lindgren & Sullivan, 2003; Sullivan, Kollberg, & Pålson, 1998; Sullivan & Lindgren, 2002) used in the classroom to help students become aware of their writing strategies and on the various classes in which we have used keystroke logging as a teaching and reflection tool in the writing, language and translation classroom.

### *2.1 Enhancing Input Saliance and Awareness Using Keystroke Logging*

One of the first steps a learner takes when becoming aware of a feature of writing or language that has up to that point not been salient, is noticing that feature's existence (Schmidt, 1990; Truscott, 1998). Once a feature has been noticed it becomes available for reflection and analysis. In order for noticing to occur, certain conditions have to be met; the learner has to be working with a task that is appropriate to their learning situation and in a learning environment with which they are comfortable.

A learner is more likely to notice a feature if it is made salient (Sharwood Smith, 2000 discusses the importance of what he refers to as 'input salience' for second-language learning). However, if the input is of a level that is too advanced for the learner, or includes a feature for which the learner is not yet cognitively ready, noticing is not likely to occur, even if the feature is made salient. Appropriate input comes from the learner's present level and the level immediately above the learner's present level. Vygotsky (1978) referred to 'zone of proximal development' and in Pienemann (1998) referred to 'readiness' when writing about language learning.

One way of providing students with appropriate input is for the teacher to make use of the student's output and, for example, discuss unclear issues in the student's own output are noticed by the student (Rijlaarsdam & Couzijn, 2000; Sharwood Smith, 2000; for the 'output hypothesis', see Swain, 1995, 1998, 2000). In writing, as suggested by Pålsson (1998) and Sullivan et al. (1998), revisions can provide hints about the learners' language level. Thus, for example, if a learner revises agreement incorrectly, the revision may indicate that the learner has noticed agreement, but has not yet mastered it. The grammatical feature agreement could, thus, come from the next level of learning, and the learner could be cognitively ready to learn this feature. An analysis of a learner's keystroke log could, therefore, provide the teacher with information about which features a learner has noticed and could be discussed as their level of salience would already be high.

A second way of providing students with appropriate input is make the keystroke log replay function directly available to the learner to examine and reflect upon individually in an in-class or out-of-class setting. The learner can write diary entries, write course work or, in fact, any document that needs to be written using keystroke logging software. The student can once they have completed their document, replay the log, and among other things, reflect upon the process and notice features of the writing process, grammatical feature about which they are insecure.

A third way of promoting noticing using keystroke logging, Peer-Based Intervention (Lindgren, 2004; Lindgren & Sullivan, 2003), combines the method of using multiple-writing opportunities to increase noticing that was proposed and investigated by Chanquoy (2001) with observational learning (Braaksma, Van den Bergh, Rijlaarsdam, & Couzijn, 2001; Braaksma, Rijlaarsdam, & Van den Bergh, 2002) and Stimulated recall (Gass & Mackey, 2000).

During observational learning, learners observe a peer composing a text. During observation, learners do not have to focus their attention on producing text, but can devote their entire cognitive resources towards observing how a text is being created. During observation, features in the observed writing process can be noticed, verbalised and discussed. During a stimulated recall session, the learner recalls an event with the help of a prompt to stimulate memories of the event and its developmental sequence.

Peer-Based Intervention makes use of all three techniques — stimulated recall, observational learning and multiple writing sessions. The replaying of the keystroke log is used as the stimulus for in-depth reflection and discussion together with a peer and/or a teacher based on a keystroke logged writing session. A learner, or learners, observes the replayed writing sessions together with the writer and after the observational learning session the writer revises the composition during a second writing opportunity. The PBI studies we have undertaken (Deutschmann, Lindgren, Steinvall, & Sullivan, 2005; Lindgren, 2004, 2005; Lindgren & Sullivan, 2003) have been conducted in learner pairs.

We have used each of these methods and based on student feedback and empirical results we have found that through verbalisation, peer and teacher feedback, PBI and keystroke log stimulated reflection learners are helped to become aware of the linguistic and extra-linguistic features necessary for text improvement, and language and writing development. For example, based on the experiences with these adult learners Sullivan and Lindgren (2002) concluded that "self-assessment and reflection upon one's own work — two key skills for the student to learn in order to become an effective life-long learner — are encouraged by the autonomous use of *Trace-it* [a key-stroke logger]" (p. 266).

We hope that this section inspires the reader who works in the classroom with students to use keystroke logging as one of the elements of their teaching. Suggestions for how to use keystroke logging in the classroom can be found in Lindgren, Stevenson, and Sullivan's (in preparation) forthcoming keystroke logging textbook.

## 3 Exploring Theory

Wengelin (this volume, Chapter 7), Spelman-Miller (this volume, Chapter 8) and Lindgren and Sullivan (this volume, Chapter 9) all report on research based on keystroke log data. This body of research has resulted in techniques and taxonomies for classifying log data and in detailed descriptions of how writers compose in a word-processing environment. This fundamental research provides an indication of the type of information that is possible to retrieve from a keystroke log and how it can be analysed. Together with the research reported in among other places (Strömqvist et al., this volume; Stevenson, Schoonen, & de Glopper, forthcoming), this fundamental research provides a base upon which to start using keystroke data, alone or in combination with other data-collection methods, to evaluate theories relating to writing, learning and linguistic processing. It is possible to view keystroke-logged data as forming a tangible collection of data with which it is possible to explore whether a posited theory has the impact on output production that the theory predicts. In this section we use Pienemann's (1998a, 1998b) Processability Theory to suggest possible ways in which one could use keystroke-logged data to explore and interrogate theory. The section begins by overviewing Processability Theory before progressing to suggest a way by which one could use keystroke logging to explore the theory. This section is a development of ideas presented in Lindgren and Sullivan (2002), and Lindgren et al. (2002).

### *3.1 Overview of Processability Theory*

Processability Theory (Pienemann, 1998a, 1998b) is built around a hierarchy of language-processing procedures and a learner's ability to process new cognitive structures is defined by the learner's readiness to proceed from one stage to the next. In Processability Theory, each new structure is viewed as building upon the structures from the earlier stages of the acquisition process. Thus, before a new process can be acquired, the lower levels of the hierarchy have to have been passed through and mastered. A result of this hierarchical view of the acquisition of language-processing skills is that Processability Theory can be used to make predictions about the order of acquisition of target language structures.

Processability Theory has its basis in empirical research on spontaneous speech production and is implemented within the framework of Lexical Functional Grammar (see Bresnan [2001] for a good introduction). The goal of Processability Theory is well summarized in Pienemann and Håkansson (1999, p. 386):

> processability theory focuses solely on the developmental problem as an explanatory issue; it is not designed to contribute anything to the question of the innate of learned origin of linguistics knowledge of the inferential processes by which linguistic input is converted into linguistic knowledge. Instead, it is the sole objective of processability theory to determine the sequence in which procedural skills develop in the learner. (p. 386)

According to Processability Theory, the second-language learner goes through predetermined processing procedures in the acquisition of the second language; these procedures are *lemma/word*, category *procedure*, *phrasal procedure*, *sentence procedure* and *clausal boundary procedure*.

The 'lemma' or 'word' level is the first level of acquisition and consequently the level that needs least cognitive processing to acquire. The first item in language acquisition is to learn single words, without knowing their lexical categories or how to put them together in a syntactically and semantically correct way.

When the learner has acquired enough words in the mental lexicon, the cognitive processing is ready to move on to the 'category procedure'. This level entails the processing of information of the category of 'lemma', such as categorising words as Nouns or Verbs and assigning additional information of, for example, gender or tense to the lemma. This does not imply that the learner has to designate the correct word-class, gender or tense to each word in the mental lexicon. The processing entails implicit processing and knowledge of the structures of the second language. Examples of language features processable in the category procedure are the regular plural 'girl-girls' and regular past tense morpheme 'ed', 'play-played'. In both cases the words have had to be encoded in the lexicon, together with additional information, as either a noun or a verb.

At the next level, the phrasal procedure, the learner is ready to process information within the phrase. This level is characterised by the agreement between the head in the phrase and other phrasal constituents. It is now possible for the learner to connect, for example, a determiner to the head in the noun phrase. The noun 'girl' can, thus, be combined with the article 'a' creating a noun phrase 'a girl' or, for example, in German, the correct phrase morphology is processable, for example, ein kleines Mädchen (a little girl).

The phrase level is followed by the sentence procedure in which information is processed between phrases. An example of this is subject–verb agreement in which processing between the subject in the noun phrase and the verb in the verb phrase is necessary in order to produce a correct utterance.

The final level of acquisition covers, the clausal boundary procedure, the processing of information between clauses. Examples of such processing are the usage of tag questions, sentence initial adverbials, relative clauses and in Swedish an awareness of the differences in word order between main and subordinate clauses.

### *3.2 Testing Processability Theory with Key-Stroke Logged Data*

Although Processability Theory has primarily been applied to spoken-language acquisition, written compositions have also formed the basis for studies that have tested processability theory's validity. Pienemann and Håkansson (1999), for example, used previously published research on written compositions by Hyltenstam (1977, 1978) and Rahkonen (1993), together with research on the acquisition of spoken Swedish, in their testing of a unified framework for the development of the Swedish second-language grammatical system that they had developed using Processability Theory principles. Keystroke logging affords a new data set that can be used to explore the validity of the predictions made using processability theory.

Pienemann and Håkansson (1997, 1999) found no counterevidence to their predictions in the 14 major empirical students of second-language Swedish that they tested against their predictions. In a follow-up study Håkansson (1997) systemically examined the spoken and written Swedish of four second-language learners of Swedish. Again she found that "no learner used structures belonging to a level higher up in the hierarchy without also using structures belonging to the lower levels" (p. 48). However, in this study Håkansson reported that the learners used structures in their written versions that they did not use in their oral productions; one of her participants moved from level three (phrasal procedure) to level five (clausal boundary). Moreover, she reported that when frequencies of correct use in obligatory contexts were considered "the whole pattern changes and the percentage of correct realization of inversion, level four, is higher than the one for agreement of morphology, which is level three" (p. 49). As the written context affords a greater opportunity for monitoring of correctness, an increase in the overall level of correctness is not surprising. Yet, the inversion of levels three and four, could indicate a difference between the order of automatized acquisition and the order of acquisition during active monitoring. A keystroke log can provide the researcher with insight into levels of automatization, levels of monitoring and amount of revision; these are not available to the researcher working with final versions of written compositions.

One possible experimental design to examine Processability Theory using keystroke logging (and, perhaps, examine Håkansson's inverted percentage correct order) is to follow the development of a group of second-language learners writing. The frequency of logging and the nature of the writing tasks would need to be decided by the research leaders together with the research participants.

The structures and frequencies of correct use in obligatory contexts in the final text can be categorised into processability levels as if the texts had not been keystroke logged. From the logged data, constructions written with no pauses or revision can be compared against those that are written with pauses and revision during creation and those that are revised at a later point in time during a revision for grammatical error sweep of the text. The techniques and approaches to classification presented in the chapters by Lindgren and Sullivan (this volume, Chapter 9) and Spelman Miller (this volume, Chapter 8) and Wengelin (this volume, Chapter 7) provide methods to help decide what are useful data points and how they can be categorized.

The categorisation of structures that considers the writing process affords the researcher the opportunity to create development profiles of the writers that only use those structures that are automated or involve immediate, fast revisions. This would result in those structures that were not-yet automated, involved considerable thought and perhaps demanded active grammatical construction revision, not forming part of the hierarchy ranking. These structures may in themselves provide a window onto when hierarchy transition is about to occur. That is, the automatized data may delimit an achieved ranking and the non-automatized data may provide an indication as to how soon the learner will move to the next level of the hierarchy.

The use of computer keystroke logging could, thus, provide data that shows that processability hierarchies applies to writing as well as to spoken-language acquisition. The use may, on the other hand, show that the deviation from the hierarchy found by Håkansson (1997) cannot be explained by creating distinctions based on how the final form of structures are arrived at during the writing process. It could be that writing and speaking with their different social functions do not adhere to the same cognitive developmental process as defined by a Processability Theory hierarchy. Keystroke logged data can assist the resolving of these issues.

This section has given the reader one suggestion as to how keystroke logging can be applied beyond fundamental and descriptive research. The ideas presented have not (yet) been tested and are to be viewed, in themselves, as suggestive and exploratory. We hope that the reader is inspired by our suggestion to use the techniques presented throughout this book to explore and interrogate a range of theories.

## 4 Looking Forward with Keystroke Logging

This volume has presented the state-of-the-art situation in keystroke logging research and in Spelman Miller (Chapter 2) and Lindgren and Sullivan (Chapter 3) provided the reader unfamiliar with writing research an introduction to this field of investigation. Then in the chapters written by Stömqvist et al. (Chapter 4), Leijten and Van Waes (Chapter 5) and Jakobsen (Chapter 6) three different keystroke-logging programs with different research motivations and research programs were presented. In Chapters 7–9, we have seen how keystroke logging can be used to study writing at different levels, and in Chapter 10 we saw, picking up on the research motivations for Translog presented in Chapter 6, how we can investigate how people work when translating documents.

At various points in this volume the contributors have mentioned ways in which they are currently developing, or ways in which they would like to develop, the capabilities of keystroke logging. We saw in Strömqvist et al. (Chapter 4) how his research group based in Lund has combined keystroke logging with eye-tracking technology. Writing interacts with reading and research that disassociates one from the other can only provide a partial, even if important, picture of the writing process. With the rapid advances in eye-tracking technology, the combination of keystroke logging with eye-tracking technology promises to become more accessible and possible to use outside of the research laboratory. The combination of data sources may assist in unravelling some of the issues surrounding revision categorisation as problematised by Lindgren and Sullivan in Chapter 9.

The combination of data sources together with keystroke logging, however, raises presentation and data interrogation issues. The collection of more data does not by itself result in a clearer picture, or a better understanding, of writing, learning or translation. The adding of speech and event-related potential (ERP) capabilities to keystroke logging systems will provide additional data, yet without, appropriate analysis and data presentation methodologies these new sources of data will cloud rather than clarify. Lindgren, Sullivan, Lindgren, and Spelman Miller (in press) have proposed that the visualisation and data-mining techniques used in Geographical Information Systems (GIS) can be adopted by the keystroke logging community:

> As well as being a tool for visualisation and data mining, the GIS technique can support analysis of the interaction of cognitive processes during writing focussing on the individual writer, differences between writers or on the writing processes in general. Depending on the research question, GIS affords the possibility to aggregate data to the level of writers, de-aggregate data in any way chosen or to display data as attributes of individuals.

Lindgren et al.'s proposal of using GIS with the afforded possibility to aggregate and de-aggregate data in many ways opens up corpus-based data-mining for both research and pedagogy. Strömqvist et al. (this volume) suggested another way of using a corpus of keystroke logged texts pedagogically:

> a searchable, web-based archive of online writing data from writers of different languages, age-groups and abilities, would present a rich source not only for researchers, but also for teachers and students. Imagine a situation where, for example, a class of English pupils in upper secondary school engage in a process-oriented writing project as part of their studying French as a foreign language. The kind of web-based archive outlined above would make it possible for the students and their teacher to identify and download age-matched writing data from French school children writing compositions in French. (p. 73)

We suggest that this idea is developed with data-mining techniques being used in the selection of texts; texts need not (only) be age-matched, but also be selected using criteria such as type of revision sequence, grammatical content and pause pattern.

One aspect of writing on the computer that has little, if any, focus in this volume is that of working with the visual aspects of the text parallel with text composition. Questions such as: How do writers work with text formatting when writing? Does it assist in text and argument development by providing time to concentrate on something else? How do different people combine writing and visual editing? Does visual editing trigger certain types of revision? Questions relating to visual editing need to be integrated into keystroke logging research rather than being seen as a peripheral aspect of composition. We look forward to this in the near future as keystroke logging develops.

Even if the use of GIS may today help researchers interrogate the gargantuan amount of data from a range of data sources, it is apparent that much research needs to be undertaken in data visualisation, with regard to inter-keystroke logging program compatibility issues, with respect to porting keystroke-logged data to a web-platform and visual editing for the full potential of combining keystroke logging with other data sources to be achieved. Yet, once this has been achieved keystroke logging and its coupled data sources will open an even more detailed and richer domain of research in writing, learning, translation, and development and testing of theory than is offered by the state-of-the-art keystroke-logging research, methods and applications that have been presented in this volume. A foundation has been laid for future interdisciplinary research use and pedagogical applications of keystroke logging. To this future we welcome all researchers, educationalists and policy makers and we look forward to fruitful cooperation.

# References


Ahlsén, E., & Strömqvist, S. (1999). ScriptLog: A tool for logging the writing process and its possible diagnostic use. In: F. Loncke, J. Clibbens, H. Arvidson, & L. Lloyd (Eds), *Augmentative and alternative communication: New directions in research and practice* (pp. 144–149). London: Whurr Publishers.

Alamargot, D., & Chanquoy, L. (2001). *Through the models of writing*. Dordrecht: Kluwer Academic Publishers.

Allal, L. (2000). Metacognitive regulation of writing in the classroom. In: A. Camps, & M. Milian (Eds), *Metalinguistic activity in learning to write* (pp. 145–166). Amsterdam: Amsterdam University Press.

Allal, L. (2004). Integrated writing instruction and the development of revision skills. In: L. Allal, L. Chanquoy, & P. Largy (Eds), *Revision: Cognitive and instructional processes* (pp. 139–156). Dordrecht: Kluwer Academic Publishers.

Allwood, J., Nivre, J., & Ahlsén, E. (1990). Speech management — on the non-written life of speech. *Nordic Journal of Linguistics*, *13*, 3–48.

Alves, F. (Ed.). (2003). *Triangulation translation. Perspectives in process oriented research.* Amsterdam: Benjamins.

Alves, R. A. (2002). *Limites e processos cognitivos na composicao escrita*. MA Thesis, Universidade do Porto: Faculdade de Psicologia e de Ciencias da Educacao.

Alves, R. A., Castro, S. L., de Sousa, L., & Strömqvist, S. (in press). The cognitive cost of execution in written composition. In: D. Galbraith, L. Van Waes, & M. Torrance (Eds), *Recent developments in writing process research. Volume I: Basic processes and word-level effects*. Dordrecht: Kluwer.

Andersson, L., Lindgren, E., Spelman Miller, K., & Sullivan K. P. H. (2001). Representation of revision: Visually demonstrating written language use (August). Poster presented at *BAAL*. Reading, UK.

Applebee, A. (1986). Problems in process approaches: Toward a reconceptualization of process instruction. In: A. Petrosky & D. Bartholomae (Eds), *The teaching of writing* (pp. 95–113). Chicago, IL: National Society of the Study of Education University of Chicago Press.

Atkinson, D. (2003). L2 writing in the post-process era: Introduction. *Journal of Second Language Writing*, *12*, 3–15.

Baurmann, J. (1989). Empirische schreibforschung. In: G. Antos & H. P. Krings (Eds), *Textproduktion* (pp. 257–277). Tübingen: Niemeyer.

Beattie, G. W. (1983). *Talk: An analysis of speech and nonverbal behaviour in conversation*. Milton Keynes: Open University.

Bereiter, C., & Scardamalia, M. (1987). *The psychology of written composition*. Hillsdale, NJ: Lawrence Erlbaum Associates.

Berman, R. A., & Slobin, D. I. (1994). *Relating events in narrative. A crosslinguistic developmental study*. Hillsdale, NJ: Lawrence Erlbaum Associates.

Bernadini, S. (2001). Think-aloud protocols in translation research. Achievements, limits, future prospects. *Target, 13*(2), 241–263.

Bertram, R., Tønnessen, F. E., Strömqvist, S., Hyönä, J., & Niemi, P. (in preparation) Compound Elicitation in Finnish: The case of writing.

Bizzell, P. (1982). Cognition, convention and certainty: What we need to know about writing. *Pre/text, 3*, 211–245.

Blankenship, J., & Kay, C. (1964). Hesitation phenomena in English speech: A study in distribution. *Word, 20*, 360–372.

Bonin, P., & Fayol, M. (1996). Producing isolated words from pictures, from orally and visually presented words: An on-line study of naming and writing. In: G. Rijlaarsdam, H. Van den Bergh, & M. Couzijn (Eds), *Current research in writing: Theories, models and methodology* (pp. 145–158). Amsterdam: Amsterdam University Press.

Boomer, D. S. (1965). Hesitation and grammatical encoding. *Language and Speech, 8*, 148–158.

Braaksma, M. A. H., Rijlaarsdam, G., & Van den Bergh, H. (2002). Observational learning and the effects of model–observer similarity. *Journal of Educational Psychology, 94*(2), 405–415.

Braaksma, M. A. H., Van den Bergh, H., Rijlaarsdam, G., & Couzijn, M. (2001). Effective learning activities in observation tasks when learning to write and read argumentative texts. *European Journal of Psychology of Education, 1*, 33–48.

Bracewell, R., Frederiksen, C., & Frederiksen, J. (1982). Cognitive processes in composing and comprehending discourse. *Educational Psychologist, 17,* 146–164.

Bresnan, J. (2001). *Lexical functional syntax*. Oxford: Blackwell Publishers.

Breetvelt, I., Van den Bergh, H., & Rijlaarsdam, G. (1994). Relations between writing processes and text quality: When and how? *Cognition and Instruction, 12*(2), 103–123.

Bridwell, L. (1980). Revising strategies in twelfth grade students' transactional writing. *Research in the Teaching of English, 14*, 197–222.

Bridwell, L., Sirc, G., & Brooke, R. (1985). Revising and computing: Case studies of student writers. In: S. Freedman (Ed.), *The acquisition of written language: Response and revision* (pp. 172–194). Norwood, NJ: Ablex.

Bridwell-Bowles, L., Johnson, P., & Brehe, S. (1987). Composing and computers: Case studies of experienced writers. In: A. Matsuhashi (Ed.), *Writing in real time: Modeling production processes* (pp. 81–107). London: Longman.

Broekkamp, H., & Van den Bergh, H. (1996). Attention strategies in revising a foreign language text. In: G. Rijlaarsdam, H. Van den Bergh, & M. Couzijn (Eds), *Theories, models and methodology in writing research* (pp. 170–181). Amsterdam: Amsterdam University Press.

Brotherton, P. (1979). Speaking and not speaking processes for translation ideas into speech. In: A. W. Siegman, & S. Feldstein (Eds), *Of speech and time: Temporal speech patterns in interpersonal contexts*. Hillsdale, NJ: Lawrence Erlbaum Associates.

Brown, G., & Yule, G. (1983). *Discourse analysis*. Cambridge: Cambridge University Press.

Butterworth, B. (1980). Evidence from pauses in speech. In: B. Butterworth (Ed.), *Language production: Vol. 1. Speech and talk* (pp. 155–176). London: Academic Press.

Caccamise, D. (1987). Idea generation in writing. In: A. Matsuhashi (Ed.), *Writing in real time: Modeling production processes* (pp. 224–253). London: Longman.

Candlin, C., & Hyland, K. (1999). *Writing: Texts, processes and practices*. London: Longman.

Cederlund, J., & Severinson Eklundh, K. (nd.). *JEdit: The logging text editor for Macintosh*. Stockholm, Sweden: IPLab, Department of Numerical Analysis and Computing Science, Royal Institute of Technology (KTH).

Chafe, W. (1980). Some reasons for hesitating. In: H. Dechert, & M. Raupach (Eds), *Temporal variables in speech: Studies in honour of Frieda Goldman-Eisler* (pp. 169–180). The Hague: Mouton.

Chafe, W. (1988). Punctuation and the prosody of written language. *Written Communication, 5*, 385–426.

Chafe, W. (1994). *Discourse, consciousness and time*. Chicago: The University of Chicago Press.

Chambers, F. (1997). What do we mean by fluency? *System, 25*, 535–544.

Chanquoy, L. (1997). Thinking skills and composing: Examples of text revision. In: J. H. M. Hamers, & M. Oovertoom (Eds), *Inventory of European programmes for teaching thinking* (pp. 179–185). Utrecht: Sardes.

Chanquoy, L. (2001). How to make it easier for children to revise their writing: A study of text revision from 3rd to 5th grades. *British Journal of Educational Psychology, 71*, 15–41.

Chanquoy, L., Foulin, J. N., & Fayol, M. (1990). Temporal management of short text writing by children and adults. *C.P.C./European Bulletin of Cognitive Psychology, 10*, 513–538.

Chanquoy, L., Foulin, J. N., & Fayol, M. (1996). Writing in adults: A real time approach. In: G. Rijlaarsdam, H. Van den Bergh, & M. Couzijn (Eds), *Theories, models and methodology in writing research* (pp. 36–43). Amsterdam: Amsterdam University Press.

Chenoweth, N. A., & Hayes, J. R. (2001). Fluency in writing: Generating text in L1 and L2. *Written Communication, 18*(1), 80–98.

Chesterman, A. (1997). *The memes of translation. The spread of ideas in translation theory*. Amsterdam/Philadelphia: Benjamins.

Clark, H. (1999). Speaking in time. In: *Proceedings of the ESCA workshop on dialogue and prosody 1999*, 1–6.

Clark. H., & Clark, E. (1977). *Psychology and language*. NY: Harcourt Brace, Jovanovich.

Cooper, M., & Holzman, M. (1983). Talking about protocols. *College Composition and Communication, 34*, 284–293.

Couzijn, M., Van den Bergh, H., & Rijlaarsdam, G. (2002). Writing processes and text quality: Effects of L1/L2. Paper presented at *SIG Writing 2002*, July, Stafford, England.

Cumming, A., & Riazi, A. (1996). Building models of adult second-language writing instruction. In: A. Archibald, & G. Jeffery (Eds), *Second language acquisition and writing: A multidisciplinary approach* (pp. 7–22). The University of Southampton.

Daiute, C. (1986). Physical and cognitive factors in revising: Insights from studies with computers. *Research in the Teaching of English, 20*, 141–159.

de Beaugrande, R. (1984). *Text production: Toward a science of composition*. Norwood, NJ: Ablex.

Dechert, H., & M. Raupach (Eds). (1980a). *Temporal variables in speech: Studies in honour of Frieda Goldman-Eisler*. The Hague: Mouton.

Dechert, H., & Raupach, M. (1980b). *Towards a cross-linguistic assessment of speech production*. Frankfurt am Main: Peter Lang.

Degenhardt, M. (2005). Camtasia and Catmovie: Two digital tools for observing, documenting and analysing writing processes of university students. In: L. Van Waes, M. Leijten, & C. Neuwirth (Eds), *Wrting and digital media*. Oxford: Elsevier.

Dennett, J. (1985). Writing technical English: A comparison of the process of native English and native Japanese speakers. *Dissertation Abstracts International, 46*, 3275A.

Deschamps, A. (1980). The syntactical distribution of pauses in English spoken as a second language by French students. In: H. Dechert, & M. Raupach (Eds), *Temporal variables in speech: Studies in honour of Frieda Goldman-Eisler* (pp. 255–262). The Hague: Mouton.

Deutschmann, M., Lindgren, E., Steinvall, A., & Sullivan, K. P. H. (2005). Peer-based intervention och keystroke logging som hjälpmedel för att stimulera språkinlärning i översättningsundervisningen. In: E. Larsson Ringqvist, & I. Valfridsson (Eds), *Forskning om Undervisning i Främmande Språk. Rapport från Workshop i Växjö 10–11 juni 2004* (pp. 65–75). Acta Wexionensia, Nr 58/2005. Växjö University Press.

Dragsted, B. (2004). Segmentation in translation and translation memory systems. An empirical investigation of cognitive segmentation and effects of integrating a TM system into the translation process. Ph.D. dissertation. CBS.

Elis, R. (1994). *The study of second language acquisition.* Oxford: Oxford University Press.

Emig, J. (1971). *The composing processes of twelfth graders.* Urbana, IL: National Council of Teachers of English.

Englund Dimitrova, B. (1994). Statistical analysis of translations (on the basis of translations from and to Bulgarian, Russian and Swedish). *Scandinavian Working Papers on Bilingualism, 9*, 87–102.

Englund Dimitrova, B. (2005) *Expertise and explicitation in the translation process* (Benjamins Translation Library 64). Amsterdam and Philadelphia: Benjamins.

Ericsson, K. A., & Simon, H. A. (1980). Verbal reports as data. *Psychological Review, 87*, 215–251.

Ericsson, K. A., & Simon, H. A. (1984/1993). *Protocol analysis: Verbal reports as data* (2nd Rev. ed.). Cambridge, MA: MIT.

Erskine, J. (1999). Group and individual differences in the local level writing strategies of adult dyslexics attending higher education. In: S. Strömqvist, & E. Ahlsén (Eds), *The process of writing — a progress report. Gothenburg Papers in Theoretical Linguistics 83* (pp. 103–118). Sweden, Gothenburg: Göteborg University, Department of Linguistics.

Faerch, C., & Kasper, G. (1983). Plans and strategies in foreign language communication. In: C. Faerch, & G. Kasper (Eds), *Strategies in interlanguage communication* (pp. 20–60). London: Longman.

Faigley, L., & Witte, S. (1981). Analyzing revision. *College Composition and Communication, 32*, 400–414.

Flower, L. (1989). Cognition, context, and theory building. *College Composition and Communication, 40*, 282–311.

Flower, L., & Hayes, J. R. (1977). Problem-solving strategies and the writing process. *College English, 39*, 449–461.

Flower, L., & Hayes, J. R. (1980). The dynamics of composing: Making plans and juggling constraints. In: L. Gregg, & E. Steinberg (Eds), *Cognitive processes in writing* (pp. 31–50). Hillsdale, NJ: Lawrence Erlbaum.

Flower, L., & Hayes, J. R. (1981). A cognitive process theory of writing. *College Composition and Communication, 32*(4), 365–387.

Flower, L., & Hayes, J. R. (1984). Images, plans, and prose: The representation of meaning in writing. *Written Communication, 1*, 120–160.

Flower, L., Hayes, J. R., Carey, L., Schriver, K., & Stratman, J. (1986). Detection, diagnosis and the strategies of revision. *College Composition and Communication, 37*, 16–55.

Flower, L., Stein, V., Ackerman, J., Kantz, M., McCormick, K., & Peck, W. (1990). *Reading-to-write: Exploring a cognitive and social process.* Oxford: Oxford University Press.

Fitzgerald, J. (1987). Research on revision in writing. *Review of Educational research, 57*(4), 481–506.

Galbraith, D. (1999). Writing as a knowledge constituting process. In: M. Torrance, & D. Galbraith (Eds), *Knowing what to write: Conceptual processes in text production* (pp. 139–160). Amsterdam: Amsterdam University Press.

Galbraith, D., & Torrance, M. (2004). Revision in the context of different drafting strategies. In: L. Allal, L. Chanquoy, & P. Largy (Eds), *Revision: Cognitive and instructional processes* (pp. 63–86). Dordrecht: Kluwer Academic Publishers.

Garman, M. (1990). *Psycholinguistics.* Cambridge: Cambridge University Press.

Garrett, M. F. (1982). Production of speech: Observations from normal and pathological language use. In: A. W. Ellis (Ed.), *Normality and pathology in cognitive functions* (pp. 19–76). London: Academic Press.

Garrett, M. F. (1990). Review of W. Levelt 1989 speaking: From intention to articulation. *Language and Speech, 33*, 273–291.

Gass, S., & Mackey, A. (2002). *Stimulated recall methodology in second language research.* Hillsdale, NJ: Lawrence Erlbaum Associates Publishers.

Gee, J., & Grosjean, F. (1983). Performance structures: A psycholinguistic and linguistic appraisal. *Cognitive Psychology, 15*, 411–458.

Gerloff, P. (1987). Identifying the unit of analysis in translation: Some uses of think-aloud protocol data. In: C. Færch, & G. Kasper (Eds), *Introspection second language research* (pp. 135–158). Clevedon-Philadelphia: Multilingual Matters.

Givon, T. (1983). Topic continuity in discourse: An introduction. In: T. Givon (Ed.), *Topic continuity in discourse. A quantitative cross-language study* (pp. 1–41). Amsterdam/Philadelphia: Benjamins.

Goldman-Eisler, F. (1961). A comparative study of two hesitation phenomena. *Language and Speech, 4*, 18–26.

Goldman-Eisler, F. (1968). *Psycholinguistics: Experiments in spontaneous speech.* London: Academic Press.

Goldman-Eisler, F. (1972). Pauses, clauses, sentences. *Language and Speech, 15*, 103–113.

Gould, J. (1978). How experts dictate. *Journal of Experimental Psychology: Human Perception and Performance, 4*, 648–661.

Gould, J. (1980). Experiments on composing letters: Some facts, some myths, and some observations. In: L. Gregg, & E. Steinberg (Eds), *Cognitive processes in writing* (pp. 97–127). Hillsdale, NJ: Lawrence Erlbaum.

Goutsos, D. (1997). *Modeling discourse topic: Sequential relations and strategies in expository text.* Norwood, NJ: Ablex.

Graham, S., Berninger, V. W., Abbot, R. D., Abbot, S. P., & Whitaker, D. (1997). Role of mechanics in composing of elementary school children: A new methodological approach. *Journal of Educational Psychology, 89*(1), 170–182.

Grabe, W., & Kaplan, R. B. (1996). *Theory and practice of writing*. London: Longman.

Graham, S., & Harris, K. R. (2000). The role of self-regulation and transcription skills in writing and writing development. *Educational Psychologist, 35*(1), 3–12.

Greene, S., & Higgins, L. (1994). "Once upon a time": The use of retrospective accounts in building theory in composition. In: P. Smagorinsky (Ed.), *Speaking about writing* (pp. 115–140). London: Sage.

Griffiths, R. (1991). Pausological research in an L2 context: A rationale, and review of selected studies. *Applied Linguistics, 12*, 345–364.

Grosjean, F. (1980). Comparative studies of temporal variables in spoken and sign languages: a short review. In: H. Dechert, & M. Raupach (Eds), *Temporal variables in speech: Studies in honour of Frieda Goldman-Eisler* (pp. 91–106). The Hague: Mouton.

Grosjean, F., & Deschamps, A. (1975). Analyse contrastive des variables temporelles de l'anglais et du francais: Vitesse de parole et variables composantes, phenomenes d'hesitation. *Phonetica, 31*, 144–184.

Grosjean, F., Grosjean, L., & Lane, H. (1979). The patterns of silence: Performance structures in sentence production. *Cognitive Psychology, 11*, 58–81.

Haas, C. (1989). Does the medium make a difference? Two studies of word processing on planning. *Research in the Teaching of English, 23*(2), 181–207.

Haas, C. (1996). *Writing technology: Studies on the materiality of literacy*. New Jersey: Lawrence Erlbaum Associates, Publishers.

Hadenius, P. (1992). Pausplatser: Positioner för tankar i skrivarbetet. *Svenskans Beskrivning, 19*, 144–151.

Hall, C. (1990). Managing the complexity of revising across languages. *TESOL Quarterly, 24*, 43–60.

Halliday, M. A. K. (1967). Notes on transitivity and theme in English, parts 1–3. *Journal of Linguistics, 3*, 37–87, 199–244, *4*, 179–215.

Halliday, M. A. K. (1985). *An introduction to functional grammar*. London: Edward Arnold.

Halliday, M. A. K. (1994). The construction of knowledge and value in the grammar of scientific discourse, with reference to Charles Darwin's The origin of species. In: M. Coulthard (Ed.), *Advances in written text analysis* (pp.136–156). London: Routledge.

Hansen, G. (Ed.). (1999). Probing the process in translation: Methods and results. *Copenhagen Studies in Language 24*. Copenhagen: Samfundslitteratur.

Hansen, G. (Ed.). (2002). Empirical translation studies. Process and product. *Copenhagen Studies in Language 27*. Copenhagen: Samfundslitteratur.

Hansen, G. (2005). *Störquellen in Übersetzungsprozessen. Eine empirische Untersuchung von Zusammenhängen zwischen Profilen, Prozessen und Produkten.* Doctoral dissertation. Copenhagen: Copenhagen Business School (To be published by Gunter Narr.)

Hawisher, G. (1987). The effects of word processing on the revision strategies of college freshmen. *Research in the Teaching of English, 21*, 145–159.

Hawkins, P. (1971). The syntactic location of hesitation pauses. *Language and Speech, 14*, 277–288.

Hayes, J. R. (1996). A new framework for understanding cognition and affect in writing. In: C. M. Levy, & S. Randsdell (Eds), *The science of writing* (pp. 1–27). Hillsdale, NJ: Lawrence Erlbaum Associates.

Hayes, J. R. (2004). What triggers revision? In: G. Rijlaardsam (Series Ed.), L. Allal, & L. Chanquoy (Vol. Eds), *Studies in writing: Volume 13: Cognitive and instructional processes* (pp. 189–207) Boston: Kluwer Academic Publishers.

Hayes, J. R., & Flower, L. (1980). Identifying the organization of the writing process. In: L. Gregg & E. R. Steinberg (Eds), *Cognitive processes in writing* (pp. 3–30). Hillsdale, NJ: Lawrence Erlbaum Associates.

Hayes, J. R., & Flower, L. (1983). Uncovering cognitive processes in writing: An introduction to protocol analysis. In: P. Mosenthal, L. Tamor, & S. Walmsley (Eds), *Research in writing: Principles and methods* (pp. 206–219). London: Longman.

Hayes, J. R., & Flower, L. (1986). Writing research and the writer. *American Psychologist, 41*, 1106–1113.

Hayes, J. R., Flower, L., Schriver, K., Stratman, J., & Carey, L. (1987). Cognitive processes in revision. In: S. Rosenberg (Ed.), *Advances in applied psycholinguistics: Vol. 2. Reading, writing, and language possessing* (pp. 176–240). Cambridge: Cambridge University Press.

Hayes, J. R., & Nash, J. (1996). On the nature of planning in writing. In: C. M. Levy, & S. Ransdell (Eds), *The science of writing* (pp. 29–55). Mahwah: Lawrence Erlbaum Associates.

Hayes-Roth, B., & Hayes-Roth, F. (1979). A cognitive model of planning. *Cognitive Science, 3*, 275–310.

Hedbor, C. (2003). *Les règles d'abord ou la production directe du français écrit? Étude longitudinale sur l'utilisation ou non des connaissances explicites par cinq élèves de différentes attitudes cognitives.* Technical Report. Lund University: Department of Romance Languages.

Hellum, I. (2000). Data i norskopplaeringa. Masters thesis, Centre for Reading Research, Stavanger University College.

Henderson, A., Goldman-Eisler, F., & Skarbek, A. (1966). Sequential temporal patterns in spontaneous speech. *Language and Speech, 9*, 207–216.

Hildenbrand, J. (1985). Carmen: A case study of an ESL writer. *Dissertation Abstracts International 46*, 3637A.

Hill, C., Wallace, D., & Haas, C. (1991). Revising on-line: Computer technologies and the revising process. *Computers and Composition, 9*, 83–109.

Holmqvist, K., Holsánová, J., Johansson, V., & Strömqvist, S. (2005) Perceiving and producing the frog story. In: D. Ravid, & H. Bat-Zeev Shyldkrot (Eds), *Perspectives on language and language development* (pp. 289–302). Dordrecht: Kluwer.

Holmqvist, K., Johansson, V., Strömqvist, S., & Wengelin, Å. (2002). Studying reading and writing online. In: S. Strömqvist, (Ed.), *The diversity of languages and language learning* (pp. 103–123). Lund Lectures in Languages and Literature I. Lund University: Centre for Languages and literature.

Holsánová, J. (2001). *Picture viewing and picture descriptions — two windows to the mind*, PhD. dissertation, Department of Cognitive Science, Lund University.

Hunt, K. (1965). *Grammatical structures written at three grade levels.* Urbana, IL: National Council of Teachers of English.

Hyland, K. (1999). Disciplinary discourses: Writer stance in research articles. In: C. Candlin, & K. Hyland (Eds), *Writing: Texts, processes and practices* (pp. 99–121). London: Longman.

Hyltenstam, K. (1977). Implicational patterns in interlanguage syntax variation. *Language Learning, 27*, 383–411.

Hyltenstam, K. (1978). Variation in interlanguage syntax. *Working Papers 18*. Sweden, Lund: Lund University, Department of Linguistics.

Håkansson, G. (1997). Modern times in L2 Swedish. On the acquisition of Swedish morphology and syntax in formal and informal settings. In: L. Diaz, & C. Pérez (Eds), *Views on the acquisition and use of a second language* (pp. 39–50). Barcelona, Spain: Universitat Pompeu Fabra.

Jakobsen, A. L. (1998). Logging time delay in translation. In: G. Hansen (Ed.), *Copenhagen working papers in LSP* (Vol. 1). *LSP Texts and the process of translation* (pp. 73–101). Copenhagen: Copenhagen Business School.

Jakobsen, A. L. (1999). Logging target text production with Translog. In: G. Hansen (Ed.) *Probing the process in translation. Methods and results, Copenhagen studies in language* (Vol. 24, pp. 9–20). Copenhagen: Samfundslitteratur.

Jakobsen, A. L. (2002). Translation drafting by professional translators and by translation students. *Traducción & Comunicación, 3*, 89–103.

Jakobsen, A. L. (2003). Effects of think aloud on translation speed, revision and segmentation. In: F. Alves (Ed.), *Triangulating translation* (pp. 69–95). Amsterdam/Philadelphia: Benjamins.

Jansen, D., Van Waes, L., & Van den Bergh, H. (1996). Effects of thinking aloud on writing processes. In: M. Levy, & S. Ransdell (Eds), *The science of writing: Theories, methods, individual differences and applications* (pp. 233–250). Mahwah, NJ: Lawrence Erlbaum Associates.

Jensen, A. (2001). *The effects of time on cognitive processes and strategies in translation.* PhD dissertation. Copenhagen Working Papers in LSP (Vol. 2). Copenhagen: Copenhagen Business School.

Jensen, A., & Jakobsen, A. (2000). Translating under time pressure. An empirical investigation of problem-solving activity and translation strategies by non-professional and professional translators. In: A. Chesterman, N. G. San Salvador, & Y. Gambier (Eds), *Translation in context. Selected papers from the EST congress, Granada, 1998* (pp. 105–116). Amsterdam: Benjamins.

Johansson, V. (2003). Developing editing. In: M. Aparici, N. Argerich, J. Perera, E. Rosado, & L. Tolchinsky (Eds). *Working papers in developing literacy across genres, modalities, and languages* (Vol. III). Barcelona, Spain: University of Barcelona.

Johns, A. (1990). L1 composition theories: Implications for developing theories of L2 composition. In: B. Kroll (Ed.), *Second language writing* (pp. 24–36). Cambridge: Cambridge University Press.

Johnson, R., & Moore, R. (1997). A link between reading proficiency and native-like use of pausing in speaking. *Applied Language Learning, 8*, 25–42.

Jones, S., & Tetroe, J. (1987). Composing in a second language. In: A., Matsuhashi (Ed.), *Writing in real time* (pp. 34–57). Norwood, NJ: Ablex.

Joram, E., Woodruff, E., Lindsey, P., & Bryson, M. (1990). Students' editing skills and attitudes towards word processing. *Computers and Composition, 7*, 55–72.

Jääskeläinen, R. (1999). *Tapping the process: An explorative study of the cognitive and affective factors involved in translating.* Joensuu: Joensuun Yliopisto.

Kaufer, D. S., Hayes, J. R., & Flower, L. (1986). Composing written sentences. *Research in the Teaching of English, 20*(2), 121–140.

Keijsper, C. (1985). *Information structure*. Amsterdam: Rodopi.

Kellogg, R. (1987). Writing performance: Effects of cognitive strategies. *Written Communication, 4*, 269–298.
Kellogg, R. (1988). Attentional overload and writing performance: Effects of rough draft and outline strategies. *Journal of Experimental Psychology: Learning, Memory and Cognition, 14*, 355–365.
Kellogg, R. (1990). Effectiveness of prewriting strategies as a function of task demands. *American Journal of Psychology, 103*, 327–342.
Kellogg, R. (1994). *The psychology of writing*. Oxford: Oxford University Press.
Kellogg, R. (1996). A model of working memory in writing. In: C. M. Levy, & S. Randsdell (Eds), *The science of writing* (pp. 57–72). Mahwah, NJ: Lawrence Erlbaum Associates.
Kieft, M., Rijlaarsdam, G., & Van den Bergh, H. (in press). Writing as a learning tool: The role of students' writing strategies. *European Journal of Educational Psychology.*
Kim, H. C. (1996). *Diagnosing and filtering typing error corrections in text revision history*. Technical report TRITA-NA-P9633, IPLab 113, Stockholm, Sweden: Department of Numerical Analysis and Computing Science, Royal Institute of Technology (KTH).
Kollberg, P. (1998). *S-notation—a computer based method for studying and representing text composition*. Licentiate thesis, Stockholm, Sweden: Department of Numerical Analysis and Computing Science, Royal Institute of Technology (KTH).
Kollberg, P., & Severinson Eklundh, K. (2001). Studying writers' revision patterns with S-notation analysis. In: G. Rijlaarsdam (Series Ed.), T. Olive, & C. M. Levy (Vol. Eds), *Studies in writing: Volume 10. Contemporary tools and techniques for studying writing* (pp. 89–104). Dordecht: Kluwer Academic Publishers.
Kowal, S., & O'Connell, D. (1987). Writing as language behavior: Myths, models and methods. In: A. Matsuhashi (Ed.), *Writing in real time: Modelling production processes* (pp. 108–132). Norwood: Ablex.
Krings, H. (1986). *Was in den Köpfen von Übersetzern vorgeht.* Tübingen: Narr.
Krings, H. (2001). Habilitationsschrift. In: G.S. Koby, G.M. Shreve, K. Mischerikow, & S. Litzer (Trans.), *Texte reparieren: Empirische Untersuchungen zum Prozeß der Nachredaktion von Maschinenübersetzungen. [Repairing texts. Empirical investigations of machine translation post-editing* processes] Kent, Ohio: Kent State U.P.
Künzli, A. (2001). Experts versus novices: L'utilisation de sources d'information pendant le processus de traduction. *Meta, XLVI*(3), 507–523.
Lansman, M., Smith, J., & Weber, I. (1990). *Using computer-generated protocols to study writers' planning strategies.* Technical Report No. TR90-033. Chapel Hill: University of North Carolina, Department of Computer Science.
Lautamatti, L. (1987). Observations on the development of the topic of simplified discourse. In: U. Connor, & R. B. Kaplan (Eds), *Writing across languages: Analysis of L2 text* (pp. 87–114). Reading, MA: Addison-Wesley.
Ledin, P. (1998). Att sätta punkt: Hur elever på låg- och mellanstadiet använder meningen i sina uppsatser. *Språk och Stil, 8*, 5–7.
Leijten, M., & Van Waes, L. (2003). *The writing processes and learning strategies of initial users of speech recognition: A case study on the adaptation process of two professional writers*. Antwerp: Faculty of Applied Economics, University of Antwerp (Research paper).
Leijten, M., & Van Waes, L. (2005). Writing with speech recognition: The adaptation process of professional writers. *Interacting with Computers, 17/5.*
Lennon, P. (1990). Investigating fluency in EFL: A quantitative approach. *Language Learning, 40*, 387–417.
Levelt, W. (1981). The speaker's linearization problem. In: H. Longuet-Higgins, J. Lyons, & D. Broadbent (Eds), *The psychological mechanisms of language* (pp. 91–101). London: The Royal Society and The British Academy.
Levelt, W. (1989). *Speaking: From intention to articulation.* Cambridge: MIT Press.

Levy, C. M., Marek, P., & Lea, J. (1996). Concurrent and retrospective protocols in writing research. In: G. Rijlaarsdam, H. Van den Bergh, & M. Couzijn (Eds), *Current research in writing: Theories, models and methodology* (pp. 542–556). Amsterdam: Amsterdam University Press.

Levy, C. M., & Ransdell, S. (1994). Computer-aided protocols of writing processes. *Behavior Research Methods, Instruments and Computers, 26*, 219–223.

Levy, C. M., & Ransdell, S. (1996a). Writing signatures. In: C. M. Levy, & S. Ransdell, (Eds), *The science of writing* (pp. 149–161). Mahwah: Lawrence Erlbaum Associates.

Levy, C. M., & Ransdell, S. (Eds). (1996b). *The science of writing*. Mahwah: Lawrence Erlbaum Associates.

Lindgren, E. (2004). The uptake of peer-based intervention in the writing classroom. In: G. Rijlaarsdam (Series Ed.), G. Rijlaarsdam, H. Van den Bergh, & M. Couzijn (Vol. Eds), *Studies in writing: Volume 14. Effective learning and teaching of writing, 2nd edition* (pp. 259–274). Dordrecht: Kluwer Academic Publishers.

Lindgren, E. (2005). *Writing and revising: Didactic and methodological implications of keystroke logging*. (Skrifter från moderna språk, No. 18). Umeå, Sweden: Umeå University, Department of Modern Languages.

Lindgren, E., & Sullivan, K. P. H. (2002). Analysing and presenting on-line revision. Paper presented at *The First Key-stroke Logging Symposium*, Umeå, Sweden.

Lindgren, E., & Sullivan, K. P. H. (2003). Stimulated recall as a trigger for increasing noticing and language awareness in the L2 writing classroom: A case study of two young female writers. *Language Awareness, 12*, 172–186.

Lindgren, E, Sullivan, K. P. H., & Eriksson, E. J. (2002). Connecting cognitive information to computer key-stroke logging in second language learning. Paper presented at *The 6th Conference of the Australasian Cognitive Science Society*, Perth, WA. Australia.

Lindgren, E., Sullivan, K. P. H., Lindgren, U., & Spelman Miller, K. (in press). GIS for writing: Applying geographic information system techniques to data-mine writing's cognitive processes. In: G. Rijlaarsdam (Series Ed.), D. Galbraith, M. Torrance, & L. Van Waes (Vol. Eds), *Writing and cognition*. Oxford: Elsevier.

Lorenzo, M. (1999). Apuntes para una discusion sobre metodos de estudio del proceso de traduccion. In: Gyde Hansen (Ed.), *Copenhagen studies in language, vol. 24: Probing the process in translation. Methods and results* (pp. 21–42). Copenhagen: Samfundslitteratur.

Lorenzo, M. (2001). Combinación y contraste de métodeos de recogida y análisis de datos en el estudio del proceso de la traducción — Proyecto del grupo TRAP. *Quaderns. Revista de traducció*, Barcelona, no. 6, 33–38.

Lorenzo, M. (2002). ¿Es posible la traducción inversa? — Resultados de un experimento sobre traducción profesional a una lengua extranjera. In: G. Hansen (Ed.), *Copenhagen studies in language, vol. 27: Empirical translation studies. Process and product* (pp. 85–124). Copenhagen: Samfundslitteratur.

Lörscher, W. (1991). *Translation performance, translation process, and translation strategies. A psycholinguistic investigation*. Tübingen: Narr.

Lundquist, L. (2002). L'anaphore associative : Etude contrastive et expérimentale de la traduction de l'anaphore associative du français en danois, *Romansk Forum XV*, No. 16.

Lundquist, L. (2003). L'anaphore associative en danois et en français – sur quoi roule-t-elle? Etude contrastive et experimentale. In: M. Herslund (Ed.). *Aspects linguistiques de la traduction* (pp. 105–124). Bordeux, France: Presses universitaires de Bordeaux.

Lutz, J. (1987). A study of professional and experienced writers revising and editing at the computer and with pen and paper. *Research in the Teaching of English, 21*, 398–421.

Maclay, H., & Osgood, C. E. (1959). Hesitation phenomena in spontaneous English speech. *Word, 15*, 19–44.

Mann, W., & Thompson, S. (1988). Rhetorical structure theory. *Text, 8*, 243–281.

Matsuda, P. K. (2003). Process and post-process: A discursive history. *Journal of Second Language Writing*, *12*, 65–83.
Matsuhashi, A. (1981). Pausing and planning: The tempo of written discourse production. *Research in the Teaching of English*, *15*(2), 113–134.
Matsuhashi, A. (1982). Explorations in the real-time production of written discourse. In: M. Nystrand (Ed.), *What writers know. The language, process, and structure of written discourse* (pp. 269–290). New York: Academic Press, Inc.
Matsuhashi, A. (1987). Revising the plan and altering the text. In: A. Matsuhashi (Ed.), *Writing in real time — modelling production processes* (pp.197–223). Norwood, NJ: Ablex Publishing company.
Matsuhashi, A., & Gordon, E. (1985). Revision, addition, and the power of the unseen text. In: S. Freedman (Ed.), *The acquisition of written language: revision and response* (pp. 226–249). Norwood, NJ: Ablex.
Mayer, M. (1969). *Frog, where are you?* New York: Dial Press.
McCutchen, D. (1996). A capacity theory of writing: Working memory in composition. *Educational Psychology Review*, *8*(3), 299–325.
McCutchen, D. (2000). Knowledge, processing, and working memory: Implications for a theory of writing. *Educational Psychologist*, *35*(1), 13–23.
Monahan, B. D. (1982). Revision strategies of basic and competent writers as they write for different audiences. *Research in the Teaching of English*, *18*, 289–304.
Moragne e Silva, M. (1989). A study of composing in a first and second language. *Texas Papers in Foreign Language Education*, *1*, 132–151.
Myers, G. (1989). The pragmatics of politeness in scientific articles. *Applied Linguistics*, *10*, 1–35.
Nickerson, R., Perkins, D., & Smith, E. (1985). *The teaching of thinking*. Hillsdale, NJ: L. Erlbaum.
Nilsson, M., & Kollberg, P. (1994). *Trace-it 2.0 user's manual.* Stockholm, Sweden: Department of Numerical Analysis and Computing Science, Royal Institute of Technology (KTH).
Nordqvist, Å. (2001). *Speech about speech—A developmental study on form and function of direct and indirect speech.* Doctoral dissertation. Gothenburg monographs in linguistics 19. Sweden, Gothenburg: Göteborg University, Department of Linguistics.
Nordqvist, Å., Leiwo, M., & Lyytinen, H. (2003). From nonsense words to space adventure: Developing a test battery to study and diagnose writing. Paper presented at the 13th European Conference on Reading, Reading-Writing-Thinking, Tallinn, Estonia.
North, S. (1987). *The making of knowledge in composition: Portrait of an emerging field*. London: Heinemann.
Nystrand, M. (1986). *The structure of written communication: Studies in reciprocity between writers and readers*. Orlando, Florida: Academic Press.
O'Brien, T. (1995). Rhetorical structure analysis and the case of the inaccurate, incoherent source-hopper. *Applied Linguistics*, *16*, 442–482.
O'Connell, D. (1980). Cross-linguistic investigation of some temporal dimensions of speech. In: H. Dechert, & M. Raupach (Eds), *Towards a cross-linguistic assessment of speech production* (pp. 23–38). Frankfurt am Main: Peter Lang.
O'Connell, D., & Kowal, S. (1980). Prospectus for a science of pausology. In: H. Dechert, & M. Raupach (Eds), *Temporal variables in speech: Studies in honour of Frieda Goldman-Eisler* (pp. 3–10). The Hague: Mouton.
Olive, T., & Kellogg, R. T. (2002). Concurrent activation of high- and low-level production processes in written composition. *Memory and Cognition*, *30*(4), 594–600.
Olson, C. B. (2002). *The reading/writing connection: Strategies for teaching and learning in the secondary classroom*. Boston, MA: Pearson Allyn & Bacon Publishers.
Owston, R., Murphy, S., & Wideman, H. (1992). The effects of word processing on students' writing quality and revision strategies. *Research in the Teaching of English*, *26*, 249–276.

Pålson, E. (1998). *Revision strategies in young foreign language writing*. Stockholm: Technical report TRITA-NA-P9802, IPLab-143, Department of Computing Science, Royal Institute of Technology.

Pelli, T., & Sinimäki, S. (2004). ScriptLogtest för dubbelteckningsförmåga hos 9-åringar [ScriptLog-based testing of 9-year-olds' ability to spell long consonants], Technical Report. Lund University: Department of Speech Therapy.

Pennington, M. C. (Ed.) (1999). *Writing in an electronic medium: Research with language learners*. Houston: Athelstan.

Perl, S. (1979). The composing processes of unskilled college writers. *Research in the Teaching of English*, *13*, 317–336.

Perrin, D. (1998). Analyzing text progression at the writer's workplace. A theory-based tool for the writing coach. *Proceedings from the 1998 European Writing Conference*. Poitiers, France: Universite de Poitiers.

Perrin, D. (2003). Progression analysis: Investigating writing strategies at the workplace. *Journal of Pragmatics*, *35*(6), 907–921.

Phinney, M., & Khouri, S. (1993). Computers, revision, and ESL writers: The role of experience. *Journal of Second Language Writing*, *2/3*, 257–277.

Pienemann, M. (1998). *Language processing and second language development: Processability theory*. Amsterdam: John Benjamin's Publishing Company.

Pienemann, M., & Håkansson, G. (1999). A unified approach toward the development of Swedish as L2: A processability account. *Studies in Second Language Acquisition*, *21*, 383–420.

Piolat, A. (1999). Planning and text quality among undergraduate students: Findings and questions. In: M. Torrance, & D. Galbraith (Eds), *Knowing what to write: Conceptual processes in text production* (pp. 121–138). Amsterdam: Amsterdam University Press.

Piolat, A., Roussey, J. Y., Olive, T., & Amada, M. (2004). Processing time and cognitive effort in revision: effects of error type and of working memory capacity. In: L. Allal, L. Chanquoy, & P. Largy (Eds), *Revision: Cognitive and instructional processes* (pp. 21–38). Dordrecht: Kluwer Academic Publishers.

Rahkonen, M. (1993). Huvudsatsfundamentet hos svenska inlärare av finska och finska inlärare av svenska [Main clause foundation in Swedish learners of Finnish and Finnish learners of Swedish]. In: V. Muittari, & M. Rahkonen (Eds), *Svenskan i Finland 2: Meddelanden från Institutionen för nordiska språk vid Jyväskylä universitet 9* (pp. 199–225).

Reinhart, T. (1981). Pragmatics and linguistics: An analysis of sentence topics. *Philosophica*, *1*, 53–94.

Reiss, K., & Vermeer, H. J. (1984). *Grundlegung einer Allgemeinen Translationstheorie*. Tübingen: Niemeyer.

Reither, J. (1985). Writing and knowing: Toward redefining the writing process. *College English*, *47*, 620–628.

Reppen, R. (1995). A genre-based approach to content writing instruction. *TESOL Journal*, *4*(2), 32–35.

Riggenbach, H. (1991). Toward an understanding of fluency: A micro-analysis of nonnative speaker conversations. *Discourse Processes*, *14*, 423–441.

Rijlaarsdam, G., & Couzijn, M. (2000). Stimulating awareness of writing in the writing curriculum. In: A. Camps, & M. Milian (Eds), *Metalinguistic activity in learning to write* (pp. 167–202). Amsterdam: Amsterdam University Press.

Rijlaarsdam, G., Couzijn, M., & Van den Bergh, H. (2004). The study of revision as a writing process and as a learning-to-write process. Two prospective research agendas. In: G. Rijlaarsdam (Series Ed.), L. Allal, L. Chanquoy, & P. Largy (Vol. Eds), *Revision: cognitive and instructional processes* (pp.189–207). Dordrecht: Kluwer Academic Publishers.

Rijlaarsdam, G., Van der Bergh, H., & Couzijn, M. (Eds). (1996). *Effective teaching and learning of writing: Current trends in research. Studies in writing* (Vol. 2). Amsterdam: Amsterdam University Press.

Roca de Larios, J., Murphy, L., & Marin, J. (2002). Critical examination of L2 writing process research. In: G. Rijlaarsdam (Series Ed.), S. Ransdell, & M. L. Barbier (Vol. Eds), *Studies in writing: Volume 11. New directions for research in L2 writing* (pp. 11–48). Dordrecht: Kluwer Academic Publishers.

Rothe-Neves, R. (2003). The influence of working memory features on some formal aspects of translation performance. In: F. Alves (Ed.), *Triangulating translation. Perspectives in process oriented research* (pp. 97–119). Amsterdam: Benjamins.

Russo, J. E., Johnson, E. J., & Stephens, D. L. (1989). The validity of verbal protocols. *Memory and Cognition, 17*, 759–769.

Sanders, T., Janssen, D., Van der Pool, E., Schilperoord, J., & Van Wijk, C. (1996). Hierarchical text structure in writing products and writing processes. In: G. Rijlaarsdam, H. Van den Bergh, & M. Couzjin (Eds), *Theories, models and methodology in writing research* (pp. 473–492). Amsterdam: Amsterdam University Press.

Scardamalia, M., & Bereiter, C. (1983). The development of evaluative, diagnostic and remedial capabilities in children's composing. In: M. Martlew (Ed.), *The psychology of written language: A developmental approach* (pp. 67–98). New York: Wiley.

Schilperoord, J. (1996). It's about time. *Temporal aspects of cognitive processes in text production*. Amsterdam: Rodopi.

Schilperoord, J., & Sanders, T. (1999). How hierarchical text structure affects retrieval processes: Implications of pause and text analysis. In: M. Torrance, & D. Galbraith (Eds), *Knowing what to write: Conceptual processes in text production* (pp. 13–30). Amsterdam: Amsterdam University Press.

Schmidt, R. (1990). The role of consciousness in second language learning. *Applied Linguistics, 11*(2), 129–158.

Schmidt, R. (1992). Psycholinguistic mechanisms underlying second language fluency. *Studies in Second Language Acquisition, 14*, 357–385.

Schumacher, G., Klare, G., Cronin, F., & Moses, J. (1984). Cognitive activities of beginning and advanced college writers: A pausal analysis. *Research in the Teaching of English, 18*, 169–187.

Selfe, C. (1981). *The composing processes of four high and four low-writing apprehensives: A case study.* Austin, TX: University of Texas. PhD dissertation.

Selfe, C. (1984). The predrafting processes of four high- and four low-apprehensive writers. *Research in the Teaching of English, 18*, 45–64.

Severinson Eklundh, K. (1992). Problems in achieving a global perspective on the text in computer based writing. *Instructional Science, 21*, 73–84.

Severinson Eklundh, K. (1994). Linear and non-linear strategies in computer-based writing. *Computers and Composition, 11*, 203–216.

Severinson Eklundh, K., & Kollberg, P. (1992). *Translating keystroke records into a general notation for the writing process*. IPLab Report 59, Royal Institute of Technology, Stockholm, Sweden.

Severinson Eklundh, K., & Kollberg, P. (1996a). A computer tool and framework for analysing online revisions. In: C. M. Levy, & S. Randsdell (Eds), *The science of writing* (pp. 163–188). Mahwah, NJ: Lawrence Erlbaum Associates.

Severinson Eklundh, K., & Kollberg, P. (1996b). Computer tools for tracing the writing process: From keystroke records to S-notation. In: G. Rijlaarsdam, H. Van den Bergh, & M. Couzijn (Eds), *Current research in writing: Theories, models and methodology* (pp. 526–541). Amsterdam: Amsterdam University Press.

Severinson Eklundh, K., & Kollberg, P. (1999). *Emerging discourse structure: Computer-assisted episode analysis as a window to global revision in University Students' Writing*. IPLab-159. Stockholm, Sweden: Department of Numerical Analysis and Computing Science, Royal Institute of Technology (KTH).

Severinson Eklundh, K., & Kollberg, P. (2003). Emerging discourse structure: Computer-assisted episode analysis as a window to global revision in university students' writing. *Journal of Pragmatics*, *35*(6), 869–891.

Sharwood Smith, M. A. (2000). Attentional mechanisms and the language acquisition device. In: B. Englund Dimitrova, & K. Hyltenstam (Eds), *Language processing and simultaneous interpreting* (pp. 25–44). Amsterdam: John Benjamin's Publishing Company.

Silva, T. (1993). Toward an understanding of the distinct nature of L2 writing: The ESL research and its implications. *TESOL Quarterly*, *27*(4), 657–677.

Sleurs, K., Jacobs, G., & Van Waes, L. (2003). Constructing press releases, constructing quotations: A case study. *Journal of Sociolinguistics*, *7*(2), 192–212.

Smagorinsky, P. (1994). *Speaking about writing*. London: Sage.

Solheim, O. J., & Uppstad, P. H. (2003). *Spelling Quantity in Norwegian*. Technical report. Centre for Reading Research, Stavanger.

Sommers, N. (1980). Revision strategies of student writers and experienced adult writers. *College Composition and Communication*, *31*, 378–388.

Spelman Miller, K. (1999). Investigating academic writing on-line; a study of temporal aspects of text production. In: M. Pennington (Ed.), *Writing in an electronic environment: Research with language learners* (pp. 159–182). Houston, TX: Athelstan.

Spelman Miller, K. (2000a). *Writing on-line: Temporal features of first and second language written text production*. Unpublished doctoral thesis. University of Reading, UK.

Spelman Miller, K. (2000b). Academic writers on-line: Investigating pausing in the production of text. *Language Teaching Research*, *4*, 123–148.

Spelman Miller, K. (2002). Units of production in writing: Towards a discourse perspective. In: S. Burgess (Ed.), *Revista canaria de estudios ingleses*. Tenerife: University La Laguna.

Stenström, A-B. (1994). *An introduction to spoken language interaction*. Longman, London.

Stevenson, M., Schoonen, R., & de Glopper, K. (forthcoming). Revising in two languages: A comparison of writing revisions made by high school students in Dutch and English.

Stratman, J., & Hamp-Lyons, L. (1994). Reactivity in concurrent think-aloud protocols: Issues for research. In: P. Smagorinsky (Ed.), *Speaking about writing* (pp. 89–112). London: Sage.

Strömqvist, S. (1996). Discourse Xow and linguistic information structuring in speech and writing. *Gothenburg Papers in Theoretical Linguistics 72*. Sweden, Gothenburg: Göteborg University, Department of Linguistics.

Strömqvist, S. (1999). Production rate profiles. In: S. Strömqvist & E. Ahlsén (Eds), *The process of writing — a progress report. Gothenburg Papers in Theoretical Linguistics 83* (pp. 53–70). Sweden, Gothenburg: Göteborg University, Department of Linguistics.

Strömqvist, S. (2000). A note on pauses in speech and writing. In: M. Aparici (Ed.), *Developing literacy across genres, modalities and languages: Working Papers, Volume III* (pp. 211–224). International Literacy Project, Universitat de Barcelona.

Strömqvist, S., & Ahlsén, E. (Eds). (1999). *The process of writing — a progress report. Gothenburg Papers in Theoretical Linguistics 83*. Sweden, Gothenburg: Göteborg University, Department of Linguistics.

Strömqvist, S., Ahlsén, E., & Wengelin, Å. (1999). The production process in speech and writing. In: Aisenman, R. (Ed.), *Working papers in developing literacy across genres, modalities and languages. Volume 1* (pp. 1–20). Tel Aviv University: Department of Linguistics.

Strömqvist, S., Ahlsén, E., Wengelin, Å., Grönqvist, L., & Hagman, J. (1999). Types of analyses. In: S. Strömqvist, & E. Ahlsén (Eds), *The process of writing—a progress report. Gothenburg Papers in Theoretical Linguistics 83* (pp. 35–48). Sweden, Gothenburg: Göteborg University, Department of Linguistics.

Strömqvist, S., & Karlsson, H. (2002). *ScriptLog for Windows — User's manual*. Technical Report. University of Lund: Department of Linguistics, and University College of Stavanger: Centre for Reading Research.

Strömqvist, S., & Malmsten, L. (1998). *Scriptlog Pro 1.04 — User's manual*. Technical report, Sweden, Gothenburg: Göteborg University, Department of Linguistics.

Strömqvist, S., Crasborn, O., Eklund, M., Godelier, M., Karadimas, D., Kieven, E., Renn, J., Uneson, M., Wittenburg, P. (2004a). State-of-art review on humanities, social sciences, and cultural heritage knowledge bases. http://echo.mpiwg-berlin.mpg.de/home/publicRelation/reports and http://www.ling.lu.se/projects/echo/state_of_art/index.html.

Strömqvist, S., Nordqvist, Å., & Wengelin, Å. (2004b). Writing the frog story — developmental and cross-modal perspectives. In: S. Strömqvist, & L. Verhoeven (Eds), *Relating events in narrative—typologiocal and contextual perspectives* (pp. 359–394). Mahwah, NewJersey: Lawrence Erlbaum Associates Publishers.

Strömqvist, S., & Verhoeven, L. (Eds). (2004). *Relating events in narrative—typologiocal and contextual perspectives*. Mahwah, NJ: Lawrence Erlbaum Associates Publishers.

Sullivan, K. P. H., Kollberg, P., & Pålson, E. (1998). Trace-it — a computer tool with application to the second language classroom. BABEL. *Journal of the Australian Federation of Modern Language Teachers Associations Inc*, *33*(1), 22–28.

Sullivan, K., & Lindgren, E. (2002). Self-assessment in autonomous computer-aided second language writing. *ELT Journal*, *56*(3), 258–265.

Swain, M. (1995). Three functions of output in second language learning. In: G. Cook, & B. Seidlhofer (Eds), *Principle and practice in the studies of language: Studies in honour of H.G. Widdowson* (pp. 125–144). Oxford: Oxford University Press.

Swain, M. (1998). Focus on form through conscious reflection. In: C. Doughty, & J. Williams (Eds), *Focus on form in classroom second language acquisition* (pp. 15–63). Cambridge: Cambridge University Press.

Swain, M. (2000). The output hypothesis and beyond: Mediating acquisition through collaborative dialogue. In: J. P. Lantolf (Ed.), *Sociocultural theory and second language learning* (pp. 97–114). Oxford: Oxford University Press.

Swerts, M. (1998). Filled pauses as markers of discourse structure. *Journal of Pragmatics*, *30*, 485–496.

Thompson, G. (1996). *Introducing functional grammar*. London: Arnold.

Thompson, G., & Thetela, P. (1995). The sound of one hand clapping: The management of interaction in written discourse. *Text*, *15*, 103–127.

Thorson, H. (2000). Using the computer to compare foreign and native language writing processes: A statistical and case study approach. *Modern Language Journal*, *84*(2), 155–170.

Tirkkonen-Condit, S. (2002). Process research: State of the art and where to go next? *Across Languages and Cultures*, *3*(1), 5–19.

Tobin, L. (Ed.). (1994). *Taking stock: The writing process movement in the 90s*. Portsmouth, NH: Heinemann.

Tommola, J. (1986). Translation as a psycholinguistic process. In: L. Wollin, & H. Lindquist (Eds), *Translation studies in Scandinavia* (pp. 140–149). Lund: Gleerup.

Torrance, M. (1996). Strategies for familiar writing tasks: Case studies of undergraduates writing essays. In: G. Rijlaarsdam, H. Van den Bergh, & M. Couzijn, (Eds), *Current research in writing: Theories, models and methodology* (pp. 283–298). Amsterdam: Amsterdam University Press.

Torrance, M., & Jeffery, G. (1999). Writing processes and cognitive demands. In: M. Torrance, & G. Jeffery (Eds), *The cognitive demands of writing: Processing capacity and working mmemory in text production* (pp. 1–12). Amsterdam: Amsterdam University Press.

Torrance, M., Thomas, G., & Robinson, E. (1994). The writing strategies of graduate research students in the social sciences. *Higher Education*, *27*, 379–392.

Toury, G. (1986). Monitoring discourse transfer: A test-case for a developmental model of translation. In: J. House, & S. Blum-Kulka (Eds), *Interlingual and intercultural communication. Discourse and cognition in translation and second language acquisition Studies* (pp. 79–94). Tübingen: Narr.

Toury, G. (1995). *Descriptive translation studies and beyond*. Amsterdam/Philadelphia: Benjamins.

Trimbur, J. (1994). Taking the social turn: Teaching writing post-process. *College Composition and Communication, 45*, 108–118.

Truscott, J. (1998). Noticing in second language acquisition: A critical review. *Second Language Research, 14*(2), 103–135.

Van Gelderen, A. (1994). Prediction of global ratings of fluency and delivery in narrative discourse by linguistic and phonetic measures — oral performances of students aged 11–12 years. *Language Testing, 11*, 291–319.

Van Gelderen, A., & Oostdam, R. (2002). Improving linguistic fluency for writing: effects of explicitness and focus of instruction. *L1 Educational studies of Language and Literature*, 2(3), 239–270.

Van Gelderen, A., & Oostdam, R. (2004). Revisions of form and meaning in learning to write comprehensible text. In: G. Rijlaarsdam (Series Ed.), L. Allal, L. Chanquoy, & P. Largy (Vol. Eds), *Studies in writing: Volume 13. Revision: Cognitive and instructional processes* (pp. 103–124). Dordrecht: Kluwer Academic Publishers.

Van der Pool, E. (1996). A text-analytical study of conceptual writing processes and their development. In: G. Rijlaarsdam, H. Van den Bergh, & M. Couzijn (Eds), *Current research in writing: Theories, models and methodology* (pp. 456–472). Amsterdam: Amsterdam University Press.

Van Waes, L. (1991). *De Computer en het Schrijfprocess. De Invloed van de Teksverwerker op het Pauze — en Revisiegedrag van Schrijvers*. Enschede: Universiteit Twente.

Van Waes, L. (1992). The influence of the computer on writing profiles, In: H. P. Maat, & M. Steehouder (Eds), *Studies of functional text quality. Utrecht studies in language and communication 1* (pp. 173–186). Amterdam: Rodopi Publishers.

Van Waes, L., & Schellens, P. J. (2003). Writing profiles: The effect of the writing mode on pausing and revision patterns of experienced writers. *Journal of Pragmatics, 35*(6), 829–853.

Van Wijk, C. (1999). Conceptual process in argumentation: A developmental perspective. In: M. Torrance, & D. Galbraith (Eds), *Knowing what to write: Conceptual processes in text production* (pp. 31–50). Amsterdam: Amsterdam University Press

Vygotsky, L. S. (1978). *Thought and language*. Cambridge, MA: MIT Press.

Wagner, Å., Hansen, K., & Uppstad, P. H. (2005). Bilingual literacy: Narrative performance in bilingual students. In; Cohen, J., McAlister, K., Rolstad, K., & MacSwan, J. (Eds), *ISB4: Proceedings of the 4th International Symposium on Bilingualism*. Somerville, MA: Cascadilla Press.

Warren, E. (1997). The significance of pauses in written discourse: A comparison of native speaker and learner writing. In: A. Archibald, & G. Jeffery (Eds), *Second language acquisition and writing: A multidisciplinary approach* (pp. 152–177). The University of Southampton.

Weingarten, R., Nottbusch, G., & Will, U. (2004). Morphemes, syllables and graphemes in written word production. In: T. Pechman, & C. Habel (Eds), *Multidisciplinary approaches to language production*. Mouton de Gruyter: Berlin, New York.

Wengelin, Å. (2001) Disfluencies in writing — are they like in speaking? In: *Proceedings from Disfluency In Spontaneous Speech (DISS'01)*, Edinburgh University, Edinburgh.

Wengelin, Å. (2002). *Text production in adults with reading and writing difficulties*. Doctoral dissertation. Sweden, Gothenburg: Göteborg University, Department of Linguistics.

Wengelin, Å. (in press). The word level focus in text production by adults with reading and writing difficulties to appear. In: D. Galbraith, M. Torrance, & L. Van Waes (Eds). *Recent developments in writing process research: Basic processes and word-level effects*. Amsterdam: Elsevier.

Wengelin, Å., & Strömqvist, S. (2000). Discourse level writing in dyslexics — methods, results, and implications for diagnosis. *Scandinavian Journal of Logopedics, Phoniactrics and Vocology, 25*(1), 22–28.

Wengelin, Å., & Strömqvist, S. (2004). Text-writing development viewed through on-line pausing in Swedish. In: R. Berman (Ed.), *Language development across childhood and adolescence* (pp. 177–190). Philadelphia: John Benjamins.

Wiktorsson, M. (2000). The production rate of *prefabs* — a pilot study. In: M. Aparici, (Ed.), *Developing literacy across genres, modalities and languages: Working papers, Volume III*, (pp. 211–224). International Literacy Project, Universitat de Barcelona.

Wiktorsson, M. (2003). Learning idiomaticity. A corpus-based study of idiomatic expressions in learners' written production. *Lund Studies in English 105.* Lund University.

Will, U., Weingarten, R., Nottbusch, G., & Albes, C. (1992). Linguistic units, hierarchies and dynamics of written language production. *Cognition, 42*, 261–286.

Williamson, M. M., & Pence, P. (1989). Word processing and student writers. In: B. K. Britton, & S. M. Glynn (Eds), *Computer writing environments: Theory, research and design* (pp. 93–127). Hillsdale, NJ: Lawrence Erlbaum Associates.

Witte, S. (1983). Topical structure and revision: An exploratory study. *College Composition and Communication, 41*, 313–341.

Witte, S. (1987). Pre-text and composing. *College Composition and Communication, 38*(4), 397–425.

Witte, S. (1992). Context, text, intertext: Toward a constructivist semiotic of writing. *Written Communication, 9*, 237–308.

Witte, S., & Cherry, R. (1986). Writing processes and written products in composition research. In: C. Cooper, & S. Greenbaum (Eds), *Studying writing: Linguistic approaches* (pp. 112–153). Newbury Park, CA: Sage.

Wittenburg, P., Johnson, H., Buchhorn, M., Brugman, H., & Broeder, P. (2004) Architecture for distributed language resource management and archiving. In: X. Fátima Ferreira, R. Costa, R. Silva, C. Pereira, F. Carvalho, M. Lopes, M. Catarino, & S, Barros (Eds), *Proceedings from the 4th International Conference on Language Resources and Evaluation (LREC2004-Lisbon)*, pp. 361–364.

Wollin, L., & Lindqvist, H. (Eds). (1986). *Translation studies in Scandinavia.* Lund: Lund University Press.

Yau, M. (1989). *A Quantitative Comparison of L1 and L2 Writing Processes*. Paper presented at the 23rd Annual TESOL Convention, March, San Antonio, Texas.

Zamel, V. (1983). The composing process of advanced ESL students: Six case studies. *TESOL Quarterly, 17*, 165–187.

Zesiger, P., Orliaguet, J., & Monoud, P. (1994). The influence of syllabic structure in handwriting and typing production. In: C. Faure, P. Keuss, G. Lorette, & A. Vinter (Eds), *Advances and handwriting and drawing: A multidisciplinary approach* (pp. 389–401). Paris: Europia.

Zimmermann, R. (2000). L2 writing: Subprocesses, a model of formulating and empirical findings. *Learning and Instruction, 10*, 73–99.

# Author Index

# Subject Index

# Contributors

*Birgitta Englund Dimitrova*
Institute for Interpretation and Translation Studies, Stockholm University, SE-106 91 Stockholm, Sweden, birgitta.englund@tolk.su.se

*Kenneth Holmqvist*
Humanistlaboratoriet, Centre for Languages and literature, Lund University, Box 201, SE-221 00 Lund, Sweden, Humlab@sol.lu.se

*Arnt Lykke Jakobsen*
Department of English and Center for Innovation in Translation and Translation Technology, Copenhagen Business School, Dalgas Have 15, DK-2000 Frederiksberg, Denmark, alj.eng@cbs.dk

*Victoria Johansson*
Centre for Languages and literature, Lund University, Box 201, SE-221 00 Lund, Sweden, victoria.johansson@ling.lu.se

*Henrik Karlsson*
Oribi AB, Paradisgatan 1, SE-223 50 Lund, Sweden, henrik.karlsson@oribi.se

*Mariëlle Leijten*
Department of Management, University of Antwerp, City Campus, Prinsstraat 13, E-2000 Antwerp, Belgium, marielle.leijten@ua.ac.be

*Eva Lindgren*
Faculty of Teacher Education, Umeå University, SE-901 87 Umeå, Sweden, eva.lindgren @fceduc.umu.se

*Kristyan Spelman Miller*
Department of Applied Linguistics, The University of Reading, Whiteknights, PO Box 217, Reading, RG6 6AH, UK, k.s.miller@reading.ac.uk

*Sven Strömqvist*
Centre for Languages and literature, Lund University, Box 201, SE-221 00 Lund, Sweden, sven.stromqvist@ling.lu.se

*Kirk P. H. Sullivan*
Department of Philosophy and Linguistics, Umeå University, SE-901 87 Umeå, Sweden, kirk@ling.umu.se

*Luuk Van Waes*
Department of Management, University of Antwerp, City Campus, Prinsstraat 13, E-2000 Antwerp, Belgium, luuk.vanwaes@ua.ac.be

*Åsa Wengelin*
Centre for Languages and literature, Lund University, Box 201, SE-221 00 Lund, Sweden, asa.wengelin@ling.lu.se